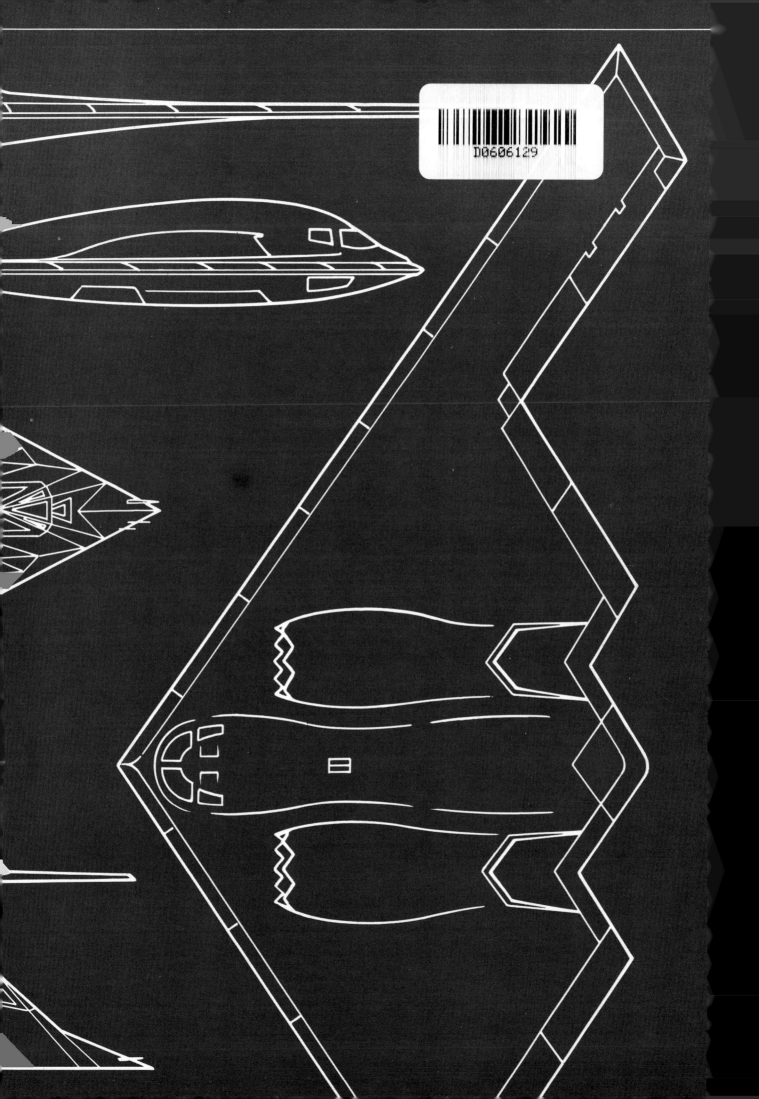

STEALTH

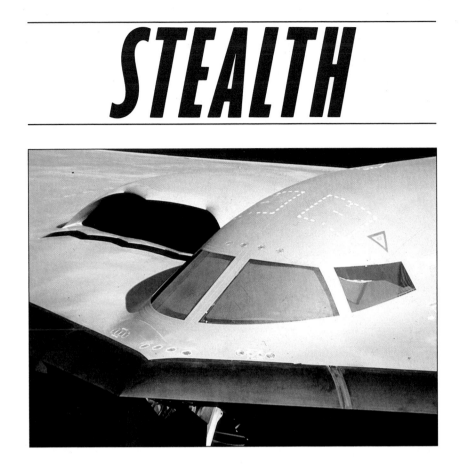

STEALTH

DOUG RICHARDSON

ORION
BOOKS

New York

A SALAMANDER BOOK

Copyright ©1989 by
Salamander Books Ltd.

Published in the United States
by Orion Books, a division of
Crown Publishers, Inc. 201
East 50th Street, New York,
New York 10022

Published in Great Britain by
Salamander Books Ltd.

ORION and colophon are
trademarks of Crown
Publishers, Inc.

Manufactured in Italy

Library of Congress
Cataloging-in-Publication
Data available.
Library of Congress Catalog
Card No. 89-062784

ISBN 0-517-57343-1

10 9 8 7 6 5 4 3 2 1

First Edition

**Dedicated to the memory of
Lee Begin**

CREDITS

Editor: Graham Smith.
Designer: Nigel Duffield.
Colour artworks: Stephen
Seymour, Terry Hadler and
the Maltings Partnership.
(©Salamander Books Ltd).
Profiles ©Pilot Press.
Diagrams: Geoff Denney
Associates.
Filmsetting: The Old Mill
Colour reproduction:
Magnum Graphics Ltd.
Printed in Italy.

THE AUTHOR

Doug Richardson is a defense
journalist specializing in the
fields of aviation, guided
missiles and electronics. He
was formerly defense editor
of *Flight International*, editor
of *Military Technology and
Economics*, and editor of
Defense Materiel.
   He has written several
books, including *The
Illustrated Guide to Electronic
Warfare, The AH-64 Fact-File,
The F-16 Fact-File*, and *An
Illustrated Survey of the West's
Modern Fighters*. He has also
contributed to *The
Intelligence War* and
*Advanced Technology
Warfare*.

Contents

Left: It's big, it's beautiful, and it's stealthy. Northrop's B-2 displays the clean lines which also spell low drag and fuel efficiency.

Previous page: A USAF F-117A Senior Trend stealth fighter with gear down approaches Tonopah during a daylight mission.

INTRODUCTION

From the earliest times when men could recount the past, the tales which the poets sang included those telling of heroes and mighty warriors. The stories reflected a simple world in which enemies were overthrown by the manly virtues of strength, courage and force of arms. The poets were less kind to those who sought to achieve their end by trickery or stealth; Homer's "wily Odysseus" is less favourably depicted than valiant warriors such as Hector and Achilles.

In all these stories, deception and stealth are seen as evil or ill-intentioned, an opinion widely held in many societies. Throughout history, armies have not hesitated to execute enemies found guilty of wearing false colours, while in mediaeval Japan the black-robed ninja was much feared.

With the arrival in the 1930s and early 1940s of the cinema swashbuckling heroes, deception suddenly became innocent sub-plot, as Errol Flynn's Robin Hood and his Merry Men dressed as simple peasants in order to sneak into Nottingham. Such innocence was not to last. Wartime commandos, saboteurs, special forces and fifth columnists soon restored deception to its traditional rôle. In Tolkien's saga of elves and hobbits, the power of invisibility is given not by Gandalf's benevolent magic but by an evil ring of power. In the "Star Trek" TV series, it's the Klingons who equip their space vessels with invisibility-shrouding "cloaking devices". Such trickery is beneath the honour of the steely-jawed crew of the Starship Enterprise. Concealment by shape-changing reached its dramatic but gory cinematic climax in John Carpenter's 1982 movie "The Thing", a remake of the earlier black-and-white classic directed by Howard Hawks.

Yet in the late 1970s, the concept of stealth and deception suddenly became respectable. Within the aviation community, rumours began to circulate of a new and highly-secret technology which would make aircraft

and missiles near-invisible to radar systems.

The Washington-based magazine *Aviation Week and Space Technology* was once described by an ex-astronaut as being "... to airplane and space people what *Rolling Stone* is to rock musicians". Around the aerospace industry, it is sometimes known as "Aviation Leak" because of its long record of being first into print with sensitive items of aviation news. (In 1947 it published the first news of Chuck Yeager's then-classified pioneering supersonic flight.)

LEAKS

For aerospace professionals, *Aviation Week* is essential reading. For anyone attempting to tell the story of stealth technology, it is an essential source. Its name will appear again and again throughout this book.

In the struggle for opinion and support among the key members of the defence community, aerospace industry executives, Pentagon "top brass", US politicians and the inevitable consultants and analysts, the US military often turn to the magazine as an ideal vehicle for judiciously-timed leaks. In 1980 just such an operation seemed to be under way, as stories of stealth appeared in its pages and in several US newspapers, lifting the veil on the new technology. Following a series

Above: **President Carter inspects a SAC B-52. In 1977 he decided to re-equip these old bombers with air-launched cruise missiles.**

of stealth-technology stories in *Aviation Week,* President Carter and US Defense Secretary Harold Brown finally confirmed that radar-invisible stealth aircraft had been test flown but ordered a security clampdown on the entire topic.

It is simple to declare a brand-new technology secret but when the secret consists largely of a blend of existing technologies it is more difficult. Such is the case with stealth. For three years following these early revelations, very little useful information on stealth was published. Behind the scenes however, the new technology was creeping out of the closet.

Like so many "modern" ideas, stealth technology first appeared in the world of nature. The simplest stealth technique is that of camouflage. Any child will be able to list examples from the animal world such as the polar bear's white fur, the stick insect's ability to mimic a twig and the colour-changing capabilities of the chameleon.

Other examples of "low observable technology" can be found in nature. Many large marine predators such as killer whales, sperm whales, dolphins and

Below: Until the unveiling of the F-117A late in 1988, most analysts predicted that the aircraft would rely on rounding, wing/body blending and extensive use of RAM. Thanks to tight security, the concept of using faceting as a means of RCS reduction remained secret.

Above: When first released, this Testor/Italeri kit of the "F-19" was seen by some observers as a potential breach of security.

porpoises, search for their prey by means of a form of sonar. They emit beams of sound waves and measure how long the echo takes to return from "targets". To cope with this threat, some fish and cephalopods, such as squid and octopuses, have evolved "stealth" defences. The bodies of some fish and squid are poor reflectors of the whale's sonar waves, the result of their not having an air-filled swim bladder (a good sonar target) for depth control. One scientist has even speculated that the mucus on their skin may be a sound absorber, a natural prototype for the radar-absorbing materials (RAMs) carried by stealth aircraft.

CLASSIFICATION

Much the same concepts lay behind the new and secret stealth technology — avoid radar-reflective structural features and absorb the incoming energy — but they were shrouded in secrecy. Since the mid-1970s, all new work on scattering, shaping and RAMs had been highly classified (some observers would argue excessively so).

Despite this, a substantial amount of information remained in the public domain. Engineers and scientists working in the field could hardly be expected to surrender their files and personal libraries for security vetting, or to de-programme their brains.

Given the amount of information in the public domain, it was inevitable that stealth would begin to creep out of the closet. In 1982,

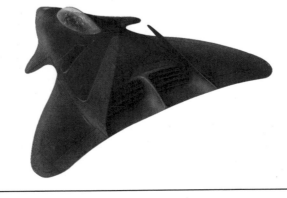

Right: Inward canted tail fins, plus "venetian blind" exhausts were seen as likely "F-19" features. In practice, the F-117A tail surfaces were tilted outwards (an equally effective low-RCS shape), but these engine exhausts are not too unlike those actually used by Lockheed.

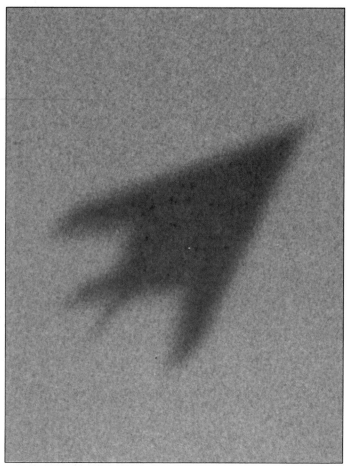

Above: **Taken by a ground-based photographer, this unauthorised picture of the F-117A revealed the true leading edge angle of the aircraft's highly-swept wing.**

Professor Allen E. Fuhs of the US Naval Postgraduate School began to lecture on the subject of radar cross-section (RCS) while on a sabbatical to NASA's Ames Research Center. A short course on the subject was introduced at Georgia Tech in January of the following year.

STEALTH MODELS

In a special electronics supplement pubished in September 1984 by the journal *International Defense Review* my former *Flight* colleague Bill Sweetman pushed back the bounds of what was in the public domain in a six-page article simply entitled "Stealth". He returned to the subject again in 1985 with a three-page article, "The Vanishing Air Force", in the August issue of *International Defense Review* and again on "Stealth" in the pages of the November edition of *Interavia*.

By this point, Bill was rapidly becoming a one-man stealth industry whose detective work was not always appreciated by those

Right: **The B-2 was assembled at Palmdale, so could not be kept under wraps indefinitely. Even so, guests at the rollout were allowed only a frontal view.**

attempting to keep stealth technology under wraps. Behind the scenes, however, he was preparing the manuscript of an entire book on the subject.

Before it saw print, two textbooks on the subject appeared. Professor Fuhs's RCS lectures were printed in 1985 by the American Institute of Aeronautics and Astronautics in a volume soon dubbed "The No-See-Um Book", while the Georgia Tech course resulted in Eugene F. Knott, John F. Shaeffer and Michael T. Tuley publishing their massive textbook *Radar Cross Section: its prediction, measurement and reduction.*

These were both highly theoretical treatments of the subject, but 1986 saw the appearance of a popular account in the form of Bill Sweetman's *Stealth Aircraft — secrets of future airpower.* Stealth technology had "come in from the cold".

In July 1986 toy stores around the USA began to sell a plastic construction kit which claimed to depict the Lockheed "F-19" stealth

fighter. "Attention all foreign spies", announced the 26 July edition of *The Washington Post,* "if you want to know what the Air Force's supersecret stealth fighter jet looks like, try your local toy store". The $9.95 model was a product of the Testor Corporation of Rockford, Illinois. Within a few weeks it had registered orders of around 100,000.

Following the release of the Testor model, a Pentagon official told Congress that it was inaccurate and that any aircraft built to that shape would crash. Model designer

John Andrews retaliated by claiming that the model was "80 per cent accurate" and that more than 100 copies had been sold by a model shop close to the Lockheed plant where the real aircraft was being built.

FIRST LOOK

Testor national field sales manager, Steve Kass, denied that classified information had been used to design the model. "Everything we got, you can get out of any library", he explained to a *Washington Post* reporter. The

model revealed no information which had not already been published in trade journals, he claimed.

By late 1988, the veil of secrecy had to be relaxed. As this introduction was being written, in the autumn of 1988, Northrop was preparing to roll out the first prototype of its B-2 Advanced Technology Bomber and the Pentagon had just released the first photograph of the legendary Lockheed "stealth fighter", giving the world at large a first look at one of the new generation of aircraft designed specifically to operate in the radar-equivalent of Tolkien's "land of darkness, where the shadows lie".

In the 1920s and 1930s, the nations of Western Europe were apprehensive about the threat posed by the primitive but near-unstoppable piston-engined bombers of the day. Within a few years, radar was to give the fighter an ascendancy over the medium- and high-altitude bomber. At first sight it might seem that stealth technology has simply restored the *status quo* but, in practice, the situation is more complex. Applied to bombers, fighters and even missiles, stealth is completely re-writing the book of air combat operations and tactics.

In Bram Stoker's gothic classic *Dracula*, vampire hunter Professor Van Helsing describes the difficulties which his party will experience in their attempts to locate and destroy the evil Count. "He can, within limitations, appear at will, where and when, and in any of the forms which are to him ... he can grow and become small; and at times he can vanish and come unknown. How then are we to begin our strife to destroy him?" It is a good description of the problems faced by would-be vampire hunters but is almost equally applicable to the problems faced by future air defences which must cope with a range of stealthy attackers.

This book will attempt to describe the stealth technology used to make aircraft and missiles "grow and become small" or to "vanish and come unknown". It will also look at the technologies that will be needed "to begin our strife to destroy him".

DECEIVING THE EYE

When the first military aircraft were fielded, little thought was given to colour schemes which might help reduce detection. The fact that they flew at all seemed more than adequate. Like their civil counterparts, military aircraft had no paint finish to speak of but were a pale yellow, the result of applying fabric-tautening dope and protective varnish to the linen or cotton covering.

Some work on reducing visibility had been done prior to the war. This had not been done by the application of deceptive colouring but rather by the even more obvious approach of trying to make the aircraft near-invisible by covering its wooden framework not with doped fabric but with a transparent skin. It may surprise those working with today's highly-classified stealth aircraft to learn that the first attempts to build aircraft of this type date back to the era of their great-grandparents.

In 1913 the United States War Department carried out experiments intended to assess the feasibility of building an aircraft which would be invisible to the naked eye when flying at an altitude of 1,000ft (300m). In an attempt to meet what by any standards must be seen as an impossible target, the

Below: **US First World War air ace Eddie Rickenbacker poses alongside his French-built Spad fighter. Although more complex than the contemporary British camouflage scheme shown above, the colour finish on the aircraft was probably no more effective as an anti-detection measure.**

wings of an aircraft were manufactured with what a contemporary newspaper account described as "a material of a semi-transparent nature, composed partly of celluloid". Other trials involved the use of the same material in the "understructure" of airships. A secondary goal of the work

was to give aircrew a better view of the ground.

In 1914 the magazine *Flight* reported similar experiments. "Only the framework is dimly visible, and this and the outline of the motor and the pilot and passengers present so small an area for rifle or gun fire, that at the rate of speed at which aeroplanes are flown today, accurate aiming at such surfaces becomes nearly impossible."

CAMOUFLAGE

British troops had adopted khaki uniforms as a result of casualties to long-range rifle fire in the South African wars, so this colour was the logical choice for an aircraft finish. When the state-owned Royal Aircraft Factory (forerunner of the Royal Aerospace Establishment) developed a pigmented compound intended to protect the fabric covering of aircraft from the adverse effects of strong sunlight, the colour chosen for the resulting Protective Covering (PC) No. 10 was of the khaki type. The exact shade used is a matter of some debate, involving fading

Right: RAF Handley Page Hampden in typical early WWII bomber camouflage. The white ring is omitted from the wing roundels.

Below: This replica of the late WWI Sopwith Snipe has only nominal camouflage, heavily compromised by roundels and white lettering.

Below: The winning side can ignore camouflage rules. The bold insignia on this Bf 109E spoil the effect of the splinter green finish.

Bottom: For a brief period prior to the United States' entry into WWII, traditional tail stripes were retained despite the new olive drab.

memories and faded paint samples, and seems to have ranged from a greenish khaki to what can best be described as chocolate brown.

French aircraft started the First World War without camouflage. Early Nieuport fighters carried the company's standard silver-grey finish, for example. A nominally "standard" French camouflage scheme was later adopted, a distinctive finish made up of green and two or even three shades of brown. This was often retained by French built aircraft taken into Royal Flying Corps or US Army service. Describing the Spad XIII C.1 in a 1960s monograph, C.F. Andrews summed up the French attitude to camouflage: "The variations of French camouflage patterns during 1917 and 1918 have been somewhat obscure".

The Germans took a different approach. Initial experiments involved applying two or three shades of colour to the aircraft by

means of paints or distempers but this was soon superseded by a scheme in which camouflage colouring was printed on the fabric used to cover the aircraft. This approach allowed the use of camouflage patterns too complex to be cost-effectively applied by hand. The pattern chosen was a complicated one, a dense network of hexagons in four or five colours, and there is no evidence that this "lozenge fabric" was any more effective than the RFC's single-colour PC No. 10.

NIGHT COLOURS

Bomber units operating by night adopted specialised colour schemes. Black seemed the obvious choice for an aircraft intended to operate under the concealment of darkness, but nobody seems to have realised that to be effective such a finish must be matt so that reflections from searchlight beams be minimised. So disappointing

were the results of tests on black aircraft that few service machines were painted in this manner. The huge Handley Page 0/400 — a twin-engined biplane of 100ft (30.5m) wingspan developed to meet Commodore Murray Sueter's requirement for a "bloody paralyzer of an aeroplane" — was finished overall in PC No. 10 compound.

A better paint finish for night operations emerged in early 1918. Developed by the Experimental Station at Orford Ness, Suffolk, the grey-green varnish known as "Nivo" was optimised for use on moonlit nights and had a surface sheen intended to match that of open water. It was too late for large scale wartime use.

With the arrival of peace, camouflage was soon abandoned by most squadrons in favour of brighter colours. The inter-war years were to prove the zenith in the art of aircraft decoration and nowhere was this more true than in Britain's Royal Air Force (RAF), successor to the Royal Flying Corps. A generation of pilots serving in what they sometimes termed "the best flying club in the world" flew silver-doped biplanes adorned with highly-conspicuous squadron markings. In the United States, the Army Air Corps preferred to leave aircraft in their natural finish but added brightly-coloured tail stripes and squadron insignia.

TONING DOWN

By the mid 1930s, Britain faced the growing air strength of a reborn German *Luftwaffe* which would soon re-equip with modern monoplane fighters and bombers. As the likelihood of war increased, bright colours gave way to drab low-visibility schemes.

Early WWII German Colours

1930s American Bomber Scheme

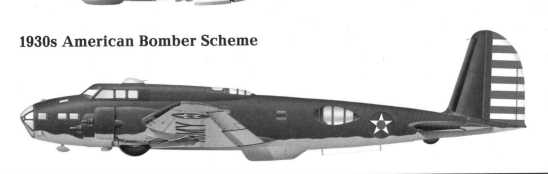

Reconnaissance Spitfires

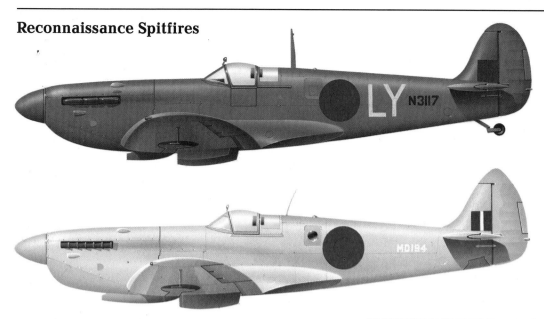

Top: **As WWII progressed, the Royal Air Force developed special low-visibility schemes. This recce Spitfire sports a blue finish.**

Above: **A pink colour was also found to be effective at high altitude, helping to match the aircraft with the sky background.**

black area was extended initially over the entire lower half of the aircraft then to all but the upper surfaces in 1941. From 1943 onwards, Coastal Command aircraft were finished in white, expect for the upper surfaces which were dark slate grey/extra dark sea grey.

NEW COLOURS

The most novel colours were those applied to high-altitude photo-reconnaissance aircraft. These were finished in a single colour overall, varying from several shades of blue to pink. Night fighters of the RAF and USAAF were also painted black overall.

The US Army Air Force entered the war using its olive

Camouflage was re-introduced. The basic RAF scheme involved upper surfaces painted in two colours — dark green and dark earth, applied in large areas with curving outlines.

At the same time, the RAF's night bomber units bade farewell to "Nivo". Tests had shown that the varnish's surface sheen reflected too much light if the aircraft were illuminated by a searchlight. Upper surfaces were finished in dark green and dark earth, while the undersides received a matt black known as RDM2. The low-visibility roundel was retained, however, and also applied to the wings of camouflaged aircraft which operated mainly by day.

Other nations similarly toned down their aircraft. The United States opted for olive drab upper surfaces and sides and grey or azure undersides. The US Navy's pale grey or even bare metal gave way to finishes based on blue or grey. A typical scheme had upper surfaces in non-specular blue/grey and under surfaces in non-specular light grey.

For much of the war, the *Luftwaffe* used a distinctive two-tone "splinter" colour scheme for the upper surfaces of its aircraft. This used two shades of green — dark green *(dunkelgrün)* and a very dark green *(schwarzgrün)* applied in large patches with angular outlines. Undersides were painted in light blue *(hellblau).*

As the war progressed, camouflage finishes on both sides were improved and new schemes devised to suit

various specialised rôles or geographical regions. In the UK, the basic "Temperate Land" dark green/dark earth finish was altered in 1941 with sea grey replacing dark earth. This basic finish was supplemented by a combination of dark slate grey and extra dark sea grey ("Temperate Sea") better suited to the over water rôle, while aircraft assigned to the North African campaign and the Middle East were finished in a combination of dark earth and middle stone ("Middle East"). Undersurfaces were finished in grey or blue, depending on the geographical area in which the aircraft was operating.

RAF night bombers retained their dark green/dark earth upper surfaces but the matt

Above: **Red outer wings and large red stars make nonsense of the white winter camouflage applied to these Soviet MiG-3 fighters.**

Right: **This 1918 photo of the Royal Navy battleship *Revenge* shows the disruptive "dazzle" camouflage scheme.**

drab paint scheme, albeit without the brightly-coloured unit insignia and tail marking of the pre-war era. Tail stripes had been deleted from camouflaged aircraft in 1940. It was to retain this scheme until 1944.

The bright colours applied to some areas of *Luftwaffe* aircraft slowly disappeared and new paint schemes attempted to reduce the visibility of aircraft. For day operations the *hellblau* undersides were frequently retained but often merged gradually into the green upper surfaces.

Bombers assigned to the night-time *blitz* against the UK often carried hastily improvised camouflage. On the undersides, black replaced

German Nightfighter Colours

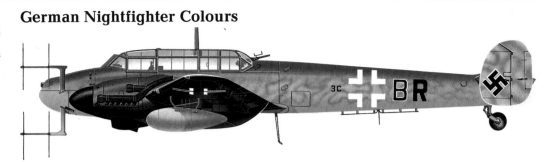

***Above:* Painstaking research resulted in the bizarre mottled blue/grey paint scheme used on WWII *Luftwaffe* night fighters.**

***Below:* As USAAF strength rose and that of the *Luftwaffe* faded, US fighters and bombers flew combat missions in metal finish.**

the traditional *hellblau* and was often carried up over the fuselage sides. In some cases, the fuselage crosses were toned down or even painted out completely.

New camouflage colours were devised to match the aircraft to their theatre of operation. For the North African campaign, a sand brown colour with a distinctly pinkish cast was used on upper surfaces. This worked well over the desert but, on aircraft operating in areas where scrub was common, this basic colour was often overlaid with areas of dark green. These varied in size from large sections of the aircraft down to small patches. Given the right circumstances, the effect of the latter was to make the aircraft near-invisible when seen from above.

WINTER COATS

Winter operations on the Russian front again demanded a custom paint job — in this case all-white upper surfaces intended to reduce visibility over a snow-covered landscape. As the spring saw areas of green breaking through the snow and ice, it is hardly surprising that many white-finished aircraft sported green patches. A non-drying glyptal paint was developed to aid the application and

removal of such temporary colour finishes.

For early night fighter operations, the *Luftwaffe* adopted an all-black finish similar to that used on Allied night fighters. So obvious did the virtues of black colouring seem that throughout the war the RAF and US Army Air Force never fielded a successor. Given the growing magnitude of the RAF's night bomber campaign against German cities, the *Luftwaffe* could not be so complacent and had to launch a research programme to test low-visibility paint schemes for night use.

One suspects that much to their surprise, they found that the ideal finish was very far from the traditional black. Tests showed that the night sky over Western Europe still contained sufficient light to silhouette a black-painted bomber when seen from the side or below. As the tests proceeded, lighter shades replaced black until aircraft were flying in an odd-looking scheme or overall pale blue with mottled grey. This was soon widely applied to nocturnal hunters such as the Ju 88 and He 219.

DAZZLE SCHEMES

At best, these traditional camouflage schemes could only delay visual detection. A more subtle approach involves applying markings intended to deceive the eye into wrongly identifying what it is seeing. The first military application of the concept had been during the First World War when Royal Navy warships sported what became known as "dazzle" camouflage. This took the form of large jagged panels of bold colouring and was intended to break up the vessel's visual outline. It could also help create a false perspective. Painted-on bow waves could complete the illusion, seen though a submarine periscope, giving the attacking U-boat a false idea of the warship's true course and speed. The idea was taken to its extreme in the Second World War when

Japanese aircraft carrier *Zuiho* had its flight deck painted to represent a light cruiser.

With the end of the Second World War, camouflage was once more abandoned, with most air forces flying in natural metal finish. Navies stayed with camouflage for their carrier-based aircraft. Britain's Fleet Air Arm settled for medium blue upper surfaces, while the USN adopted light greys.

POST WAR

In 1955 the USN threw caution to the wind, adopting upper surfaces of non-specular light gull grey and lower surfaces finished in glossy insignia white which formed the background for brightly-coloured unit markings reminiscent of the 1920s and 1930s.

With the escalating Cold War, the UK re-adopted camouflage in 1947. Fighters once more sported grey and green upper surfaces. The new Canberra light bombers started life in 1951 with grey upper surfaces and black under sides. Soviet aircraft operating in North Korea followed suit, the result of Allied air superiority.

For the main part, the USA and Soviet Union stayed with natural metal for both fighters and bombers. This was a particularly good choice for supersonic aircraft since it reduced drag and posed no abrasion problems. In the late 1950s, the RAF fielded the Lightning in natural metal but the long-range V-bombers carried an all-white anti-flash finish designed to minimise

Above: **For almost a decade, USN F-14 Tomcats relied on a basic grey and white finish, and carried brightly-coloured unit insignia.**

Below: **Like Britain and the Soviet Union, France operated its first-generation Mach 2 warplanes in natural metal finish.**

the thermal effects of nuclear explosions. With the US Navy operating aircraft from its carriers in bright paint schemes reminiscent of the inter-war years, the concept of camouflage seemed to be nearly forgotten.

Two factors restored the need for visual stealth in the 1970s. One was the downing of Gary Powers's Lockheed U-2 spyplane over Soviet territory on 1 April 1960 and the other was the outbreak of the Vietnam War.

Early Vietnam War operations were flown by

Above: The Vietnam War saw the US re-adopt camouflage, but the schemes used were little improved over those of two decades earlier.

uncamouflaged aircraft, but the growing threat posed by the North Vietnamese fighter force resulted in the re-introduction of camouflage. Upper surfaces of USAF fighters and fighter-bombers were given a three-tone treatment of Forest Green, Medium Green and Tan Brown, while the undersides were finished in the much lighter Very Pale Grey.

During the war, the USAF gradually reduced the size of the national insignia applied to its aircraft, the final version being only 15in (38cm) high.

Left: As these RAF Harrier GR3s show, the art of applying temporary winter camouflage schemes is still very much alive.

Another change applied to some aircraft later in the war, intended to reduce the demarcation between the insignia and the camouflage scheme, was the deletion of the blue outline from the "wings" of the insignia.

Other nations followed the US lead in readopting camouflage. Several broad patterns emerged, setting the style for many of today's colour schemes.

GREY AND GREEN

Camouflage finishes were not always the result of careful research or study. When the Indian Air Force hastily camouflaged its fighter force during the December 1981 war with Pakistan, considerable "artist's licence" seems to have been granted to those who wielded the paint brushes. Great variations in

Above: The "air superiority blue" finish used on prototype and early-production F-15 Eagles proved unsuccessful.

interpreting the new standard finish were displayed by the men who worked on individual aircraft, or even on different parts of the same aircraft. Some aircraft sported two-tone dark green and grey/green for example, while others displayed a finish reminiscent of the 1940s *Luftwaffe* "mirror" camouflage.

When the F-15 Eagle first entered service in the mid-1970s, it was finished all over in air-superiority blue. National insignia were small in size and had no border. It was short lived. The skies may be blue over Texas but grey is closer to the normal in Western Europe. Pale blue gave way to the grey-based "Compass Ghost" finish. This uses two different tones of grey in an arrangement known as "counter-shading" in which the lighter tone is applied to the parts of the aircraft likely to be in shadow.

The year 1983 saw the introduction of low-visibility markings for the USN. Overall grey replaced the long-established gull grey and insignia white, while national and unit insignia shrank in size and were applied in a medium grey only.

In 1979 the RAF tested an alternative to its then-current dark green and grey with light grey undersides. This took the form of an all-grey scheme retaining standard-sized national and squadron markings. Radomes remained black. This period also saw the introduction of the pale brown "hemp" finish on larger aircraft such as the Nimrod, Victor and C-130 Hercules. The latest RAF scheme sees tactical fighters given an all-green finish. This was first seen on the Harrier GR5 (British version of the AV-8B) and BAe's second Hawk 200 prototype single-seater.

Research into multicoloured camouflage continued. During the JAWS (Joint Attack Weapon System) trials of the A-10 in 1977, the Second World War *Luftwaffe* concept of temporary finishes was taken to its logical extreme. Aircraft were regularly repainted to match the

Right: **This mottled camouflage was just one of those tested on the A-10 during the 1977 Joint Attack Weapon Systems trials.**

current terrain and weather conditions.

In the early 1980s, the USAF recognised that its Vietnam-era scheme was not ideal for NATO low-level operations. As an interim measure, the pale grey of the undersides was replaced by the three colours used on the upper surfaces instead, creating a completely "wrap-around" finish.

Eventually the USAF settled on what it termed "European One" — a "wrap-around" scheme using medium green,

Below: **Dark tones on well-lit areas, plus lighter tones elsewhere are a feature of the USAF's current "Compass Ghost" finish.**

dark green and dark grey. This entered service in 1983, gradually replacing the older colours as paint stocks for the latter were used up. At the same time, Phantoms assigned to air defence were painted in the pale blue and grey finish used for other interceptors.

Experience showed that the USAF fighters spent more time at altitude than at low level. Since the green and grey scheme had been designed for low-level use, it was thus far from the optimum. Two permutations suitable for medium-altitude use were tested in the mid-1980s. "Hill Gray I" combined medium grey and dark grey upper surfaces with light grey undersurfaces, while "Hill Gray II" was a "wrap-around" medium grey and dark grey finish. By 1987, USAF aircraft assigned to air-defence and multiple operations were beginning to appear in "Hill Gray II". Earlier schemes had involved a separate colour for the aircraft undersides but this new finish was applied over the whole airframe.

FERRIS SCHEMES

Given the number of colour schemes which have been tried, abandoned and, in some cases, retried, it is hard to avoid the conclusion that camouflage is at least in part a matter of fashion. As a limited number of colours and ideas are regularly changed, little effort seems to be going into novel alternatives. The "dazzle" experiments of the early 1940s have not really been pursued. One of the few individuals to explore the unusual has been US aviation artist Chris Ferris.

Camouflage has been a subject of great interest to Ferris. One of his paintings of

Above: **The USN went visually stealthy in 1983 with an all-over grey scheme, plus low-visibility national markings.**

Right: **Aviation artist Chris Ferris devised this novel paint scheme for the F-4 Phantom, but it was never adopted for service.**

Below: **F-14s test another Ferris paint scheme. More recent experience suggests that luminescence is more important than colour.**

a pale blue F-15 against a grey sky background was specifically intended to point out the folly of that aircraft's initial finish. Both the F-14 and the F-15 have been tested in a camouflage scheme devised by Ferris with upper surfaces finished in a medium blue whose jagged edges are vaguely reminiscent of "dazzle" camouflage.

Ferris considers that an all-over grey would have been better in Vietnam than the three-tone treatment which was actually used. Canada seems to have taken his point; today's CF-18 Hornet fleet is camouflaged in a dull non-specular grey, while the tone used for the national insignia and other markings offers little contrast. One neat touch of deceptive camouflage is the false canopy painted on the underside, a feature intended to encourage tactical errors by the opposition during air combat manoeuvres.

SMOKE AND LIGHT

Some effort has been expended on active optical camouflage — the use of lights and sensors to adjust the luminance of the airframe to match the background. Work on what were nicknamed "Yehudi lights" started in the USA after the Second World War. Various models of piston-engined aircraft including the B-24 Liberator and SBD Dauntless

naval bomber were fitted with an experimental arrangement of lamps built into the wing leading edge. "Yehudi lights" are also reported to have been tested in the engine inlets of some F-4 Phantoms during the Vietnam War. Studies have shown that at longer ranges it is more important to match the luminance than the actual shade of colour.

Most modern jet engines are virtually smokeless but this was not the case 15 or more years ago. Early-model B-52 bombers and KC-135 tankers tended to lift off from the runway amidst dense clouds of smoke which would send today's environmental pressure groups scampering for their protest banners. Jet fighters of the 1950s and 1960s were almost as bad. This could be a major weakness in air combat. Experience in the skies over North Vietnam soon taught the USAF and USN that engine smoke could effectively pinpoint their fighters in combat.

Smoke emission was to remain a bugbear of the Phantom throughout the Vietnam War. Smoke output peaked sharply when the engine was run at full military power. To avoid this effect during combat operations,

pilots would sometimes run with one engine on afterburner and the other throttled back. This resulted in the same total thrust as two engines at full military power, while the close spacing of the Phantom's engine bays minimised the effects of thrust asymmetry.

TRAILS

Several programmes were to attempt to reduce the smoke output of the Phantom's J79 engines. The USN replaced the J79-GE-8 engine used in its early F-4B and RF-4B Phantoms with the lower-smoke J79-GE-10B. The USAF's solution was developed in the 1970s under a programme known as "Seek Smoke". Originally devised for the Imperial Iranian Air Force, this modification works by slightly increasing the jetpipe temperature. The modification kits were built for Iran but never delivered. Following the Iranian Revolution, they were passed to the USAF and production has continued to meet the needs of the large USAF and Air National Guard F-4 fleet.

Contrails are another unwanted phenomenon which can betray an aircraft's position. More accurately known as "condensation trails", these are formed at altitude by the condensation or even freezing of the water vapour created as a by-product when jet fuel is burned.

During trials in 1962 of the first Teledyne Ryan Firebee reconnaissance drones (a programme which will be described in a later chapter), test interceptions by USAF and USN fighters showed how easily contrails could guide an attacker, so work was started in that year on a "no-con" system. This involved two QC-2C drones equipped with a system which injected a chemical agent into the exhaust. It was not very successful; the best method of eliminating contrails proved to be giving the drone the ceiling performance needed to fly above the altitudes at which contrails form.

AIRFIELDS

Similar measures may be needed in stealth aircraft such as the F-117A and B-2. Details of anti-contrail measures are scarce. Like the 1962 experiments, most are thought to involve the use of chemical additives in the exhaust. These alter the size of the water droplets that form in the atmosphere.

Since a combat aircraft spends most of its time on the ground, where it is vulnerable to sneak attack, low-visibility aircraft ideally require low-visibility airbases. Application of camouflage to the airfield from which military aircraft operate was a Second World War development. One of the first experiments in heavily camouflaging military bases was conducted in the United States. In 1940 Brigadier General Thomas M. Robins, then assistant chief of the US Army's Corps of Engineers, was responsible for building a new airfield at Windsor Locks, Connecticut. To illustrate what camouflage could do, Robins worked with Lt Colonel John Bragdon to build the new base to conform to the principles of visual deception rather than the formal arrangements which the conventional military mind would regard as neat and tidy.

Airfield buildings were positioned among existing buildings present at the site. The latter, like the natural vegetation, were left in place wherever possible. Roads followed normal ground contours rather than taking direct routes, fuel tanks were buried and barracks were built to resemble the tobacco-drying sheds common on

Above: **Smoke pours from the engines of an F-4C. Combat experience in Vietnam showed that smoke trails could betray an aircraft.**

Below: **Good camouflage discipline is essential when deploying V/STOL fighters such as these Royal Air Force GR3s off-base.**

Bottom: **Lockheed's Burbank plant vanishes under protective camouflage in the early 1940s. Fake "trees" help maintain the illusion.**

Below: **Almost two decades after the Six Day War, aircraft could still be found parked in unprotected lines during major exercises.**

nearby farms. To break up the outlines of the field's three runways, their surfaces were painted to match the shape and colour of nearby fields and to create the illusion of being crossed by many paths or roads.

HIDDEN FACTORIES

Other efforts saw the camouflage treatment of US aircraft factories on the west coast. The most famous instance was Lockheed-Vega's Burbank works which was exposed to the full talents of Hollywood's special-effects men. The entire site, including buildings and parking lots, disappeared under a giant camouflage shelter which incorporated fake houses, gardens, roads and even parked cars. To maintain the illusion, the positions of the "cars" were regularly changed, while the "houses" even had fake "washing" hung out to dry once a week. An idea of the cost and complexity of the illusion can be gleaned from the fact that the bill for its removal after the war came to $200,000. A similar scheme saw Boeing's vital Seattle

Right: **The Swedes place great emphasis on off-base operations. Their "Base 90" programme has emphasised the use of roads as airstrips.**

plant disappear under a fake camouflage "town".

Researchers in the USA have investigated methods of applying an up to date version of such techniques to NATO's highly-vulnerable air bases in Western Europe. The aim is to fool not just the human eye but also infra-red and radar sensors. Some of the techniques being studied were revealed in 1985 when the London newspaper *Sunday Times* reported that the US Government was funding secret trials in the UK of methods of reducing the visibility of airfields. The report linked this work with the development of US stealth aircraft. "If all goes according to plan, invisible NATO aircraft could be landing at invisible airfields all over Europe within a decade", wrote defence correspondent James Adams.

Some of the techniques used were a re-run of the 1940s work. Trees were planted to break up the outline of buildings and perimeter fences, while all concrete surfaces, including the runways, were treated with a chemical solution

intended to give them an IR signature similar to that of the surrounding grass.

The article also described how the Royal Air Force base selected for the tests had been equipped with water sprinklers which would be used to douse hangars and other major facilities with water if the airfield was about to be attacked. This would reduce the IR signature of the genuine targets, while heaters inside inflatable decoy hangars would create alternative realistic visual and thermal targets.

As radar-invisible stealth aircraft enter service in growing numbers, air defences will place increasing reliance on alternative sensors. These will include long-range electro-optical television systems mounted on interceptors and SAM fire-control units in addition to the more traditional "Mark 1 eyeball". Far from having been made obsolete, the visual countermeasures described in this chapter are likely to grow in importance as the effectiveness of radar and thermal sensors are degraded.

RADAR AND RADAR CROSS-SECTION

To the latin speaking inhabitants of northwestern France in the Dark Ages, the region was the end of the known world. Looking out over the often angry sea which stretched to the horizon and beyond, they named it *"finis terrae"* — the end of the land. In the centuries which followed, this peninsula thrusting out into the Atlantic Ocean became a navigational landmark for mariners — Cape Finisterre.

A short drive from the cape today will bring you to the site where the 16th Century French castle builder Vauban erected a fort intended to guard this strategic point. In fact, the site is now guarded by barbed wire and is prohibited to tourists; its ramparts are now protected against a threat the like of which its builder could never have dreamed.

The upper part of the stone battlements are now covered with blankets of thick rubber-like material. Known to the electronics industry as Radar Absorbent Material (usually abbreviated to RAM), the coating is designed to absorb radar energy, ensuring that the old fort does not reflect the radar energy radiated by the nearby Mengam electronic-warfare test site run by electronics giant Thomson-CSF.

Inaccessible though Vauban's battlements may be, they are a good starting off point for a study of the most secretive of 20th Century military technologies — "stealth" — the art of making aircraft, missiles and other military systems invisible to radar. Let us return for a moment to the threat against which Vauban's fortress was designed, the traditional sailing ship armed with broadside-firing cannon. As will have been seen by anybody who has watched old movies, the standard naval cannon (or at least the Hollywood version) fired a spherical cannonball about 8 inches (20cm) in diameter.

How big would such a cannonball have looked to a radar at Vauban's fortress, had it been so equipped in Napoleonic times. The most

Above: **Most radars operate at microwave frequencies, and must have a direct line of sight to the target. If over the** horizon, the latter will be masked by terrain, so raising the antenna improves long-range coverage.

obvious answer is of course the area of a circle of 8 inches (20cm) in diameter. To save the reader from reaching for a pocket calculator while muttering the schoolboy formula "Pi times R squared", the area in question is 0.35 square feet ($0.032m^2$).

Substitute a metal plate 7in (18cm) square, and you'd have the same physical cross-section, but the radar cross-section could be anything from less than a tenth of a square metre to several hundred square metres, depending on the frequency of the radar. Welcome to the strange world of stealth, a universe where nothing is

quite what it seems even before the electronic wizards have begun practising their super-secret electronic trickery.

RADAR WAVES

The key to understanding stealth is to understand how radar works and in particular how radar signals are reflected from aircraft structures. The following "crash course" on these subjects will strike a radar or stealth engineer as grossly oversimplified but it will attempt to cover in a single chapter subjects to which a stealth technology textbook

would devote 400 pages, while at the same time steering clear of the sort of mathematics and numerical analysis which would satisfy only the expert.

A radar wave is a form of electromagnetic radiation, as are the lower frequencies used for radio and TV and the higher frequencies such as infra-red energy and visible light. The basic theory of such waves was first described in the 19th Century by Clerk Maxwell who predicted their properties long before the technology needed to prove him right became available. The early pioneers of radio were starting from a blank sheet of paper, they were trying to find a method of creating and detecting waves whose existence had been foreseen by Maxwell.

An electromagnetic wave consists of two components — an electric field and a magnetic field — positioned at right angles to one another and whose values rapidly fluctuate in strength, rising to a peak, falling away to zero, then rising to a peak in the opposite direction before falling back towards zero. The entire process then repeats over and over again. The whole electromagnetic wave travels (engineers would say "propagates") in a direction at right angles to the electric and magnetic fields. Think of the latter as the vanes on a dart or arrow; the direction of propagation will then be along the length of the shaft.

FREQUENCY

In any book on radio or radar, let alone stealth technology, the terms "frequency" and "wavelength" are unavoidable. Both describe methods of measuring the rate of this cyclic variation. "Frequency" is a measurement of the number of times this cycle occurs in every second. Until the 1960s, it was expressed in cycles, kilocycles (thousand of cycles), megacycles (millions of cycles) or even gigacycles (thousands of millions of cycles) per second. The self-explanatory term "cycles per second" was replaced by the totally artificial term "Hertz" during the 1960s (after the German physicist Heinrich Hertz, 1857-94) in the interests of international standardisation, so in this book we refer to megahertz (MHz) and gigahertz (GHz).

"Wavelength" is an older concept. The wave propagates at 90 degrees to its electric and magnetic fields. The wavelength is the distance between two successive peaks in either of these fields. It's a useful measurement, being directly related to the physical size of components such as antenna elements — which is why it was widely used in the early days of radio. The two are directly inter-related. Increase the frequency and the wavelength is reduced. Decrease the frequency and the wavelength increases.

RADAR BEAMS

As the reader is probably aware, radar sets illuminate their target with a beam of high-frequency radar energy and detect the resulting reflections. A good analogy is the Second World War searchlight. Lost in the night sky, a bomber was virtually invisible from the ground. Once caught in the beam of a searchlight, it became visible and could be engaged by anti-aircraft gunfire.

Only two countermeasures were available to aid the aircraft, one passive and the other active. For most of the war, all air arms engaging in

Right: **Above the main antenna of this Thomson-CSF TRS-22XX radar is an upper unit for the interrogation of aircraft-mounted civil or IFF transponder systems.**

Below: **As frequency rises, wavelength falls, as do the dimensions of antenna feeds and waveguides.**

Wavelengths

Frequency	Wavelength
100kHZ	3,000m
1MHz	300m
10MHz	30m
100MHz	3m
1GHz	20cm
10GHz	3cm
100GHz	3mm
velocity of light = 300×10^6 m/s approx	

Right: **The wavelength of a signal is the distance between successive peaks. The higher the frequency, the shorter the wavelength.**

Below: **An electromagnetic wave has two components at right angles — an electric field (shown in blue), and a magnetic field (shown in red).**

Waveforms

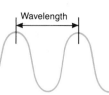

Wavelength

Magnetic and Electric Components of a Wave

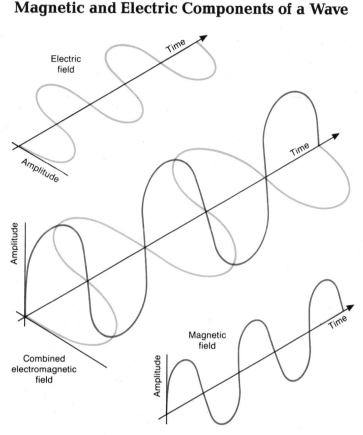

Electric field
Time
Amplitude

Amplitude
Time

Combined electromagnetic field

Magnetic field
Time
Amplitude

night bombing painted the underside of their aircraft black, so as to minimise the amount of light reflected should they be caught momentarily in a searchlight beam. If caught and followed by the beam, the aircraft's only hope was to manoeuvre violently in the hope of slipping out of the narrow beam of light. If successful, once outside of the beam it was once more cloaked in darkness.

Both measures were partially countered by having several searchlights concentrate their beams onto any target detected by one of their number. Aircrew dreaded being "coned" by a group of searchlights. The cluster of beams interesecting on the coned aircraft illuminated a large volume of sky in the aircraft's immediate vicinity, while the additional light from every beam joining the cone increased the light level illuminating the aircraft, and thus the amount reflected back to the ground for the AA gunners to see.

REFLECTIONS

When British scientists started work on radar in 1935, they realised the importance of target reflectivity. If the new method of aircraft detection (then known as Radio Location) was to work effectively, it was essential that the reflection be as strong as possible. The illuminating signal would have to be as powerful as possible, given the state of radar technology as it existed then, while the frequency used would have to be one which the aircraft would reflect strongly.

Use of the word "reflect" simplifies a more complex process. The radar energy does not just bounce the way a squash ball does off the court wall. When an electromagnetic wave meets an electrical conductor, such as a wire, it creates within that conductor electrical and magnetic currents at the same frequency. That is how a radio antenna works — the electromagnetic wave from the distant transmitter induces a tiny current within the antenna which the radio receiver then amplifies. At the transmitter, the process works in reverse. The transmitter feeds an electrical current of the appropriate frequency into the antenna. This current creates an electromagnetic wave which then radiates outwards from the antenna. The process

Reflection of Radar Energy

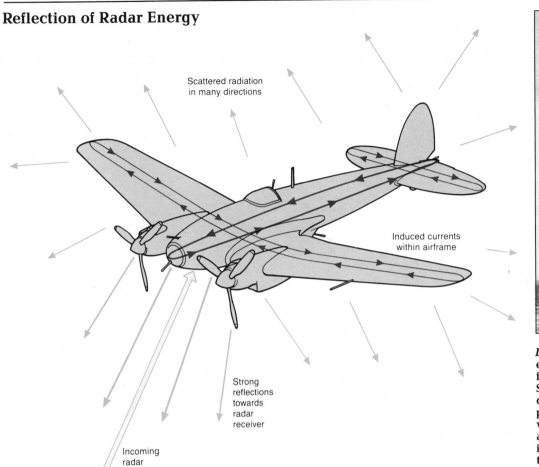

Scattered radiation
in many directions

Induced currents
within airframe

Strong
reflections
towards
radar
receiver

Incoming
radar
signal

Left: **The scientists and engineers who developed the first radars just before the Second World War found it difficult if not impossible to predict how a radar wave would reflect from an aircraft. It seemed to scatter in all directions. No simple theory could explain what was happening.**

works both ways — a current in a conductor can create an electromagnetic wave, and an electromagnetic wave can create a current in a conductor.

This is the central principle of the phenomenon which causes an aircraft or any other target to reflect radio energy. When the radar wave hits the target, it induces electric and magnetic currents within that object. By the act of flowing, these currents in turn cause an electromagnetic wave to be created. It is this latter wave which the radar sees as a reflected echo.

From work on antenna (aerial) design, the engineers who developed Britain's first radars already knew that a wire whose length corresponded to half the wavelength of the radio signal would re-radiate strongly. Assuming that the wing of a metal aircraft would behave in the same way as a simple wire, this suggested that the optimum frequency would be that which had a wavelength twice the length of the wing of a typical bomber of the period.

At that time the latest generation of German bombers was beginning flight tests and the equivalent British types were about to

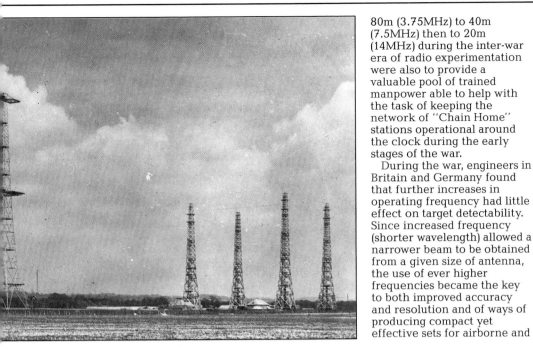

80m (3.75MHz) to 40m (7.5MHz) then to 20m (14MHz) during the inter-war era of radio experimentation were also to provide a valuable pool of trained manpower able to help with the task of keeping the network of "Chain Home" stations operational around the clock during the early stages of the war.

During the war, engineers in Britain and Germany found that further increases in operating frequency had little effect on target detectability. Since increased frequency (shorter wavelength) allowed a narrower beam to be obtained from a given size of antenna, the use of ever higher frequencies became the key to both improved accuracy and resolution and of ways of producing compact yet effective sets for airborne and

other applications in which space and weight were at a premium.

Soon after the war, security restrictions on the massive amount of research and development which had been invested in radar technology were relaxed, allowing the publication of several textbooks, culminating in the classic *Radiation Laboratory* series, a collection of definitive textbooks prepared by the Radiation Laboratory of the Massachusetts Institute of Technology to record the contemporary state of the art.

CROSS-SECTION

Reading these and other early radar textbooks books shows how far the engineers of the early 1940s had progressed in studying the complex processes by which radar energy is reflected by an aircraft. "It is essential to realise that the cross-section of a given target will depend not only on the wavelength, but also upon the angle from which the target is viewed by the radar", wrote E.M. Purcell in the 1947 *Radiation Laboratory* volume on radar systems engineering. "The fluctuation of [radar cross-section] with 'target aspect' as it is called, is due to the interference of reflected waves from different parts of the target ... . Only for certain special cases can [radar cross-section] be calculated rigorously; for most targets [it] has to be inferred from the radar data."

To define the radar cross-section of a target, the radar engineer calculates the size of a sphere which would reflect the same amount of radar energy as the aircraft he has measured. The RCS in square metres is then the area of a circle of the same diameter as this imaginary sphere.

A Taylorcraft light aircraft had an RCS of 170sq ft (16m²), Purcell and collaborator A.J.F. Siegert reported, while a B-17 bomber had an RCS of 800sq ft (74m²). (Since those early days, RCS has by convention been measured in metric terms, so the corresponding imperial/US units will no longer be given in the text which follows.)

"Only a rough estimate of the cross-section of such targets as aircraft or ships can be obtained by calculation", they warned. "Even if one could carry through the calculation for the actual target (usually one has to be content with considering a simplified model) the

Above: **The first British "Chain Home" early-warning radar stations were based on short-wave and television broadcasting technology.**

Below left: **On 26th February 1935, Sir Robert Watson-Watt used this primitive receiver to make the first detection of an aircraft target.**

fly; so a good idea of the dimensions of wingspans of likely targets was available.

Although a follow-on generation of heavier bombers with wingspans of around 100ft (30m) or more could already be envisaged, the radar engineers decided to regard 80ft (25m) as a good compromise value, fixing the frequency of their equipment at 6MHz, where the wavelength would be 50m.

CHAIN HOME

Unfortunately, these frequencies proved unreliable due to ionospheric refraction. Wavelengths/frequencies of 26m/11.5MHz and eventually 13m/23MHz were both tried, before the latter was found satisfactory and was adopted as the basis for the pioneering "Chain Home" radar network.

The use of 23MHz for "Chain Home" had been unduly conservative from a theoretical viewpoint. From the practical point of view, it was nearly ideal, since the power transmitters and sensitive receivers required could be developed using the experience gained by short-wave radio equipment. The amateur radio enthusiasts who had steadily reduced operating wavelengths (increased frequencies) from

Below: **Early research into radar reflectivity showed that the apparent echoing area — known as the radar cross section (RCS) and** calculated as an imaginary sphere — varied widely with changing aspect angle. A small change in angle could effect the observed RCS.

Variation in RCS with Angle

Viewing angle   Possible RCS

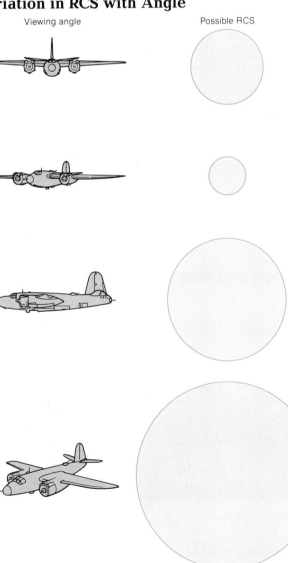

comparison of calculated and observed cross-section would be extremely difficult because of the strong dependence of the cross-section on aspect.''

RCS VARIATIONS

To illustrate this, they reported on tests made using a B-26 bomber. In many cases, the level of radar energy reflected could vary by as much as 15dB when the viewing angle was changed by only a third of a degree.

The decibel (dB) is a unit of measurement much used in electronics. It is often found in technical articles on anything from hi-fi to electronic warfare. The key to understanding it is to realise that it describes a ratio between two values and that it is calculated logarithmically and not arithmetically. An increase of 3dB amounts to an arithmetic doubling, for example, while an increase of 10dB represents a tenfold increase.

What Purcell and Siegert were saying in ''scientific shorthand'' was that a third of a degree change in viewing angle could affect the measured RCS of the B-26 buy a factor of up to 32. Post-war research has shown that in practice the RCS of real-world targets can fluctuate by up to 80dB (up to a million).

One factor influencing RCS was propeller position, they reported, while the effect of propeller rotation both increased and modulated the radar return. Tests had shown that shutting down the starboard engine of the test B-26 reduced RCS in the sector from 2 to 5 o'clock by a massive amount. Much research in the 1950s and 1960s was devoted to studying the exact mechanisms by which electromagnetic beams were reflected by objects of various shapes and sizes.

Much of the results remain classified to this day but the little information which has leaked suggests that, although the individual phenomena which caused reflection from different types of basic shape were becoming better understood, the problem of calculating and predicting RCS remained close to unsolvable.

Two factors resulted in the eventual breakthrough. One was the Vietnam War, where US military aircraft and their crews had been exposed to radar-directed air-defences.

The other was the development of the supercomputer. These giant and incredibly fast machines

Variation in RCS with Propeller Position

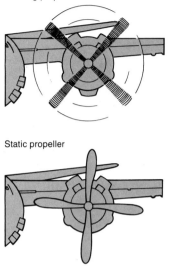

Rotating propeller

Widely varing RCS

Static propeller

Static RCS
(at one angle and frequency)

Above: **Wartime researchers trying to understand RCS even found that stopping and starting an engine and its associated propeller could markedly affect the radar cross section of a bomber.**

Right: **In the 1930s, UK radar designers tried to match wavelength with the wingspan of typical bombers.**

Typical Wingspans of 1930s Bombers

Aircraft	First flight	Wingspan
Dornier Do 17	1934	59ft (18m)
Heinkel He111	1935	74ft (22.4m)
Armstrong Whitworth Whitley	1936	84ft (25.6m)
Bristol Blenheim	1936	56ft (17.1m)

Above: **The development of radar-guided AA weapons such as the SA-2 Guideline created new interest in methods of reducing RCS.**

had been developed for two basic applications — codebreaking and computer simulation of the intricate processes and reactions at the heart of a nuclear or thermonuclear explosion. As soon as enough of these costly machines had been built to satisfy at least partially the needs of the codebreakers and nuclear weapon designers, radar engineers applied their massive capability to those thorny problems of RCS prediction.

To understand the different ways in which an aircraft or missile reflects radar energy, a good starting point is the principle stated earlier in this chapter. ''When the radar wave hits the target, it induces electric and magnetic currents within that object. By the act of flowing, these

Right: **A radar wave which strikes a flat metal plate such as a fin, reflects in much the same way as a light beam reflects from a mirror. Like a**

transmitted beam, this reflected energy forms a main beam, flanked by several smaller beams known as sidelobes.

currents in turn cause an electromagnetic wave to be created. It is this latter wave which the radar sees as a reflected echo."

This is what radar and stealth engineers call the scattering process, the newly created wave being known as the "scattered field". Stealth technology is the art of controlling that scattering so as to minimise the amount of energy returned to the radar.

The wavelength of a radar wave can have three possible relationships with the dimensions of the target — it can be much bigger, roughly the same size or much smaller. In each case, a different type of scattering will take place.

SCATTERING

If the wavelength is much larger than the dimensions of the target, all parts of the target are illuminated by the same part of the wave and the result is what is known as Rayleigh scattering. Under such conditions, only gross size and shape of the target are important and RCS is roughly proportionate to target size. Since a frequency of around 100MHz is the lowest normally used for radar, the longest military significant wavelength which a target will receive is thus around 3m. In most cases, this will be smaller than the target, so Rayleigh scattering is of little importance, although it could be significant when predicting the RCS of small details such as gun muzzles, vents, grilles and protrusions.

In cases where the wavelength is close to the target dimensions, resonant scattering is observed. This, it

Reflection

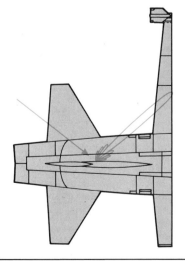

Diffraction

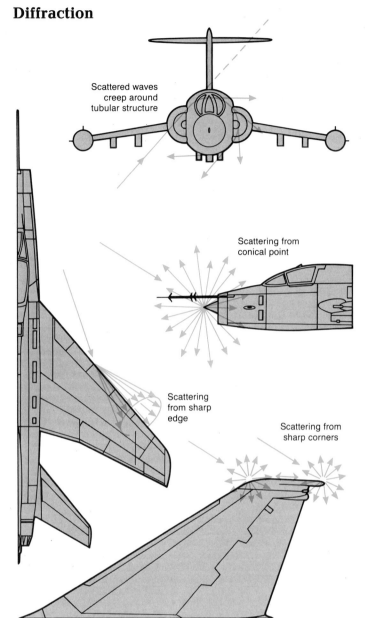

Scattered waves creep around tubular structure

Scattering from conical point

Scattering from sharp edge

Scattering from sharp corners

Above: **Radar waves grazing a circular structure can creep around its circumference, while waves striking a** conical point, a sharp edge such as a leading edge, or a corner are scattered by a process known as diffraction.

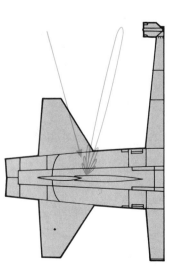

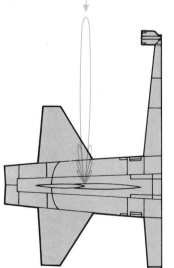

may be remembered, is what the British tried to achieve with the original choice of "Chain Home" operating frequency. Target behaviour under such resonant and near-resonant cases (known as the Mie region) is the most difficult to predict. The phase of the incident wave changes several times along the length of the target. Overall geometry of the target is important, since every part of the target affects every other part. Resonance may occur between specular reflected waves and creeping waves. The resulting Mie-region RCS is very dependent on aspect angle and can fluctuate massively.

When the wavelength is very much smaller than the target, interactions between the latter's different parts are minimal and the target can be treated as a collection of independent scattering centres. The incoming wave acts in a manner similar to light and the laws of optics, so stealth engineers use geometric optics (GO) to help them predict the RCS of a target.

The smallest target for most radars will be a jet fighter or a cruise missile. A light fighter is normally about 45ft (14m) in length, while a modern cruise missile is often around 21ft (6.5m) in length. The radar signals directed against them will have wavelengths of between 0.75in and 10ft (2cm and 3m). In most cases, the target will be 10 or more wavelengths long, making high-frequency scattering the most important component of the overall RCS.

INTERACTIONS

With high-frequency scattering, every part of the target scatters energy independently of the rest of the structure. This in theory would make it relatively easy to estimate the effect of each and, by integration, the scattered field and thus the RCS of the entire target. In practice, the interaction between all the individual scatterers which make up a complex shape such as an aircraft is so complex as to require the use of powerful computers.

Just as a curved surface on an aircraft will exhibit a reflection in sunlight, that surface will have a similar radar reflection. This is termed specular reflection and is a strong component of RCS. When a radar wave is reflected from a flat surface — another form of specular reflection — it behaves rather like a beam of light striking a mirror, or a squash ball bouncing off the walls of the squash court. The angle of incidence equals the angle of reflection. A simple example of this is when a child "skips" a stone across the surface of a pond. The stone descends towards the water at a shallow grazing angle of 10 or 15 degrees (the angle of incidence) then after striking the water begins to rise at the same 10 to 15 degree angle (the angle of reflection).

The reflected energy does not confine itself to a single beam or lobe. Diffraction results in the formation of sidelobes which send smaller amounts of energy off in a number of directions slightly displaced from the axis of the main lobe.

DIFFRACTION

This simple theory breaks down completely when dealing with such discontinuities as edges, tips and corners or changes in slope or curvature. Here the re-radiated field is the result of a process known as diffraction. It depends on the shape of the feature in question, the direction from which it is being illuminated, the position of the observer and the polarisation of the radar wave. To calculate the result, engineers rely on the geometric theory of diffraction (GTD).

Below: **Aircraft fuselages, external stores and even the metal skin of the wing or fins can all provide a habitat for travelling waves.**

Typical Radar Wavelengths

Frequency	Application	Wavelength
150MHz	Long-range surveillance	6.5ft (2m)
2GHz	Surveillance	6in (15cm)
10GHz	Tracking	1.2in (3cm)

Surface waves of electric and magnetic current flowing along the structure of an aircraft or missile in response to the arrival of radar energy pose further problems for the stealth designer. These surface waves come in several forms. Rounded targets such as cylinders or spheres suffer from creeping waves. As its name suggests, the creeping wave flows around the skin of a target. Starting from the point where the radar wave just grazes the edge of the curved surface (known as the "shadow boundary"), the currents creep round onto the

Travelling Waves

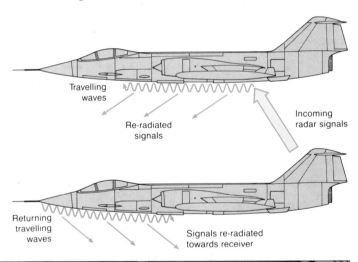

Travelling waves

Re-radiated signals

Incoming radar signals

Returning travelling waves

Signals re-radiated towards receiver

Above: **A combat aircraft is likely to be illuminated by many different radars, and a wide range of wavelengths.**

Right: **Radar waves grazing a long metallic structure such as this MiG-21 fuselage and its external tanks induce travelling waves in the skin.**

Below: **Travelling waves re-radiate radar energy away from the radar. On reaching a discontinuity or the end of the structure, they are reflected, and now add this energy to the total RCS observed by the receiver.**

side not illuminated by the radar, then back towards the opposite edge. Once at the opposite edge, they then re-radiate energy back towards the radar. If the object around which they are creeping is more than 10 or 15 wavelengths in diameter, they are of little importance.

TRAVELLING WAVES

Much more troublesome are what are known as travelling waves which affect long slim objects such as missile airframes, fuel tanks and underwing stores, or even the entire fuselage of a slender aircraft such as the F-104 or TR-1. Radar energy striking such a target at low angles of incidence, that is to say close to head on, create what engineers call a surface travelling wave. This is an electric and magnetic current which heads down the length of the target object.

As it does so, it will emit its own electromagnetic field, a signal which heads in the same general direction as the illuminating radar signal. The principle of "angle of incidence equals the angle of reflection" still applies. Since this reflected signal is directed away from the illuminating radar, it adds nothing to the target RCS and is of no immediate concern to the stealth designer.

The problem comes when the travelling wave reaches the far end of the object along which it is flowing. Having nowhere to go, it is reflected back up along the body, still emitting its own

electromagnetic field. Unfortunately, this time the reflected energy is directed back towards the illuminating radar, adding to the target's overall RCS.

In the case of an aircraft fuselage illuminated from the forward sector, similar surface waves will be set up. As these travel backwards along the fuselage, they may meet discontinuities such as seams, gaps, changes in surface material or sudden changes in shape.

In terms of traditional aircraft engineering, such features are common and pose no problems. For example, mid-1960s vintage MiG-21s were notorious for large gaps between individual fuselage panels. On a stealth aircraft, such surface discontinuities must be eliminated. If the surface wave cannot continue along its route, it will reflect backwards along the fuselage as did the travelling wave, adding its own unwanted contribution to aircraft RCS. All discontinuities such as edges, gaps and corners are good scatterers of radar energy.

When an aircraft is illuminated from the rear sector, fuselage travelling waves can become a major problem. Moving forward along the fuselage, they eventually arrive at the nose, where they are reflected back down the fuselage, adding to the rearward RCS.

As we have already seen, the largest RCS component is specular reflection. On a typical aircraft, creeping and

travelling waves will account for around 1m^2 of the total. As RCS-reduction measures reduce specular reflection, these lesser sources become more important, so must be treated.

DIHEDRALS

A major headache for the stealth designer is the dihedral, a radar-reflective area created whenever two metallic surfaces are positioned at 90 degrees to

one another. An incoming radar signal entering the right angle formed by two such surfaces will carry out a "double-bounce" manoeuvre, the geometry of which ensures that the signal will be returned in exactly the same direction as the incoming. To see a simple analogy, drive a ball towards the corner of a pool table. It will bounce off one edge of the table, then off the adjacent edge, and emerge heading back towards the player.

To continue the analogy, if you sawed the corner off the pool table leaving a 12in (30cm) wide gap in place of the pocket, then drove the ball back towards the corner (but not directly into the gap) it would still carry out a similar bounce manoeuvre from the sides and re-emerge. This illustrates the fact that the two surfaces of a corner reflector need not meet; they only need be at 90 degrees with respect to one another.

CORNERS

Armed with this knowledge, the reader should have no difficulty is identifying radar-reflective corner reflectors on a modern warplane. Horizontal stabilisers are often at right angles to the vertical fin, underwing pylons are at right angles to the wing lower surface, cruciform wings and fins of missiles and bombs fit the bill nicely, while common features such as wing fences and stiffening ribs add their share of 90 degree corners.

Let three surfaces meet at 90 degrees and an even more dangerous triple-bounce manoeuvre is possible, returning a strong radar signal over a wide range of aspect angles. This junction of three surfaces is called a

Typical Dihedral Reflector

Incoming radar signal

Reflection directly back towards radar receiver

"Double bounce"

Left: **Two surfaces at 90 degrees can turn a radar signal through 180 degrees, providing a strong echo. Three surfaces meeting at right angles are even more effective at enhancing the reflection.**

corner reflector. In some non-aerospace applications corner reflectors are deliberately created. For example metal corner reflectors a few feet (less than a metre) in size are often fitted to the masts of sailing boats to help coastguard radar detect them.

No aircraft has such an external feature but canopies are transparent to radar waves and cockpits contain many box-like objects and 90 degree corners. Accidental creation of a corner reflector is only too easy.

To see a corner reflector in action, watch when driving at night for the reflective "cats eyes" often used as road markers. These are designed to catch the light from the car's headlamps, returning it directly to the driver. The more powerful the headlamps, the brighter the "cat's eyes" will shine. That is how a corner reflector behaves when seen by a radar.

CAVITIES

The corner reflector is just one of the features which the stealth designer terms a "re-entrant structure" — an object which traps and strongly reflects radar energy. Substitute the word "cavity" for "re-entrant structure", pick up a photo of your favourite warplane and you'll begin to take a jaundiced view of intakes, jet pipes, suck-in doors, air scoops and other vents, gun muzzles and other common features. All are prominent radar targets.

Bear in mind the fact that radomes, canopies and other transparencies are also radar-transparent and a new set of re-entrant structures can be found. The cockpit and any electro-optical (EO) fairings are prime candidates, while

Above: **Hidden from sight under nose radomes, radar antennas are designed to handle 'friendly' signals, but also add to RCS.**

Below: **Count the 90 degree angles on this Tornado interceptor and its weapons — each will add its share to the total radar signature.**

In theory at least, all you have to do is add up the RCS from a dozen or so major shapes, plus dozens if not hundreds of smaller ones to get the RCS of the complete aircraft. In practice, all these individual returns interfere with one another.

Remember how the components of an electromagnetic wave continually swing from positive to negative and back again? If all the hundreds of individual reflected signals were all in step with one another (engineers would say "in phase" with one another), such simple addition would work. Unfortunately for the stealth engineer they are not; when one is peaking in the positive direction, others are approaching their peak or dying away to zero, while yet more are doing the same thing in the negative direction. In engineering parlance, they are "out of phase" with one another. To complicate matters further, the polarisation of each individual return may be changed by the reflection process, while the reflectivity of each individual scatterer will vary with frequency, each member of the hierarchy of basic shapes is behaving in a different frequency-related manner.

The summation of all the individual reflections from a complex target is made even more chaotic by the effect of changes in viewing angle. Two individual reflections which

are in phase to the observer (and thus boosting each other's strength) will be out of phase if the observer moves, while further movement will bring them back in phase, then out of phase again, and so on. Signals which are out of phase with each other will interfere with one another. If they are of opposite phase, one will tend to cancel out the other — a process known as destructive interference. Take into account the fact that literally hundreds of signals are involved, then it is little wonder that the total fluctuates violently.

Such then are the complex and intractable rules of radar reflection. Given their compexity, it is little wonder that as late as 1981, in *IEEE Transactions on Antennas and Propagation*, Edward M. Kennaugh was to describe how "As measurement capabilities improved, investigation of the variation of RCS with these parameters [target aspect, radar frequency and wave polarisation] provided the radar analyst with a plethora of data, but few insights into this relation." Despite his pessimism, enough was understood to allow engineers to devise methods of reducing RCS, creating design rules which would make stealth aircraft possible. The next chapter examines some of the materials, design concepts and construction methods used in the creation of stealth aircraft, RPVs and missiles.

behind the radome lurks an ideal reflector in the shape of the radar antenna, particularly if the latter is of the traditional paraboloid "dish" type. On some aircraft, the radar antenna is deliberately slewed to an extreme angle when the radar is not being used, so as to reduce its contribution to the head-on RCS.

Above: **This Grumman A-6 Intruder has a typical collection of exposed cavities, inlets, vents and grilles — all highly reflective.**

Below: **One of the biggest radar-reflective cavities on any aircraft is the cockpit and its cluttered consoles. This is a MiG-29 Fulcrum.**

RCS CALCULATIONS

In the Middle Ages, students of the occult drew up long lists of demons and spirits, solemnly documenting their relative positions and powers in a sort of satanic hierarchy.

Stealth engineers have their own version of the "Hierarchy of Hell", with the three-surface corner reflector cast in the rôle of the major villain. Such lists detail all the common geometric shapes in order of descending radar reflectivity. Directly beneath the three-surface corner reflector is its two-surface cousin, followed by the flat plate, cylinder, sphere, straight edge, curved edge, cone, followed by various types of curvature. It may seem at first sight about as pointless as the listing drawn up by their mediaeval predecessors, but it is in fact a list of many of the basic shapes into which a larger and more complex target may be broken down.

DESIGNING A STEALTH AIRCRAFT

Creation of a stealth aircraft or missile requires that the visual, radar, thermal and acoustic signatures be reduced. There are other more exotic signatures, some of which have potential as the basis for anti-stealth sensors, but these are the most important.

To achieve a militarily significant reduction in RCS, four techniques may be used: (1) avoid design features which will create strong reflections in the direction of the radar; (2) use non-metallic materials; (3) absorb rather than reflect the incoming radar energy; (4) mask or cancel out any remaining reflections.

No single approach will provide enough RCS reduction. The first, second and third of these techniques are already used in different degrees by existing stealth aircraft and missiles; the fourth could be in use already and will certainly come to play a more significant rôle in future aircraft designs.

Earlier we used the analogy of comparing a radar system with a searchlight. In one respect, this analogy was badly flawed — the searchlight illuminated its victim so that other air-defence weapons could detect the reflected light. Once the powerful beam had lit the target aircraft, the reflected light could be seen by anti-aircraft gunners on the ground and even by the crews of any friendly nightfighters operating within visual range.

REFLECTIONS

In the case of almost all present-day radars, the sensor which is looking for the reflected echo uses the same antenna as was used to send out the illuminating pulse. Only the reflected energy which returns directly to the radar is usable. Energy which redirected in other directions will do nothing to betray the target.

Careful control of aircraft shape plays a vital part in reducing RCS at microwave frequencies by directing the scattered signal away from the radar which is trying to

receive it. On early stealth aircraft, including the Lockheed F-117A, it was the main RCS-reduction measure.

To avoid directing reflected energy back to the hostile radar, the stealth designer tries to observe a series of rules. One of the most important is to avoid the use of large flat vertical surfaces. No attempt was made when designing the B-52 to keep RCS to a minimum, so that aircraft's slab sides and relatively straight lines make it a prominent radar target. If vertical fins or fuselage sides must be used, these should be canted inward. Canted fuselage sides may be seen on the Boeing AGM-86B ALCM and on Teledyne's Model 324 and 350 RPVs, while the same company's AQM-91A Compass Arrow RPV shows an example of inward-canted tail surfaces. Many early-1980s artists' impressions of stealth fighters also incorporated inward-tilted vertical fins.

Two approaches may be taken to eliminate reflections from the fuselage. The most obvious is to curve the

Left: The use of two-dimensional afterburner nozzles (as seen here on a Lockheed ATF artwork) may help reduce IR signature.

fuselage surfaces, preferably in two dimensions — a technique used on the SR-71 and B-1 bomber. For best results, this curvature should be concave (inward); convex (outward) curvature would be reflective. The designer should avoid discontinuities such as corners and abrupt changes of shape/profile, blending and smoothing all wing/fin and surface junctions. This removes geometric discontinuities which would result in wave scattering.

FLAT CANOPY

There remain limits to what can be done with curvature, especially given the fact that most practical designs demand convex curves. An early morning walk along a fighter flight-line on a sunny day will show just how effectively curved surfaces such as fuselage sides and cockpit canopies can reflect the sunlight over a range of aspect angles. Radar waves would also reflect in a similar manner.

The first aircraft to try to eliminate this problem in optical terms was the US Army's Bell AH-1S Cobra. On the earlier AH-1G and AH-1J, the canopy used conventional rounded transparencies but

Left: **Features of the B-52 which create high RCS include the slab-sided fuselage, and the engine pods and pylons.**

Above: **Light glints from the curved fuselage of a Mirage 2000. Radar energy can be reflected in the same manner, increasing RCS.**

Above: The angular "flat-plate" canopy on this AH-1S uses faceting to reduce optical glint. A similar technique can also be employed to reduce RCS.

Below: The wing leading edge of an aircraft can be a strong radar reflector but increased sweep angles will direct radar reflections away from the critical head-on sector. Use of a changing sweep angle, such as on the crescent wing of the Handley Page Victor, can scatter the reflected energy over a wide range of angles.

the version adopted for the -1S was of flat-panel design, consisting of seven surfaces. Each individual section reflected sunlight in one direction only, making the overall design less likely to betray the aircraft's position.

The wing leading edge can be a strong reflector in the forward sector. Given that the reflected energy from an incoming head-on radar signal will leave a wing leading edge at an angle equal to twice that of the leading-edge sweep angle at the point of "impact", increasing the sweep angle will increase the amount by

which the reflected energy is shifted away from the forward sector, thus reducing the chances that it will be detected by the receiver of the head-on radar. At high angles of sweep, most of the reflected energy is deflected at angles away from the critical forward sector.

FACETING

On most aircraft, the leading and trailing edges are straight or near-straight, so the reflected energy will be concentrated over a narrow range of angles. By curving

the leading edge, or using compound sweep, the designer can arrange that the reflected energy is not all returned in the same direction but is weakened by being spread over a range of harmless directions.

Since wing and horizontal leading/trailing edges are good radar reflectors, the angles used on the wing and stabiliser leading and trailing edges must either be kept common (scattering the radar energy in a few carefully-chosen directions) or made as different as possible (so as to "dump" the reflected energy in several pre-planned sectors).

As wing sweep is increased, the delta wing becomes more attractive but, by its long chord, will provide an opportunity for travelling waves to be set up. These can in turn be minimised by rounding the wingtips, minimising the reflective discontinuity which the travelling waves will meet when they reach the trailing edge of the wing.

These are the basic rules which defined the configuration of the first stealth aircraft. Both the Lockheed (XST/F-117A) and Northop (B-2) teams came up with the same solution in terms of wing planform —

The RCS Effects of Wing Sweep Angle

Moderately swept

Highly swept

Delta

Crescent

straight leading edges which would re-direct the radar energy well away from the frontal sector, plus a moderate sweep angle which would keep the chord short enough to avoid the worst effects of surface travelling waves. Lockheed opted for a faceted fuselage — probably the only practical configuration given mid-1970s technology — and eliminated horizontal and vertical tail surfaces by adopting a "V" configuration. Faceting would have imposed a significant range penalty on a long-range bomber, so Northrop backed a combination of curvature and advanced RAM for its flying wing design and relied on a sophisticated flight control system which would allow the elimination of all vertical surfaces.

Faceting on the F-117A

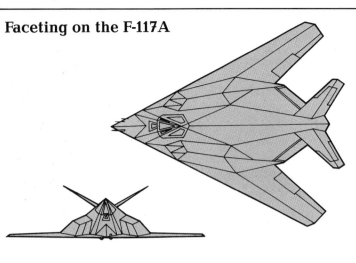

CAVITIES

Creation of a practical stealth aircraft or missile requires meticulous attention to detail if RCS is to be minimised. Cavities such as air intakes, known to stealth engineers as "re-entrant structures", have a high RCS. Prediction of the RCS of a cavity is difficult and depends on what is in the cavity. As a first order approximation, the stealth engineer can assume that the RCS will be similar to that of a flat plate of equivalent size.

On a high-flying reconnaissance aircraft or maritime patrol aircraft, the threat may be primarily from below, allowing high-RCS features such as inlets and exhausts to be moved onto upper surfaces where they will be screened from below by the wing. On a low-level strike aircraft, the main threat may well prove to be look-down/shoot-down radars, forcing such reflective features onto the aircraft's underside.

In cases such as an air-superiority fighter where attack could come from above or below, shaping starts to get tricky. In his massive textbook *Radar Cross-Section Reduction* Eugene F. Knott poses the question "What rationale can be taken if all threat directions are equally likely?" His answer is not comforting — "It is a question that has not been satisfactorily answered."

Conventional ramp-type inlets often give a head-on observer a good view of the engine fan or compressor face, so are near-ideal radar reflectors. A quick look down the intake of a MiG-29 at the 1988 Farnborough air show gave me a good look at the front face of the powerful R-33 turbofan and the realisation that a reduced RCS was far from being a significant design goal when Belyakov and his team developed this agile and effective fighter aircraft.

Above: **The Lockheed F-117A Senior Trend stealth fighter makes extensive use of faceting in order to reduce RCS. Its shape remained secret until late in 1988.**

Below: **The huge inlets of the AV-8A (and other members of the Harrier family) will give radars a good view of the front face of the Pegasus turbofan engine.**

Above: **The inlets of the B-1A were designed for Mach 2 dash performance, so incorporated variable ramps intended to match the airflow to the engine.**

Intakes may be designed to use half-cone centre-bodies of the sort used on the Mirage fighter. Efficient and light, these would block much radiation, preventing it from reaching the engine. Further measures which would prevent radars from "seeing" the highly reflective front face of the jet engines include long sinuous serpentine or even zig-zag air trunking in which radar energy could be trapped inside the inlet, then bounced back and forth and damped by radar-absorbent material (RAM).

In the 1940s, the US National Advisory Committee for Aeronautics (NACA) developed flush inlets. Visible from a smaller range of angles than a conventional inlet, these could be a viable alternative to conventional designs. Tested in 1950 on the first of two experimental YF-93A prototypes, these were replaced on the second aircraft by conventional lateral intakes. The sole current application is on the McDonnell Douglas Harpoon anti-ship missile.

In the early 1960s, Teledyne Ryan reconnaissance drones were flown with wire-mesh screens over their prominent "shark's mouth" air inlets. This worked well against long-wavelength threats such as Soviet

surveillance radars but would be difficult to implement against modern centimetric radars. To be effective, the mesh must be smaller than a small fraction of a wavelength. A quick look at the window of a microwave oven will show just how small a centimetric mesh must be.

COCKPITS

One of the most troublesome cavities on an aircraft is the cockpit. Virtually as transparent to radar energy as it is to light, the canopy or windshield allows radar energy access to the cluttered and radar-reflective cockpit interior. One way of preventing this is to apply a thin layer of gold to the canopy transparency, a technique already used on the canopy of the EA-6B Prowler to protect the crew from the powerful signal emitted by the aircraft's jammers. This will have a minimal effect on visibility but will be "seen" by the radar as being an electrically conductive surface rather than a transparency — virtually an extension of the aircraft's skin. Indium-tin is another possible canopy coating which is reported to allow 98

per cent transmission of visible light.

Aircraft radomes are custom designed to match the operating frequency of the radar they cover but are also transparent to a much wider band of frequencies, exposing the antenna to hostile radars. An antenna makes two contributions to RCS. One is the scattering due to its structure, the other is more subtle and due to its function-related shape. Radar energy arriving at a conventional paraboloidal "dish" antenna will be gathered and focussed onto the antenna feed in exactly the same way as the

would be to devise a "band-pass" radome transparent only to the relatively narrow band of frequencies used by the stealth aircraft's own radar. A more intriguing possibility is that of an electrically-switchable radome. This takes the band-pass concept a stage further by arranging for suitable electrical impulses to turn the band-pass characteristic off and on in much the same way that electrical impulses can be used to darken or extinguish the characters on the LCD display on a digital watch. For most frequencies, and for even the band-pass frequency whenever the radar was not being used, the radome would be opaque.

TRAVELLING WAVES

Travelling waves and other surface waves flowing on the skin of an aircraft or missile can give rise to re-radiation of energy if they meet discontinuities such as seams, gaps between panels, changes in surface material or sudden changes in shape. In designing and building a stealth aircraft, care must therefore be taken to ensure that all gaps and seams are eliminated either by closing the gap with an electrically conducting material (the approach used on the B-1B) or by working to tight tolerances to eliminate gaps (as on the B-2).

Above: **The B-1B is optimised for high-subsonic cruise, so the inlets were redesigned as simpler fixed-geometry units with engine-concealing anti-radar baffles.**

Below: **Side-fuselage flush intakes (seen here on the experimental North American YF-93 derivative of the F-86 Sabre) prevent radar from "seeing" the engine inlet.**

Right: **The antennas, equipment racks and LRUs within the radome of this Tornado IDS may act as hot spots when illuminated by enemy radar.**

echo return signal. Not being at the frequency for which the feed was designed, it will reflect, travelling back along the same route and being sent off on its unwanted way by the main reflector.

Flat planar-array antennas of the type used in more recent designs are less of a problem but measures must still be taken to reduce their RCS. The design used on the

B-1B is deliberately canted downward to reduce its signature, relying on electronic beam steering to direct the radar energy ahead of the aircraft rather than in the direction the planar antenna is facing.

In the long run, the antenna must be concealed from hostile radars by mounting it within a special radome. One possibility for stealth aircraft

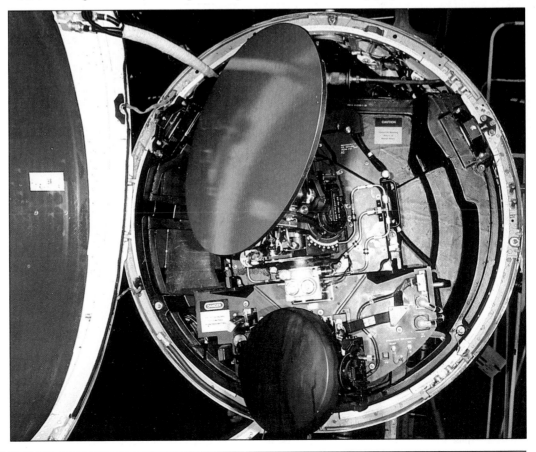

Wing slats and flaps can create such gaps, particularly when used for manoeuvring. When an aircraft such as the F-14 Tomcat sets its wing geometry to the combat manoeuvring position, gaps exist between the wing, the slat and the flap. When the wing is illuminated by radar energy, such gaps will help reflect a signal. This is particularly true if the aircraft is illuminated from head-on or the rear quarter, when surface waves moving across the wing chord will meet one of those gaps.

ADAPTIVE WING

A much better way of altering wing geometry is the Mission Adaptive Wing (MAW) which Boeing is testing on an F-111 testbed. Developed under the USAF's Advanced Fighter Technology Integration (AFTI) programme, the adaptive wing has no conventional ailerons, flaps, slats or spoilers but incorporates flexible leading and trailing edges able to bend into the required position without leaving gaps. The MAW leading edge can move from 1 degree upwards to 20 degrees downwards, while the trailing edge can move from 1 degree upwards to 18 degrees downwards.

RCS reduction was never stated as a programme objective but the timescale of the flight tests would have provided MAW technology in time to allow incorporation into the Advanced Tactical Fighter (ATF) but was perhaps too early for the US Navy's A-12 strike aircraft.

A travelling wave flowing along a fuselage will eventually meet an unavoidable discontinuity — the point at which the structure physically ends, for example, at the tip of a radome or the end of a jetpipe or exhaust. The best way of dealing with it is to attenuate the wave before it reaches the end of the structure. This is often done by applying radar-absorbing material to the surface.

Stealth designers must also eliminate small exposed cavities such as gun muzzles, sensor windows or refuelling receptacles. Most features of this sort should be screened by small doors but the cannon muzzle would probably require a small frangible panel of metallised plastic.

Above: **The mechanism within the US-designed Mission Adaptive Wing (MAW) is classified, but this photo gives a good view of the unit's flexible upper skin.**

Below right: **Internal weapons carriage reduced the drag of the Convair F-102 Delta Dagger. On stealth aircraft, internal ordnance storage also reduces RCS.**

Below: **Unlike conventional leading edge slats and trailing edge flaps, the Mission Adaptive Wing leaves the upper and lower skin surface unbroken. Travelling waves flowing within the wing skin as the result of illumination by radar thus never meet gaps which would cause them to re-radiate energy and increase the apparent RCS.**

Mission Adaptive Wing

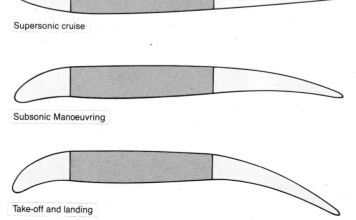

Supersonic cruise

Subsonic Manoeuvring

Take-off and landing

Other conventional features which radar sees as scatter-inducing discontinuities are small fairings, protrusions, grills, domes and wingtip fairings. If allowed to protrude, even rivets and other fasteners can act as radar reflectors. Conventional airflow and pressure sensors can be strongly reflective. These must be designed for minimal radar signature and if

Above: **As part of the Advanced Fighter Technology Integration programme, this F-111 was used to flight test the variable camber Mission Adaptive Wing.**

necessary treated with absorbent material.

The move towards stealth technology in the Soviet Union must be demanding a re-think by Soviet engineers who in the past have often resorted to external fairings as a means of accommodating features such as control surface bell-cranks which a Western designer would have buried within the airframe.

This need to keep the aircraft as clean as possible effectively rules out the use of traditional types of external stores such as missiles, bombs and equipment pods. External fuel tanks are less of a problem — they would be dropped before coming into range of a hostile radar just in the way that Korean War Sabres dropped tanks before tangling with agile MiGs.

All EW and EO systems must be carried internally, perhaps on interchangeable pallets, while ordnance must be carried in internal weapon bays or in semi-buried

conformal locations. The latter might even be covered with expendable radar-absorbing fairings which could be dropped just before weapon release.

WEAPONS CARRIAGE

If any other type of underwing store is needed, it would have to be carried in a radar-absorbent container. A clue to how this may be done can be seen in surface-ship installations of the Harpoon anti-ship missile. This is mounted on the vessel in a cylindrical storage container/launcher. As the

round leaves the tube at launch, its wings and fins unfold to their flight position. Delete the solid-fuel tandem booster (which would not be needed for air launch) and make the tube slightly greater in diameter to allow for radar-absorbent material, add streamlined nose and tail caps and you've got a stealthy air-launched Harpoon installation.

Missiles and small-sized bombs could probably be carried in a large underwing container treated with radar-absorbent material and fitted with "bomb doors" or frangible panels on the

Possible Stealth Weapons Carrier

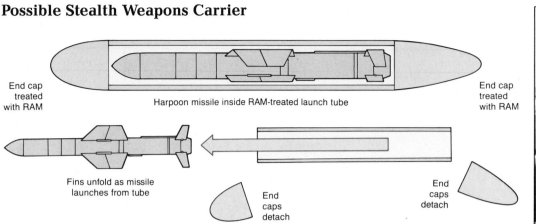

End cap treated with RAM

Harpoon missile inside RAM-treated launch tube

End cap treated with RAM

Fins unfold as missile launches from tube

End caps detach

End caps detach

underside — a stealthy version of the carriers currently used for light practice bombs.

Another RCS-reduction feature of stealth aircraft is the use wherever possible of composite materials rather than metal. Several types of composite materials are now used in aircraft construction. All consist of fibres bonded by a matrix material. The first successful composite material was glass-fibre reinforced plastic (GRP). Made from glass fibres impregnated with phenolic resin, it was introduced in the 1940s. Its main aerospace application came much later in the manufacture of helicopter rotor blades.

COMPOSITES

The most common type of composite material used in aerospace is graphite-epoxy, tapes or cloth woven from carbon fibres and embedded in a matrix of epoxy resin. Kevlar is an example of another type of composite which is based on aramid fibres. Some composites, known as "mixed modulus" types, use a mix of fibre types selected to create the required strength and elasticity in the finished product.

The fact that stealth aircraft are made from composites has already taken a deep hold in aviation folklore. After all, composites are not metal and do not show up on radar. Such, at least, is the popular theory. What may prove surprising is that the use of composites is not one of the most significant RCS-reduction measures. The wartime deHavilland Mosquito light bomber was made of wood but nobody ever suggested that it had stealth capabilities.

The sad truth is that building an aircraft from materials through which radar energy may pass simply gives the radar a good view of the

aircraft's "innards" — in the case of the Mosquito, engines, fuel pumps, electrical wiring and the primitive avionics of the time. The Mosquito undoubtedly did have a lower RCS than a four engined Lancaster or Halifax but this was not militarily significant. The aircraft's survivability came from its high performance rather than any reduction in RCS.

The rôle played by composites in reducing RCS is a more subtle one. Carbon is a poor conductor of electricity, being widely used in the manufacture of resistors used by the electronics industry. Epoxy resin is an insulator. As a result, the electrical conductivity of composite materials is low. Radar energy arriving at a composite panel or structure has a hard job setting up the electrical and magnetic currents which re-radiate the energy and form troublesome creeping and travelling waves.

By 1981, Northrop had more than 30 funded contracts worth close to $50 million to develop advanced composites technology. In the early 1980s, the company built experimental structures which were then subjected to a long-term study to investigate the effect of thermal "spikes", radiation from nuclear explosions and laser energy.

RAM CONCEPTS

New types of composite material were developed in the 1970s and 1980s. One recent breakthrough is the use of fibres to reinforce a metal matrix. In 1987 Lockheed was reported to be leading an industrial team which was manufacturing the first large sheets of metal-matrix composites — whiskers of silicon carbide in an aluminium matrix. Although this material is stronger and stiffer than aluminium and is virtually guaranteed a place

Above: **Many types of missile are already fitted with folding wings and fins so that they can be fired from tubular storage/launch tubes. If the tube and its end caps were to be treated with RAM, stealth aircraft could carry such weapons as low-RCS external stores.**

Right: **The de Havilland Mosquito light bomber was built from wood but this had surprisingly little effect on the aircraft's RCS.**

Below: **Composite manufacturing techniques used on the B-2 were the result of Northrop R&D efforts in the early 1980s.**

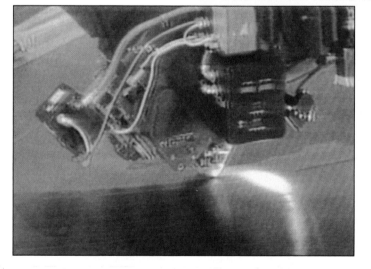

in future combat aircraft, its conductivity will not be much different to metal, bad news for stealth designers.

In the struggle to minimise RCS, a more useful ally will be reinforced carbon-carbon (RCC). This is created by baking and carbonising a matrix containing carbon fibres. As a material it is strong and exceptionally heat-resistant. Used in the manufacture of missile re-entry vehicles and the nose and wing leading edges of the US Space Shuttle, it could be used to built low-RCS exhaust

systems. To the stealth engineer, the importance of RCC is that it combines these physical virtues with another useful property — the ability to absorb radar energy.

Once the main reflection problems are identified, engineers can modify the design and employ special materials at vulnerable points. Reflections may be reduced by means of radar-absorbent materials — the radar equivalents of the black finish used on the undersides of Second World War night bombers.

There are two broad classes of RAM — resonant and broadband. Resonant absorbers are designed for use at a specific frequency but maintain some effectiveness over a range of frequencies on either side of this nominal operating point. Broadband RAM maintains its effectiveness over a much wider range of frequencies.

The simplest type of resonant RAM is the sandwich-type absorber. This operates on the same principle as the blue-tinged anti-reflection optical coatings applied to the lenses of cameras, optical instruments and even spectacles. When the light strikes such a lens, a portion is reflected by the coating. The remainder passes through the coating and strikes the front face of the lens. A portion is reflected, while the remainder enters the lens.

RESONANT ABSORBER

There are now two reflections to consider. Careful choice of coating material ensures that the amounts reflected by the coating and the glass are similar. The coating is arranged to have a thickness equal to one quarter of a wavelength of visible light. As a result, the reflection from the glass surface has travelled an extra distance totalling half a wavelength by the time that it re-emerges from the coating and meets the reflection from the front surface of the coating. That vital half-wavelength difference makes the two waves of light out of phase with one another. As one wave rises above zero, the other falls below zero by an equal and opposite amount. One is the exact opposite of the other and the two cancel each other out, a process known as destructive interference. In theory, all of the reflection should vanish, but the cancellation is never perfect, so some minimal reflection remains.

The earliest resonant RAM materials used the same principle. The Salisbury Screen consisted of a thin sheet of resistive material held at a quarter wavelength distance ahead of a metal backing plate by a low dielectric spacer. Dielectric materials have the property of resisting an electric current, while allowing electrostatic or electromagnetic forces to pass freely. In the Salisbury Screen, this often takes the form of a specially-designed foam or honeycomb material. Another type of absorber known as a Dallenbach Layer consists of a quarter-wavelength thick slab of electrically lossy material applied to a metal backing plate. Exposing a radar signal to a slab of lossy material is rather like exposing a marathon runner to a strong headwind. The slab does not conduct electrical currents, but does have the ability to dissipate a significant portion of any electric energy to which it is exposed. A radar wave arriving at the front surface of the lossy material meets a change in electrical impedance which gives rise to the front-surface reflection.

Principles of Resonant RAM

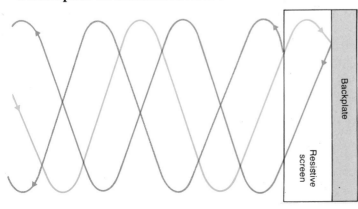

Left: **The Salisbury Screen is the simplest type of resonant RAM. A resistive screen is positioned in front of the back plate. The resistivity of the screen is such that 50 per cent of the incoming radar wave (shown in blue) is reflected from the screen surface, while the remainder passes through to reflect from the back plate. If these two surfaces are positioned quarter of a wavelength apart, the reflections from the screen (mauve) and back plate (red) cancel one another.**

Below: Rockwell engineers applied RAM to key areas of the B-1B in the effort to significantly reduce RCS. The wing root area was a source of reflections and required careful redesign. A thin dark strip of RAM is visible on the wing of this aircraft in construction.

Above: Small dark patches on the unpainted skin of this B-1B around the nose-mounted control vane indicate the presence of RAM.

Right: RAM made from pyramid-shaped elements lines the walls of this anechoic test chamber at the University of Eindhoven.

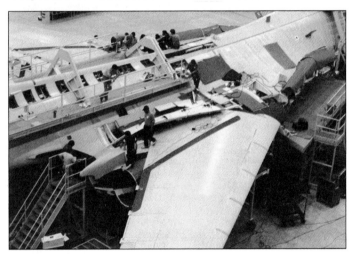

Although widely used for many applications such as damping the radar returns from buildings at airports or harbours (applications in which a single or at most a few frequencies need to be countered at minimal cost), interference absorbers are narrow-band and physically bulky, so are not very useful for applications such as stealth aircraft.

DIELECTRIC RAM

In more practical types of resonant (narrow-band) absorber, two effects are used to soak up the incoming radar energy — destructive interference between the reflections from the surface and the backing, and attenuation of the wave by the dielectric material. This type of material is known as a dielectrically-loaded absorber.

The goal of the RAM designer is to create a material the front surface of which will admit a radar wave rather than reflect it. Once within the RAM, the radar wave should then be absorbed, dissipating its energy in the form of heat. For decades, component manufacturers have fabricated electrical resistors from carbon, so it is hardly surprising that the same material should form the basis of many types of RAM. When radar waves strike such a RAM, its limited conductivity causes losses, as does the effort which the molecules must make while attempting to follow the alternating fields. This is known as "lossy dielectric" RAM.

Had dielectric RAM been the sole solution, stealth technology might never have left the laboratory. Luckily a second type of RAM has been developed which proved much easier to apply to many types of aircraft structure. Known as magnetic RAM, this is based on magnetic material such as compounds of iron, ferrites (ceramic compounds of ferromagnetic materials) or carbonyl iron. These materials are often embedded in sheets of natural or synthetic rubber which can easily be glued into position.

A resonant absorber based on magnetic materials works in much the same way as its dielectrically-loaded counterpart, combining destructive interference with attenuation. Here the energy is dissipated as the magnetic dipoles within the material move in response to the impinging radar wave. The amount of lossy material and binder is selected in order to provide the optimum electromagnetic characteristics for the range of frequencies which the designer is trying to counter.

Most readers who own a cassette recorder or video recorder will be familiar with the brand name TDK. The

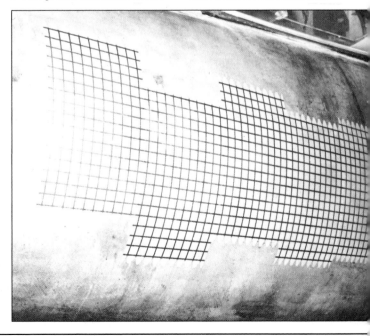

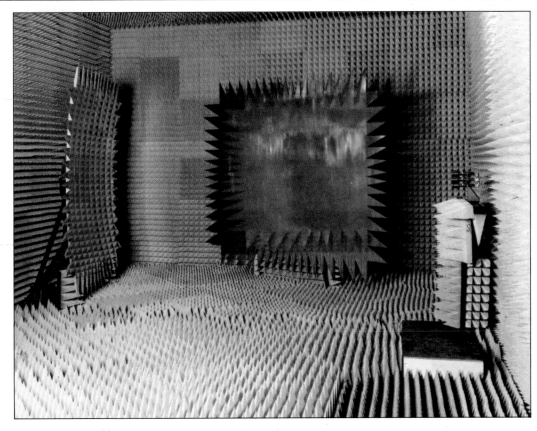

that the incoming wave meets sheets of decreasing resistivity. This type of screen, known as a Jaumann absorber, can have two, three, four or even six layers. Since all layers are spaced by the same amount, the total thickness of the screen is increased accordingly. Its bulk makes it unsuitable for most airframe applications.

One early practical application of the Jaumann absorber was a RAM developed during the Second World War by the German Navy for the treatment of submarines. It consisted of seven layers of carbon-impregnated paper, each of increasing conductivity, separated by layers of foam plastic dielectric. It was effective at the 3cm and 10cm frequency band, but was 2.5in (6.35cm) thick and rigid. As a result, it was never deployed on operational U-boats.

PYRAMID ABSORBER

Once again, a more practical solution can be found based on dielectrically-loaded and magnetically-loaded materials. What the ideal RAM should do is to gradually match the impedance of the air to that of the metal aircraft skin. If this were achievable, the incoming radar wave would never meet a change in impedance sharp enough to cause a reflection.

First attempts at creating graded material involved dipping mats of curled animal hair into a conductive mixture of carbon and neoprene. The mixture clung to the hair but, as the newly-dipped mats were laid out horizontally to dry, the mixture tended to flow downwards, creating a rough and ready dielectric gradient. The resulting material was largely used in the laboratory and on the walls of the first anechoic (reflection-free) radio test chambers developed for indoor antenna testing.

A more practical method of grading the dielectric is to mould the material into a pyramid the apex of which is pointed in the direction of the radar wave. As the wave moves forward and thus down the axis of the pyramid, it exposes itself to more of the dielectric material. This technique is ideal for use in the construction of anechoic chambers, whose pyramid-studded walls are a conspicuous feature of modern photographs showing indoor antenna or RCS tests. The dielectric used here is carbon-loaded foam.

company is the world's largest manufacturer of magnetic recording tape. It owes this lead to Doctor Yogoro Kato of Tokyo Industrial University, who passed the patents for the newly invented ferrite to a venture capitalist in 1932. This co-operation resulted in the founding of TDK.

FERRITE ABSORBER

In the 1970s, the company teamed with NEC to study methods of reducing the metal contamination of water discharged by Japanese steel mills. Having learned how to precipitate this metal waste as

low-grade ferrite, they tried to find a commercial application for what was essentially a waste product.

An application which suggested itself was the creation of RAM. By mixing magnetic material with an epoxy liquid, NEC tried to develop a paint which could be applied to the structure of metal bridges to reduce their reflectivity as seen by radar. A 1979 trial proved disappointing; the paint coating applied to the bridge did absorb a limited amount of radar energy but not over a wide enough range of frequencies.

Narrow-band absorbers can be designed to operate at any frequency but, for any practical stealth applications, a broader coverage is needed. One way of accomplishing this is to make a multilayer absorber, each layer of which is designed to resonate at a different frequency. One simple example is the multilayer Salisbury Screen. The addition of extra resistive sheets and spacers broadens the range of frequencies on either side of the nominal design frequency. For best results, the resistivity of each sheet is arranged to be lower than the one ahead of it, so

Left and Below: **In his book** ***Dragon Lady,*** **author Chris Pocock revealed how U-2 aircraft were fitted with panels of radar-absorbing**

Salisbury Screen (fuselage sides below and ahead of the cockpit) and Eccosorb (below the inlets) during late-1950s stealth experiments.

Decibels

dB	Absorption
3	50%
6	75%
8	87%
10	90%
20	99%
30	99.9%

Above: **The decibel (dB) is a unit frequently used by stealth engineers when measuring radar absorption.**

Right: **This assembly-line view of an SR-71 engine nacelle and outer wing clearly shows how triangular patches of RAM were built into the wing leading edge, a measure intended to reduce overall RCS.**

A pyramidal absorber of this classical type is impractical for aircraft use, except in a two-dimensional form buried within wing/fin leading or trailing edges. This type of material was used in the wings of the Lockheed SR-71 and can be clearly seen in some photographs of aircraft under construction.

Pyramidal or hair-mat RAM may be satisfactory for laboratory use, or for the treatment of large structures, but is far too bulky for most aerospace applications. When creating more practical designs, the RAM designer achieves the desired dielectric grading by forming the material from layers of dielectric. If a limited number of radar bands must be countered, a multilayer narrow-band RAM may have one of its layers designed to cope with one band and a second to deal with the other. A typical modern example of this is Plessey's dual-band S- and X-band RAM.

RAM PRODUCTS

Wide-band RAMs are normally created by adding a carbon-loaded plastic material to the base such as polyurethane foam. This creates the required "lossy dielectric". The thicker the material, the better the absorption. Maximum values of 90 to 99.9 per cent are possible.

Plessey has produced a range of broad-band materials based on an impregnated polyurethane foam. Known as the LA series, this covers

frequencies from 4 to 100GHz.

Emerson & Cuming offers the AN series of flexible foam sheet broad band absorbers and the similar but water- and fuel-proof AW series. Both come in a range of thicknesses, depending on frequency coverage, and are intended to provide 20dB or more absorbency. For example, AN-74 maintains this level of performance for almost the entire range from 4 to 18GHz, dipping briefly to around 18dB in the 13GHz region.

These are relatively thick materials but thinner and easier to use materials have recently been announced. Plessey's ADRAM (Advanced Dielectric RAM) is a limited-range broad-band sheet material intended to counter both specular reflections and surface waves. Normally available in sheets of between 0.04 and 0.16in (1 and 4mm)

Above: **The composite wings of Japan's new SX-3 (FS-X) fighter will make extensive use of locally-developed radar-absorptive material.**

Below left: **The radar reflectivity of the ferrite paint used on the Lockheed TR-1 can be varied by changing its thickness.**

thickness, it maintains its performance at high angles of incidence. Used as a broad band absorber, it gives an absorption of 6dB or more between 6 and 35GHz, maintaining better than 20dB between 10 and 12GHz.

Plessey also offers a thin magnetically-loaded material which might be applied to an airframe. Known as SWAM, it consists of a flexible elastomer sheet between 0.02 and 0.06in (0.5 and 1.5mm) in thickness. Absorption peaks at 15dB in the 10 to 12GHz area of the spectrum but remains at 6dB or better down to 6GHz and up to 16GHz.

MAGNETIC ABSORBER

Very little information has been released on the characteristics of ferrite paint — often referred to as "iron ball" paint in press reports of stealth technology. Advanced Absorber Products' AAP-021 is a polyurethane-cased sprayable coating, a heavy grey liquid which dries tack free in 40 minutes and hardens in 12 to 24 hours. Its RAM properties depend on the thickness to which it is applied. A 0.03in (0.76mm) coat will reduce the reflected energy by an amount increasing from 3dB at 6GHz to 13dB at 18GHz.

Being based on iron-like material, magnetic RAM is heavy. It also has a tendency to oxidise, a process which degrades its effectiveness. Oxidation is particularly severe at temperatures of more than 900°F (500°C), creating problems when

hypersonic aircraft or ballistic missile re-entry vehicles are being considered for RAM treatment.

Offsetting these disadvantages are the fact that it is thin and that it maintains its effectiveness down to sub-gigahertz frequencies. A Salisbury Screen intended to operate at 100MHz would be 29in (75cm) thick, even a dielectric absorber would be many inches thick. A magnetic RAM able to operate at the same frequency might be only a tenth of the thickness of its dielectric counterpart. Different magnetic materials have their peak efficiency at various frequencies but by layering them one on top of another a broader-band absorber will be created. Ferrite paint may also act as an electrical bonding agent between panels.

Magnetic RAM is most effective at lower frequencies, dielectric types at the highest frequencies. The logical approach is therefore to combine the two, creating hybrid RAMs effective over the highest possible range of frequencies.

A typical advanced multilayer RAM of the type in service in the late 1980s

apparently consists of three layers. The outer and inner layers are partly radar reflective and act rather like a Salisbury Screen. The central layer, made from lossy dielectric material, is intended to help contain the energy reflected from the innermost layer for long enough for cancellation to occur. It also acts as a traditional lossy dielectric absorber.

CIRCUIT ANALOGUE

Another type of RAM can be created by replacing the resistive sheet used in Salisbury or Jaumann absorbers with one on which conductive material is arranged in geometric patterns such as thin strips, grids, crosses or more complex shapes. The result is known as a Circuit Analogue (CA) absorber. The material offers a higher performance within a given volume than simpler types of absorber but must be custom-designed for each application, a task normally handled by a powerful computer.

CA absorber technology is probably the principle behind one new method of producing stealthy canopies. The easiest way of creating a canopy for a stealth aircraft was mentioned earlier — application of a thin film of gold or indium-tin to the transparent material. This conducting film keeps the radar energy out of the cockpit but will tend to reflect it. A more recent technique involves making the entire transparency absorb radar energy. This is done by embedding within it a network of thin wires cut to dipole (half-wavelength) size. When combined with an inner conductive layer, this treatment probably turns the entire transparency into a CA absorber.

Circuit Analogue Absorbers

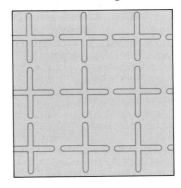
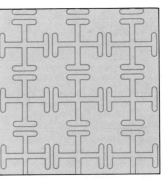

Above and Above right: **By printing conductive geometric patterns on suitable base material, engineers can create Circuit Analogue (CA)** RAM, **a highly effective radar absorber, but one which must be custom-designed by computer to suit each new apsorption application.**

Most RAM used in stealth aircraft falls into one of two categories — sheets or other off-the-shelf bulk materials for general use and custom-designed components made from RAM material. Although RAM solves many RCS problems, it also creates its own constraints. Its weight will reduce aircraft performance and its bulk may prove troublesome in volume-restricted applications such as missiles. Its purchase and machining and installation cost will make the aircraft more expensive, while its very presence may well create new servicing difficulties for ground crews, increasing direct operating costs.

By combining RAM with rigid radar-transparent substances, it is possible to create Radar-Absorbent Structural (RAS) materials, one of the most classified forms of radar absorber. Little information has been published on materials of this type. US press reports have described how RAS material based on laminated layers of glass fibre and carbon-coated plastic are used on leading and trailing edges of stealth aircraft. RAS can also be created by taking a non-metallic honeycomb, treating its surface with carbon or other lossy materials, then bonding non-metallic skins to its front and back to create a rigid panel. Honeycomb sections can absorb low-frequency radar if the individual cells are at least one-tenth of a wavelength of the radar signal.

NEW PLASTICS

In 1985, Lockheed set up a research project into conductive plastics, seeing these as a possible new material for aircraft construction. In their basic forms, polyacetylene and other conductive plastics are non-conducting. The ability to conduct electricity appears only as the result of doping the basic material with an additive. Doped polyacetylene is hardly the ideal candidate for aircraft construction. It is brittle and loses its newly acquired conductivity when exposed to air or water. One variety is even pyrophoric, bursting into flames if exposed to air.

By the end of 1987, Lockheed had devised more tractable materials, plastics which could be produced for under $1 per pound ($2.2 per kilogram), could be dissolved in solvents for processing into the required shape and could

Above and Below: **The B-2 programme makes extensive use of computer-aided design and manufacturing (CAD/ CAM) techniques. Computer screens linked to a 3D database replace drawing boards allowing the automatic manufacture of accurate components.**

be mixed with other structural plastics to create strong but electrically-conductive components.

The material was based on polyanaline, Lockheed announced early in 1988. There were still problems with stability at high temperature, the company told *Aviation Week*. Although one polyanaline compound was stable in air for more than 24 hours at 392°F (200°C), what was needed was a material able to withstand 570°F (300°C) for long periods of time.

A number of uses immediately suggested themselves. Conductive plastic could be used on composite aircraft for static control de-icing elements or even antennas, while the range of conductivity available also suggested new types of RAM. By bonding

together multiple layers of gradually increasing conductivity, engineers could create radar-absorbent skins which functioned in much the same manner as graded dielectric RAM.

A final and even more intriguing feature of these conductive plastics was that their conductivity could be switched off and on as required by applying a small voltage. They are thus likely to be a key ingredient of the electrically-switchable radomes described earlier in this chapter.

One intriguing news item in the late autumn of 1988 suggested that the new materials might have been swiftly applied to the construction of stealth aircraft. The materials used to dope conductive plastics are both reactive and toxic. In a court case brought against

Lockheed, a group of employees from the Burbank plant where the F-117A stealth fighter was being built charged that their health was being damaged by chemicals used there.

RAM created from conductive plastic was similar in principle to the more traditional varieties of dielectrically-loaded RAM but 1987 also saw the discovery of an entirely new way of absorbing radar energy. It was the result not of highly-classified "black" research in secret laboratories but was the accidental spin-off from research into the workings of the eye!

SCHIFF BASE SALTS

In a newspaper interview, Robert R. Birge, director of the Carnegie Mellon University's (CMU's) Center for Molecular Electronics, explained that his group made the discover by chance while investigating the behaviour of a class of chemicals essential to the perception of light, a part of their study of the biophysics of vision. In a paper published by the *Journal of the American Chemical Society*, Birge had described how the atoms of the molecules of a group of chemicals (known as Schiff base salts) under study at CMU underwent a slight and temporary re-arrangement when struck by light.

Birge's group believes that such momentary rearrangements of the molecules of chemicals such as rhodopsin contained in the light-sensitive cones in the retina of the eye are the key

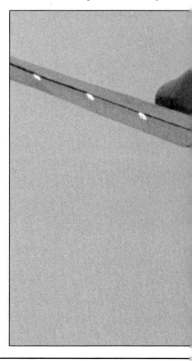

to the vision process. These trigger off a cascade of neurochemical events which result in neurotransmitters carrying light-related signals to the brain.

To help study the process, his group looked for simpler molecules which would exhibit the same process, and which would act as simple laboratory models to assist studies of the more complex chemicals in the retina. "Some of the molecules we've studied don't work very well as models for the biological perception of visible light", Birge stated in a later interview, "but they turn out to be excellent absorbers of another kind of electromagnetic radiation — radar".

The newly-discovered compounds absorbed radio frequencies as well as or better than ferrite-based materials but were only about one-tenth the weight. "Specific salts seem to absorb specific RF frequencies", Birge told the magazine *Aviation Week* in the spring of 1987. "It should be possible to modify these substances so that an ensemble of this type could absorb over the entire radar RF range."

The biggest problem in creating a usable RAM was to develop a binder material able to accept the RAM compound. With the help of a Pittsburgh-based chemical company, this had been achieved by the spring of 1987, leading Birge to predict that a coating suitable for production applications would be developed within three years. Initial evaluation by the US DoD was due to take place

Active Cancellation System

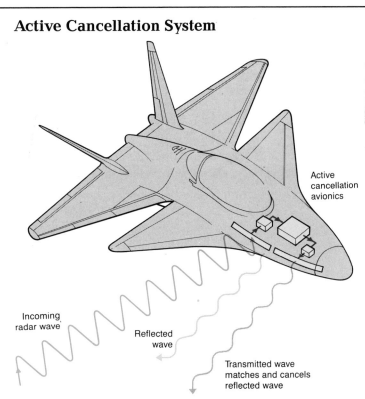

Active cancellation avionics

Incoming radar wave

Reflected wave

Transmitted wave matches and cancels reflected wave

later in 1987. There has been no subsequent news of these materials — all research on them was swiftly classified.

Following an account of his work in *Aviation Week* Birge was approached by several US Government agencies and asked to release no further information on his work. Two of these agencies (which he declined to identify) have begun research programmes based on the CMU discovery.

One intriguing but little-discussed possibility for reducing RCS is that of cancellation of the scattered signal by the transmission of a second signal of equal frequency and amplitude but

Above: **Another method of reducing RCS is active cancellation. The incoming (strong blue) radar wave is sampled by a receiving antenna. Having predicted the aircraft's reflectivity at this frequency and angle, the avionics create and transmit a false echo (mauve), a signal designed to cancel out the genuine reflection (pale blue) from the aircraft's skin.**

Below: **In redesigning the B-1A to create today's B-1B, Rockwell reduced RCS by a factor of ten, but could do little to reduce the IR output from four afterburning GE F-101 torbofans.**

of opposite phase. In theory, this could be achieved passively by creating a suitable reflector (such as an accurately-machined cavity of appropriate dimensions) designed to create the appropriate echo. In practice however, this technique (often referred to as "impedance loading") would only work at a single frequency for which the reflector had been designed, while each scattering source on the aircraft would require its own associated and matching reflector.

CANCELLATION

The only realistic method of creating the waveform needed for cancellation would be by active means. Unfortunately, the technical problems are formidable. Aircraft-mounted sensors would have to measure the frequency, waveform, strength and direction of the signal to be countered. Complex signal processing equipment whose software contained detailed information on the aircraft's radar reflectivity at a wide range of angles and frequencies would have to predict how the incoming wave would reflect, then create and transmit a suitable cancellation signal.

Cancellation would not need to be 100 per cent to be militarily useful, while the task of matching the cancellation signal to the threat could be reduced in magnitude by reducing the threat sector and frequency range to be countered. Active-cancellation systems have been discussed in technical publications and it is possible that equipment of this type is being developed for the B-2 bomber.

Given present-day sensor technology, passive IR offers the only realistic option to radar for the long-range detection of aircraft targets. With the growing use of IR sensors as a radar substitute, measures must be taken to reduce the thermal signature of a stealth aircraft.

The main sources of IR energy are hot metal components of the engine turbine and the exhaust nozzle, components which have been heated by the 1,800 — 2,300°F (1,000 — 1,300°C) efflux from the engine's combustors. The efflux leaving the tailpipe contributes relatively little — only some ten per cent of the total IR emission from a turbojet and even less from a turbofan.

Above: The tail surfaces of the Fairchild A-10 were designed to mask the engine exhausts from the seeker heads of IR-guided weapons.

If the engine uses an afterburner, the IR emission from the efflux can be increased by up to 50 times, causing it to rival or even eclipse that of the jetpipe. For this reason, all the first-generation of stealth aircraft — the XST, F-117A and B-2 — make use of non-afterburning engines.

The hot interior of the tailpipe is visible over a conical sector to the rear of the aircraft. From outside of this sector, an IR sensor will see only the outside surface of the nozzle, the temperature of which will be lower. The IR signature can be reduced by using the aircraft's aft fuselage and/or vertical tail surfaces to shield the jetpipes from view over as large a part of this sector as possible.

IR SCREENING

This approach was first used on the Fairchild A-10 Thunderbolt II attack aircraft and is a prominent feature of the "F-19" model aircraft kit released in July 1986 by the Testor Corporation. A few minutes experimentation with the assembled model shows just how well the steeply-canted tailfins act in hiding the tailpipes from view. A fighter approaching such an aircraft from the rear could be denied IR lock-on by the

Above and Below: Two-dimensional vectored thrust nozzles have a rectangular outlet and a lower IR signature than conventional round nozzles. This experimental nozzle for the F100 turbofan was developed for use on the F-15 STOL demonstrator.

Right: The jet flap/lift concept tested in the early 1960s on the Hunting 126 research aircraft probably reduced the IR signature.

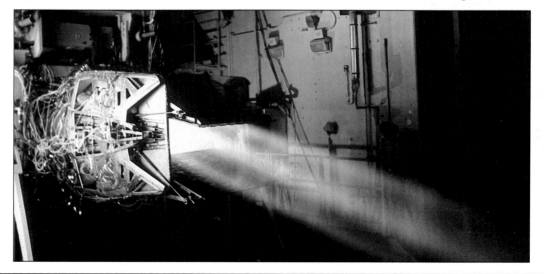

"F-19" making a sharp turn of around 45 degrees.

"Venetian blind" horizontal louvres arranged across the nozzle will restrict tailpipe visibility to a narrow range of vertical angles but would probably require cooling to ensure that they did not begin to rival the tailpipe in temperature.

Having denied an enemy IR sensor sight of the hot engine aft section, the stealth aircraft designer must also reduce other sources of IR energy. An obvious target for treatment is now the exhaust plume, which must be cooled quickly by mixing the flow of hot gas from the core with cooler by-pass air. This is already done in a turbofan engine but it can be taken a stage further in a stealth design by using additional air to provide a cool shroud around the exhaust. Diverting a large flow of air through the engine bay and around the engine will also minimise the temperature rise in the structure of the rear fuselage.

Some press reports have suggested that liquid nitrogen might be carried in stealth aircraft. It might be used at moments of high threat to chill the air used to shield the efflux, effectively surrounding the efflux with a curtain of cold gas.

Another way of reducing the IR signature is to replace the traditional circular exhaust nozzle with an elliptical or rectangular pattern. This would increase the perimeter of the plume, creating a wide "beaver-tail" of hot gases rather than a compact circular jet. It would increase the surface area of the plume, increasing the rate at which the gases cooled, and would also reduce the band of heights from which an attacking fighter could observe a strong IR signature. A two-dimensional rectangular nozzle of the type being flight-tested on the F-15 STOL Demonstrator probably has a low IR and radar signature when the engine is running in dry thrust.

AIRFRAME HEAT

As the modern all-aspect IR missile demonstrates, the airframe is also a source of detectable IR energy. This heat comes from several sources — the engine, the avionics and the thermal effects of friction with the atmosphere at high speed.

As any designer of engine bays will testify, a jet engine runs hot. Nearby structure must either be built from titanium or other temperature-resistant alloys or be shielded from engine heat. Stealth aircraft are thought to have linings within the engine bay to prevent engine heat from spreading into the structure, warming the aft fuselage and increasing the aircraft's IR signature.

At present, most aircraft simply dump the heat gathered by the cockpit and avionics cooling systems but stealth aircraft will probably rely on closed-loop cooling systems. The heat could be dumped into the fuel, a technique pioneered in the SR-71 Blackbird, or radiated at frequencies not well transmitted by the atmosphere. Another component of the IR signature is reflected or re-radiated sunlight. This can be minimised by the use of suitable surface finishes.

ENGINE NOISE

Current stealth aircraft are probably subsonic. The levels of airframe heating induced by supersonic flight would make the aircraft an easy target for IR sensors, while the noise of a roaring afterburner would betray a covert reconnaissance or strike aircraft operating at medium or low altitude.

Most of the noise created by an aircraft is generated by the engine. Remove that and the aircraft will be very hard to detect audibly. Piston-engined aircraft with muffled powerplants were developed for night reconnaissance during the Vietnam War and proved near-silent in operation at altitudes of more than a few hundred feet.

In a jet-powered combat aircraft, most of the noise is generated by the jet of hot gas from the tailpipe. The fan stages do create some noise but on a stealth aircraft little of this will escape from the long and sinuous inlet ducts needed to minimise inlet RCS. Noise suppressors of the sort fitted as "hush kits" to the low by-pass ratio engines of older airliners operate by

lagging the nacelles with sound-absorbing material and mixing the fast-moving efflux from the engine with slower-moving air. Stealth aircraft already have anti-IR engine bay liners which are also thought to play a sound-absorbing rôle. The need to mix the engine efflux with cold air has already been described as an anti-IR measure; the same technique will also provide a valuable bonus in noise reduction. It is reported that the engine noise from a taxying F-117A stealth fighter is barely audible at ranges of more than a few hundred yards (metres).

Several books discussing stealth technology have suggested that as a general rule, supersonic speeds and the use of afterburning are not compatible with low-observable operations. This had led their authors to question the wisdom of the hypersonic fighter or reconnaissance designs proposed by some aircraft companies, such as the Mach 5 methane-burning monster whose proposed configuration was released by Lockheed in the early 1980s.

Such a view overlooks one of the odder aspects of flight at high Mach numbers. As aircraft speed builds up, increasing ram pressure at the engine inlet reduces efficiency, so efflux temperature begins to fall. By Mach 3 it can be lower than that of the same engine running at military (dry) thrust. Move to Mach 3.5 and the tailpipe emission will completely dominate that from the efflux.

One unavoidable factor associated with high supersonic speed is airframe heating due to atmospheric friction. This will be a major problem in creating any "Super Blackbird" type of aircraft. Working on the assumption that the possible

Above: **This Lockheed Mach 5 concept would be a good IR target. Hypersonic stealth aircraft will have to 'dump' this unwanted thermal energy in safe directions.**

Below: **Thomson-CSF has studied the likely radar-reflectivity of the fan blades of M88 turbofan engine which will be used in the production Rafale D and M.**

threats to such aircraft will be SAMs or interceptors attempting "snap-up" missile attacks, it is possible to envisage partial solutions based on cooling systems which extract heat from the lower surface on the aircraft, re-radiating it upwards. Such a system would confound most present-day and future air defences but the Super Powers can afford to orbit space-based IR sensors such as the exerimental US "Teal Ruby". These would find upward radiation from hypersonic aircraft an easy target.

COMPROMISES

Working with these basic rules for signature reduction, the designer must tackle the problem of creating a practical stealth aircraft or missile. The design of any aircraft is essentially a matter of compromise between conflicting requirements. This is even more so when creating a stealth aircraft, since the designer must juggle a new set of rules and constraints

over and above those of the past. The price paid for low RCS may be lower performance, reduced range or a lighter payload. In 1980, Lt Gen Kelly Burke, at that time USAF Deputy Chief of Staff for Research and Development, summed up the problem of developing a low RCS design: "You don't get any desirable feature without giving up some other desirable feature."

Even within the field of stealth technology, compromises will be called for. One disadvantage of shaping as an RCS-reduction measure is that reducing the returns in one direction involves increasing them in another. No matter how surfaces are angled, there will always be directions from which they are seen at normal incidence and where their reflectivity is high.

Before the designers can shape the aircraft, the authors of the operational requirement may have to indicate the approach to be followed. Should RCS be kept

cope with the stresses caused by the high rotational speeds.

Moving all the ordnance into an internal bay and eliminating traditional underwing sensor or EW pods reduces RCS but eats into the space available for internal fuel. The use of a weapons bay may also reduce the maximum weapon load, while elimination of external pods prevents the rapid updating of the aircraft by add-ons.

HOT SPOTS

A major part of the design process is to identify at an early stage the main elements which contribute to the final RCS. To make the process of RCS reduction cost-effective, the stealth designer must identify these dominant scatterers, the features on the aircraft which make the greatest contribution to total RCS. These are known as "hot spots" or "flare spots". Stealth measures applied in these critical areas will make the largest overall difference to total RCS.

When an aircraft is viewed from the front, the largest contributor to RCS is likely to be the inlets. Being re-entrant structures, they tend to act like corner reflectors, efficiently trapping and re-radiating radar energy. Any cooling ducts or other inlets visible from the front will prove equally efficient radar reflectors. Another will be any forward-facing antennas

Above left: **Lockheed's experimental Q-Star may look crude, but this adapted sailplane proved the sound-reduction technology used on the low-noise YO-3A.**

Above: **The North American F-107A (an unsuccessful rival to Republic's F-105 Thunderchief) is the only jet fighter to have flown with a dorsal air intake.**

Below: **The MiG-25 Foxbat was optimised for high-speed dash at Mach 2.8 and no attempt was made to minimise radar signature. Its huge inlets and abundance of right angled surfaces all help reflect radar energy.**

moderately low over a wide range of viewing angles, or does the user want the RCS from a certain critical sector to be kept as low as possible at the expense of "dumping" the energy in the form of strong reflections at other less important angles? Techniques such as operational analysis may help provide the answer here by allowing hypothetical aircraft using both approaches to RCS reduction to be "flown" against the postulated enemy defences.

The powerplant and its associated inlets and nozzles create their own problems. Many stealth configurations have engine inlets mounted above the wing or fuselage to

keep them hidden from ground-based radars but any aerodynamicist will warn of the possibility of airflow problems during high angle-of-attack manoeuvres. The sort of ventral air intake flight tested on the North American F-107 was not dropped just because it looked ugly.

When radar energy strikes the compressor or fan face of a jet engine it effectively acts as a solid surface, preventing the wave from proceeding further. The most obvious way of reducing intake RCS would be to coat the first-stage blades with RAM. This would have the desired effect but is not a practical solution — the absorbent material could not

Non-Stealthy Features of MiG 25 Foxbat

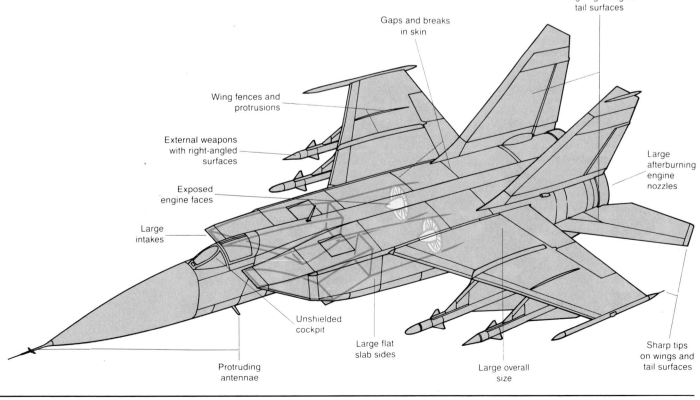

Large right-angled tail surfaces

Gaps and breaks in skin

Wing fences and protrusions

External weapons with right-angled surfaces

Exposed engine faces

Large intakes

Protruding antennae

Unshielded cockpit

Large flat slab sides

Large overall size

Large afterburning engine nozzles

Sharp tips on wings and tail surfaces

in the nose radome of the aircraft or its missiles. If a radome is not fitted, a near-spherical metal nose may also act as an efficient scatterer, while travelling waves moving along the fuselage may add their own contribution. The cockpit is another cavity which may return strong echoes.

Moving away from the centre line, the wing leading edges play a major rôle in scattering. At broadside angles the fuselage sides, vertical fin, underwing stores and pod-mounted engines become major sources. When radar waves strike wing and fin leading and trailing edges at near-grazing incidence, travelling waves can be set up, while further towards the rear sector radar returns from the wing and fin trailing edges will be observed. From behind the aircraft, the most important contributors will be the engine exhausts and any travelling waves set up along the fuselage.

RCS also varies with elevation angle. When an aircraft is viewed from the side and above, the wing/fuselage junction creates a radar-reflective 90 degree feature, while the right angle between the vertical fin and the horizontal stabiliser adds its own component. Radar waves arriving from above or below will also find the near-flat areas on the wings and horizontal control surfaces to be good radar targets.

Experience will allow designers to identify these features but their effect on overall RCS must be assessed. In the earliest stages of a hypothetical design, this can only be done using RCS prediction codes, specialised

computer software which makes use of a company's or nation's accumulated RCS expertise.

By a process of analysis, the shape of the complete aircraft is broken down into simple parts — the plates, cylinders, edges, spheres and the like whose individual RCS is predictable. Then comes the task which only a supercomputer can realistically handle — synthesis of these into a highly-complex total RCS.

There is thus no neat or easy way to predict RCS and the magnitude of the task which the designer faces is dependant on the complexity of the shape he is considering.

RCS Measurement Plot

Above: **This Lockheed concept of an ATF production line illustrates the computer-controlled technology needed when building the structure of future low-RCS fighters.**

Below right: **The complex shape of the B-2 inlet follows a precisely calculated stealthy profile, development of which caused programme delays.**

Below: **The digital computer has revolutionised the science of RCS predictiion. As this Thorn EMI polar diagram of an unidentified RPV shows, the measured RCS (red trace) is close to the forecast value (blue trace).**

It is thus no accident that one of the first applications which Thomson-CSF is applying to its RCS-prediction software suite is the design of stealthy re-entry vehicles. The sheer computer ''number-crunching'' power needed to carry out realistic RCS predictions was not available until the mid to late 1960s.

MEASUREMENTS

The next stage is to carry out measurements using an accurate model of either the whole aircraft or the areas of the aircraft identified as ''hot spots''. The latter can be tested at full-scale but, when the entire aircraft must be examined, the normal approach is to build an accurate scale model of the proposed design. This must either be made from metal or be electroplated or silver painted after construction so that its surface becomes electrically conductive. Unless a low electrical resistance is obtained all over the skin of the model, surface waves will not build up to the correct intensity.

In the 1960s and 1970s, most RCS testing was done at outdoor test ranges. These facilities consisted of

Indoor Test Chamber

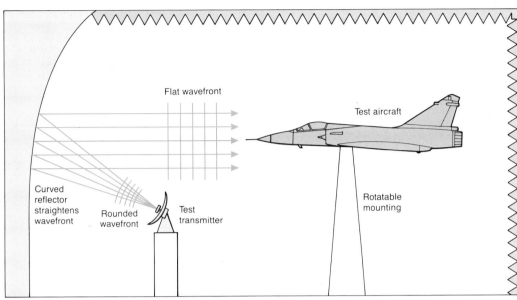

Above: **Indoor RCS test ranges shield stealth designs from prying eyes, but the radar energy reaching the target must behave as if it had travelled a long distance. The most common scheme involves collimating the energy by means of a carefully shaped reflector, so that it presents a flat wavefront. The chamber is lined with RAM to absorb excess radar energy.**

a mounting able to hold the model and turn it to any direction required for the test. The radar transmitters used to illuminate the model and the receiver which sampled the returned signal were located at a fair distance away, at least 100ft (30m), and often 1,000ft (305m) or more. The radar beam directed at the target would at least partially illuminate the terrain. To

reduce the effects of this, the ground between the transmitter site and the test position was carefully treated. One technique involved creating a berm, a vee-shaped raised area running from the transmitter to the test site. Another involved erecting a series of low lateral fences coated with RAM.

The problem with outdoor ranges is that their size makes

them expensive to build and run, while the accuracy of the test results is affected by weather. There is also a risk that the security of the design of a new aircraft may be compromised. Given a photograph of a stealth aircraft, a low-observables expert can estimate its characteristics.

Indoor test ranges allow the radar cross-section of highly-classified stealth warplanes and missiles to be tested in complete secrecy and also eliminate the effects of weather on the measurements being made.

For the designer of such test facilities, the problem is to devise a way of creating the same conditions as an outdoor range. The most obvious technique is to line the walls of the test chamber with RAM, absorbing the beam once it has passed the target and maintaining the electronic "illusion" that the target is out of doors. This is normally done using the pyramidal type of RAM material described earlier. A radar signal directed into such a chamber will almost completely disappear when it meets the wall, with less than a fraction of one per cent being reflected.

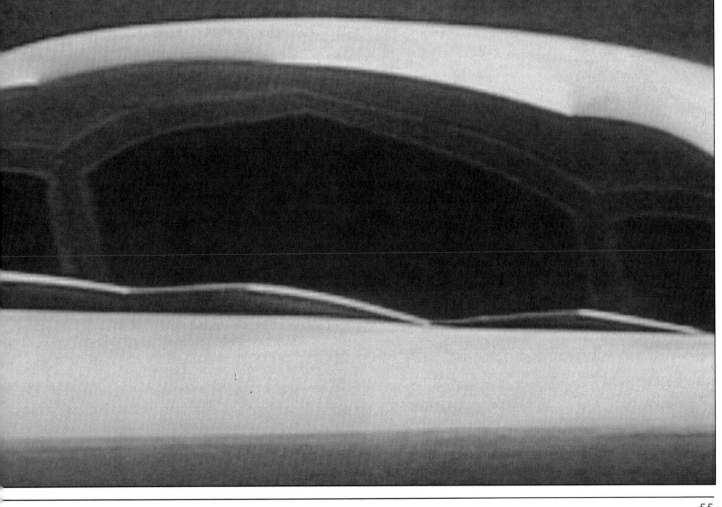

If good results are to be achieved, the wave-front must be as flat as could be obtained from an antenna a long distance away. The most common technique is to direct the radar energy from the antenna not directly at the target but indirectly, via a specially designed reflector. This collimates the energy, creating an evenly distributed signal identical to that from an antenna located a long distance away. An alternative but less common technique involves passing the radar beam through a collimating lens made of plastic but the manufacture of large enough lens structures has proved difficult.

At first, compact ranges were seen simply as convenient alternatives to outdoor ranges, useful largely for initial testing only but no substitute for definitive trials on a good outdoor range. Improvements in computers, range instrumentation and range design have now reduced or even eliminated this performance gap. In 1988, the Government Communications Systems Division of Harris, told *Aviation Week* that compact ranges could in some cases now offer ''better measurement accuracy than many of the outdoor ranges''. With the rise of stealth technology, most of the major US aircraft companies now own both outdoor and indoor test ranges.

RCS TESTING

Whether tested indoors or outdoors, the proposed design must be examined at varying radar frequencies. Whenever the wavelength being used is of the same order as the size of any feature on the aircraft, a resonance may occur, producing a larger radar echo. As different frequencies are tested, different-sized components on the aircraft will resonate when illuminated at the appropriate frequency. All the possible reflection mechanisms, such as specular reflections, edge diffraction, plus travelling and creeping waves are all frequency-dependant, creating a mass of ever changing variables. To keep the magnitude of the task within bounds, engineers will often confine their tests to the forward sector or any other direction in which RCS will be critical for the aircraft under investigation.

Many features of the proposed design can be checked with a simple plot of

3-D Radar Plot of Canberra

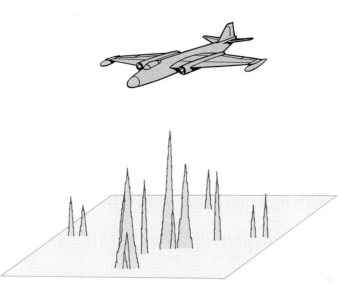

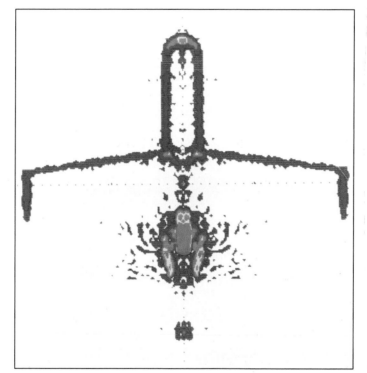

reflectivity versus range, repeated at different aspect angles. To get a really detailed radar ''look'' at a complex target requires more sophisticated test methods, usually involving synthetic aperture techniques.

The most normal use of synthetic aperture technology is in the creation of high-definition sideways-looking radars (SLRs). These obtain their near-photographic resolution by exploiting Doppler shift, the slight modification in signal frequencies caused by relative movement of the signal source and observer. (The classic example of Doppler shift is the apparent drop in pitch of the noise from a speeding train as it passes an observer standing on the railway platform.)

For RCS testing, instrumentation designers use inverse synthetic aperture radar (ISAR) technology. Instead of moving the radar, they move the target in order to create the Doppler effect. The target was normally rotated, so that its individual ''hot spots'' would display a Doppler shift, dependant on radar frequency, and any radial movement caused by their distance from the centre of rotation.

RADAR IMAGES

The end result of an ISAR test is a complex three-dimensional radar image whose basic co-ordinates are range and cross-range and where the third dimension (height) indicates reflectivity. This can be compared with the target and all sources of reflection swiftly located.

These tests allow the designers to identify all the high-reflective features of the

Top: **This three-dimensional plot identifies the main ''hot spots'' in the radar signature of a Canberra bomber. Such diagrams for current front-line aircraft are highly classified, but it's safe to predict that the Thorn-EMI facility which prepared this diagram also tests accurate models of Soviet fighters and bombers.**

Above: **MBB's Brevel RPV combines the wing span of an albatross with the RCS of a dove. This two-dimensional plot shows its radar image.**

Right: **This Northrop CAD (Computer-Aided Design) screen shows the likely configuration of the two-man cockpit of the B-2 bomber.**

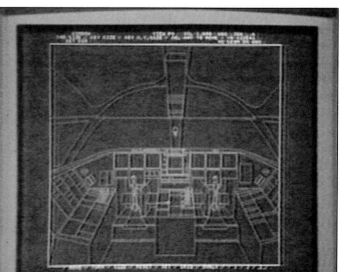

aircraft it was building or might build in the future. Built into a penthouse in its roof is a crane with a lifting capacity of 80,000lb (36,300kg) which is used to lift aircraft in and out of the chamber once the 70-ton door has been opened.

A feature of the installation was the ability to link the chamber to the company's flight-simulation and electronic systems laboratories and also to an Air Force Electronic Warfare Evaluation Simulator (AFEWES). In 1987 GD was already spending close to $1 million on control software for this "ultimate" research and test tool. When all the planned link-ups are installed (the company has been reluctant to predict when that might be), an aircraft on test in the chamber could be

manned by a crew which would have full flight-simulation facilities, working avionics and a realistic RF threat environment controlled by an operator who could react to the test aircraft's sensor and EW behaviour.

The walls of the facility are lined with pyramidal absorbers whose individual elements are between 2 and 6ft (0.6m and 1.8m) deep. At frequencies above 250GHz, the walls have an absorption rated at a staggering 60dB. In conventional terms, that means that 99.9999% of the energy striking the wall is absorbed and a mere ten-thousandth of one per-cent is reflected. That is as close to perfection as anybody is ever likely to need. Reduce the RCS of the biggest bomber ever built by such an amount and it would appear on a radar as a target no larger than a tiny insect.

SECRECY

Another advanced indoor range commissioned by Boeing in 1988 is even larger, with a test chamber measuring 225ft × 112ft (68.6m × 34m) under an 80ft (24.4m) roof. This is large enough to test many types of aircraft, or half-scale models of larger designs. Targets under test can either be mounted on a radar-invisible pylon of ogival cross-section or be suspended on a system of cables which allows the "fly-by" RCS to be measured. High measurement accuracy is a feature of the facility, as is the rigorous security demanded by "black" programmes. The foundations of one of the chamber's two test turntables are isolated from the rest of the base structure, while the support structure of the ceiling-mounted turntable is isolated from the walls by means of slip joints. In order to maintain strict "need to know" rules for models tested, a series of physically separated rooms for model storage and preparation are provided.

Once any remaining "hot spots" identified on the full scale aircraft or missile have been dealt with, the design can then be cleared for full production. All the test results and additional knowledge gathered during the development effort is then available for study, helping to refine the low-observable technologies, materials and techniques to be incorporated in the next generation of stealthy aircraft and missiles.

Above: **Superimposed on the image of a hovering Westland Lynx helicopter, this plot shows the Doppler spectrum generated by the main rotor.**

Right: **The test rig holding this B-1B tail cone has been treated with RAM to minimise interference with the EW antennas being tested.**

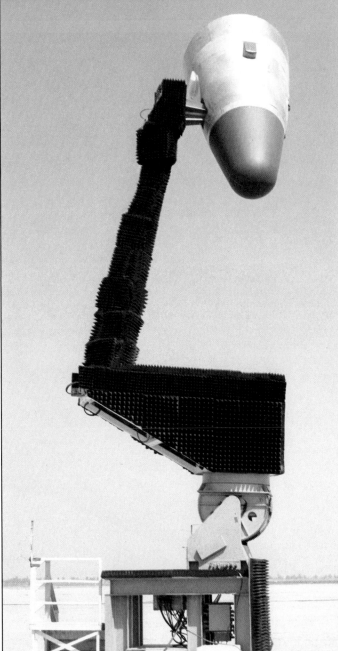

proposed design — parts of the airframe which make an unduly large contribution to total RCS and whose physical size may have little relationship to their apparent radar size. A large airframe feature may contribute little to RCS while a small one may prove to be a major scatterer. These "hot spots" must either be eliminated from the design or be treated with RAM to reduce their reflectivity.

INDOOR TESTS

Once a prototype of the aircraft has been completed, it will undergo RCS testing to verify the results of the earlier tests with scale models. Until recently, this work had to be done at an outside test range, but can now be done in a secure manner thanks to a new generation of indoor test facilities — the designation "compact range" may seem almost a misnomer for a treated chamber able to swallow an entire fighter!

In 1987, General Dynamics' Fort Worth division commissioned one of the world's largest anechoic chambers. This $9.3 million facility measured 120ft × 85ft (36.6m × 26m) and had a ceiling height of 40ft (12.2m). According to the company, it was big enough to house any

EARLY STEALTH AIRCRAFT

About once a decade or so history throws up momentous events, the sort of thing which years later can lead to reminiscences along the lines of "I can remember where I was and what I was doing when I heard the news that ...". For many readers of this book, these events are probably the assassination of President Kennedy or the shooting of John Lennon. For our parents or grandparents, it was Pearl Harbor, while a new generation will probably refer to the loss of the Space Shuttle *Challenger*.

These events are by definition memorable but few can accurately date news of a different type — the new trend which may create major changes in some aspect of the world but which arrives unbidden and unnannounced. *Glasnost* may be a household word for the late 1980s, for example, but who outside of a handful of "Kremlin watchers" could date its apparent birth?

Much the same applies to the first news of stealth technology. It seems to have crept into the public domain with virtually no publicity, a classic example of how first news of a major development can pass almost unnoticed. Legends die hard and aeronautical legends are no exception. An "official version" of the unveiling of stealth seems to have evolved and requires to be debunked before politically expedient claims become elevated to the status of history.

According to a number of 1980 pronouncements by US Government officials and even by President Carter, news of the programme had first leaked in August of that year. A subsequent official release of minimal information was depicted by the Democratic Party as a move intended to damp down future press leaks, while the Republican Party saw it as a blatant attempt by a shaky Adminstration to boost its image for the forthcoming US Presidential election.

Like many legends, it is neat, colourful and bears little relationship to reality. Reports of stealth technology had

Above: **When President Carter cancelled the B-1A bomber programme in 1977, the first XST stealth aircraft was already being built.**

Below: **The single-seat configuration identifies this "US Air Force" aircraft as a CIA A-12, predecessor of the SR-71 Blackbird.**

Right: **This Lockheed U-2R of the USAF's 9th Strategic Reconnaissance Wing is externally similar to today's Lockheed TR-1.**

been circulating for several years before the August 1980 incident. Casting my mind back over more than a decade, I cannot remember when I first heard of stealth. In much the same way as a police pathologist will give a spread of times of the likely moment of death for a murder victim, I can only reply "not before 30 June 1977 and not later than 27 May 1978".

In 1977, Friday was press day for the pages which contained regular news features in the British aviation magazine *Flight International*. On 30 June 1977, the day was going much like any other. The full quota of news stories had not yet been completed

but the remaining shortages were nothing which a lunchtime visit to the nearby Rose and Crown public house was not helping to cure (a process known to staff reporters as "lubricating the the fingertips"). Defence Editor Charles Gilson was working steadily on a large news story, while I was on the phone obtaining the regular weekly news report from the magazine's US correspondent.

At the end of a lengthy phone call and much notetaking, I realised that it was time to spoil Charles Gilson's entire day. "Carter has just cancelled the B-1", I explained. Under normal circumstances, Gilson was the ideal boss, radiating a general air of calm in a profession noted for stress and frayed tempers. On this occasion, he reacted as if I had kicked him in the seat of the pants. "He's WHAT?", was his shocked response.

STEALTH APPEARS

Rapidly consigning most of the material we had written for that week's issue to oblivion and warning the production department that our news pages would be closing for press late, we started work on a massive two-page news story. Entitled "Rockell B-1 cancelled", this explained President Carter's decision to abandon the swing-wing manned bomber programme in favour of deploying the new air-launched cruise missiles.

In the most important of my research files on which this book is based, a photocopy of the B-1 cancellation story is the first item. It's not there because of what it says but because of what it doesn't say. Nowhere in Charles Gilson's description of the reasons for the B-1 cancellation or my account of how cruise missiles would take over the Rockwell bomber's intended rôle does any mention of stealth technology or even the very idea of low-observables appear. Obviously neither Charles Gilson nor I had heard of it, since it would have formed a natural part of our report. First news that Lockheed was working on new types of aircraft came in the Fiscal Year 1977 US defence budget. The USAF announced for the first time that Lockheed was to develop and build the TR-1 variant of the U-2 family, while the Defense Research Projects Agency (DARPA) revealed that Lockheed had received a three-year development contract worth an estimated $90 million to develop and fly an undesignated new aircraft type. At that time, nobody seems to have realised the purpose of these unidentified aircraft. The first rumours of stealth technology were not to leak to the world's aviation press for sometime.

By the time that I reported the first crash of a stealth aircraft in the 27 May 1978 issue of *Flight International*, tales of radar-invisible aircraft were already in the public domain. Although the *Flight* story is only the second document in my own stealth files, the fact that I did not explain at great length within its half-page length exactly what a stealth aircraft was indicates that I was assuming that the reader was already familiar with the concept. My contemporary notes have long since vanished into *Flight* archives — I left the magazine 18 months later — but I can remember reading other (and almost certainly earlier) reports of the aircraft's existence.

SKUNK WORKS

The idea of stealth aircraft had been around for sometime in classified form. In 1953 the USAF drew up a requirement for a highly-specialised reconnaissance aircraft able to fly over Soviet targets at altitudes of 70,000ft (21,000m) or more. The aircraft would rely primarily on height for survivability but the need for stealth was also

appreciated. "No [radio or radar] emanations from the aircraft will be permitted over enemy territory", the specification insisted, while "Consideration will be given in the design of the vehicle to minimising the detectability by enemy radar". Low RCS thus became a design goal of the Lockheed U-2 and Martin RB-57 but in practice little could be done.

The earliest useful work on low-observable technology did not begin until the end of the 1950s. When drawing up plans from the spring of 1958 to the late summer of 1959 for a U-2 sucessor, Kelly Johnson's team at the Lockheed's "Skunk Works" investigated measures for RCS reduction. The go-ahead was given in August 1959 for the construction of the first prototype A-12, an aircraft which would incorporate low-RCS features such as wing/body blending and built-in RAM.

Low-observable technology was also seen as a method of improving the survivability of unmanned vehicles. In 1960, even before the jet-powered AGM-28A Hound Dog had become operational with SAC, North American was give a contract to reduce the RCS of the follow-on AGM-28B version.

RYAN DRONES

Early in 1960, Ryan Aeronautical proposed to the USAF the development of a reconnaissance version of the Ryan Q-2 Firebee target drone. The company had toyed with the idea of a reconnaissance drone in the mid-1950s but it was not until the growing deployment of Soviet SAMs in the late 1950s which threatened the future of U-2 operations that the USAF showed serious interest.

On 1 April of that year, a Soviet SA-2 Guideline missile downed the U-2 being flown by CIA man Francis Gary Powers. On 8 July, Ryan was given a $200,000 USAF contract to demonstrate the use of modified target drones for reconnaissance known as project "Red Wagon". One of the goals of this project would be to assess RCS reduction measures which might improve survivability without an extensive re-design.

A wire screen was fitted to mask the air intake from long-wavelength radars of the sort which the Soviet Union used for surveillance, blankets of RAM were fitted to the fuselage sides and the nose section was treated with what has been described as "non-conductive paint".

Test results were applied to a new stealthy design known as the Ryan Model 136. This featured a high aspect ratio unswept wing, a twin tail with inward canted verticals and a dorsal air inlet and engine installation. Work had barely started on the programme when Harold Brown (then director of Defense Research and Engineering) ordered the cancellation of "Red Wagon".

Ryan reworked its proposal, offering in the summer of 1961 a design optimised for operations along and close to the Warsaw Pact borders rather than overflight. Known as "Lucy Lee", this would have climbed from 65,000ft (19,800m) to 72,000ft (22,000m) as fuel burned off. Once more, stealth would be a feature, with the RCS being "reduced to a minimum using defraction (sic), transmission

Above: **On the original photo of this SR-71, triangular RAM panels are clearly visible on the starboard wing leading edge and chine.**

and absorption techniques". Once more, Brown declined to give the go-ahead.

Perhaps with the Brown "axe" in mind, the company had also submitted a mimimum-modification rework of the Q-2C drone as an air-launched platform for reconnaissance missions. Known as the 147A Fire Fly, this was given the go-ahead in early 1962 funded under the USAF "Big Safari" special reconnaissance programme.

The first 147A was a Q-2C modified to act as a testbed for the proposed navigation and guidance system. The remaining three were Q-2Cs with a fuselage stretch of 35in (89cm) which increased fuel capacity by 68 US gallons (257 litres). Several had extended-span wings which the USAF obtained from a US Army Q-2 project. Flight trials started in April 1962 with the first camera-equipped sortie taking place on 27 April.

On 17 May, a 147A was flown from Tyndall AFB, Florida, to test the effectiveness of the RCS-reduction measures. The crews of the five F-106 Delta Dart interceptors sent to hunt down the 147A found it virtually impossible to obtain radar lock-on, even when vectored to the drone by GCI. Final interception was carried out as tail-chase pursuits following the drone's contrail,

Above: **In an attempt to improve the effectiveness of the AGM-28 Hound Dog missile, the USAF ordered an RCS-reduction programme.**

Above: **Soviet radars such as Fan Song and its associated SA-2 Guideline missile forced the USAF to study anti-radar measures.**

Crisis. Following the loss of a U-2 over Cuba, two 147A drones were rushed to Tyndall AFB. A drone-equipped aircraft had barely started engines to begin the first mission over Cuba when the order to cancel the flight was given. The 147A was not to see action but Ryan had demonstrated that the tiny craft was ready to go to war. The company was rewarded by a contract for the definitive big-winged 147B. Flight trials of this model started in May 1963 and missions were flown to test the effectivess of the craft's RAM blankets. A year later, the 147B was rushed to southeast Asia to play its rôle in the early stages of the Vietnam War.

NEW BOMBERS

The year 1964 also saw the much-delayed first flight of the North American XB-70 bomber. Nobody watching the maiden flight on 21 September was under any illusion that the six-engined Mach 3 monster would ever see SAC service. The decision to make the programme a purely technological demonstration had been taken in 1960. In my opinion, it was a bad decision and one which would be paid in human lives in the skies over North Vietnam later in 1972. Many of the bomber crews who died over North Vietnam in the Linebacker II raids

Below: **Having proved a difficult radar target, Teledyne RPVs became useful recce platforms for the Vietnam War.**

while eight Hughes GAR-3A (AIM-4F) Falcon semi-active radar missiles failed to down the Ryan aircraft.

CUBA

During a test run over the Atlantic missile range on 5 August, Air Defense Command had launched interceptors to catch the drone. The result was embarassment all round. The fighters failed to locate the drone but an over-confident Ryan crew ran the tiny aircraft out of fuel, dropping it in the sea 65 miles (105km) off the coast. Another flight on 9 August saw the F-102 and F-106 interceptors obtaining only momentary radar glimpses of the drone and eventually pursuing a non-existent "target" across Florida and into Georgia.

On 29 August, a U-2 aircraft returned from a sortie over Cuba with photos which showed the installation of SAM sites. Although the presence of ballistic missiles would not be detected until mid-October, this was the opening move of what was to become the Cuban Missile

would be alive today had they been piloting 2,000mph (3,200km/h) B-70s rather than elderly subsonic B-52s through the skies over Hanoi and other heavily-defended targets.

In its search for a new bomber during the early 1960s, the USAF had carried out studies of concepts such as the Advanced Manned Precision Strike System, the Low Altitude Manned Penetrator, the Strategic Low Altitude Bomber and the Extended Range Strategic Aircraft. By 1965, this work had focussed on a concept known as the Advanced Manned Strategic Aircraft. A specification issued that year called for an aircraft able to fly at high subsonic speed at low level or at supersonic speed at high altitude and emphasised the need for RCS reduction. It was to result in the decision to build the Rockwell B-1.

Research into stealth technology really got into its stride in the early to mid-1970s. Run by DARPA, it was based on work already carried out in the 1960s, on what Perry would later describe as "some of our reconnaissance aircraft", and being applied to the then-new 1970s generation of US cruise missiles. It was aimed at countering the development by the Soviet Union of jam-resistant high-power monopulse ground radars and overcoming the performance of modern look-down/shoot-down radars able to observe targets flying within ground clutter.

HAVE BLUE

In the 1960s Dr Leo Windecker had designed and built an all-composite fibreglass light aircraft known as the AC-7 Eagle 1. This was a four-seat aircraft of conventional appearance, powered by a 285hp (213kW) piston engine. In 1963 he offered this to the USAF as a possible low-RCS research aircraft but the concept fell on deaf ears. When he re-proposed the idea in 1972, the concept of low-observables was coming into vogue.

The prototype Eagle was lent to the USAF for RCS tests and Windecker Aviation was given a USAF contract to build the YE-5A, a modified Eagle with internal changes such as the addition of RAM. Delivered in 1973, this was tested by the USAF and Lockheed, being used in studies of the radar reflectivity of glass-fibre

constructed airframes.

DARPA is thought to have issued a number of research contracts in early 1973, a move which may have marked the beginning of the highly-classified "Have Blue" signature-reduction programme. Late the same year, DARPA issued a Request For Proposals (RFP) for a small flying testbed able to demonstrate the feasibility of stealth aircraft. The

specification was demanding, calling for an airframe skinned in RAM and having minimal RCS in the head-on sector, a cooled engine exhaust, noise reduction measures intended to make the aircraft acoustically silent at ranges of more than a few hundred yards (metres), plus a custom-designed EW suite.

Boeing, Grumman, Lockheed and McDonnell Douglas are all reported to

Above: **Although a good radar target, the XB-70 cruised at speeds and heights beyond the reach of present-day SAMs.**

Below: **SR-71 technology was taken a stage further in Lockheed's highly-classified D-21 reconnaissance RPV programme. It proved unsuccessful, and surviving examples were retired in the late 1970s.**

have bid, a listing which strangely omits Northrop, a company which might logically have been expected to bid. Initial contracts covered research and development studies. This comprised theoretical studies, laboratory work and some flight trials using modified aircraft or unmanned scale models.

As a result of these studies, the field was soon narrowed to Grumman and Lockheed but it is likely that only the latter received a development contract in 1976. When revealing the existence of stealth technology in 1980, the US DoD did admit that "a number of different vehicles had been flight tested". Although there have been a few reports of a competitive fly-off between the Lockheed aircraft and rival designs, the DoD was almost certainly referring to adapted existing

Below: **This P-50 Barlock radar is probably a US-built replica of the Soviet original, a novel research tool in the US anti-radar effort.**

designs, plus unmanned test vehicles such as the Lockheed stealth cruise missile.

The contract awarded to Lockheed called for the construction of five XST (Experimental Stealth Tactical) technology-demonstration aircraft. Some sources suggest that only three were built, a confusion probably due to the fact that two were later lost in accidents.

Early in 1977, Defense Secretary Harold Brown and his advisers carried out a survey of all current research and development programmes in the hope of identifying key areas which might yield useful operational advantages for the US military during the new Adminstration of President Carter. A similar technology survey in the early 1970s had resulted in the US cruise missile programmes, so Brown doubtless hoped that another potential breakthrough could be found. He rapidly identified low-observable technology as a likely candidate.

EARLY STEALTH

By mid-1977, when spending was running at around $10 million a year, it was becoming obvious that RCS reductions large enough to give real military advantage were within reach. The decision was taken to increase the pace of the programme but to keep it under wraps, giving what Perry would later describe as "extraordinary" security protection "even to the point of classifying the very existence of the program".

The XST was not the aircraft now known as the "F-117A", but a much smaller design powered by a pair of non-afterburning General Electric J85 turbojets, probably the 2,750lb (1,247kg) J85-17 version used in the Saab 105 trainer. In 1983 a Pentagon official was to describe the XST as being "more a testbed for future ATB designs" than a pre-production fighter.

Unofficial reports have suggested that the XST was about 35ft (10.7m) long and 20ft (6.1m) in wingspan and of double-delta configuration, rather like the US Space Shuttle. If correct, the aircraft would be rather similar in appearance to the definitive F-117A, an aircraft with a narrow, highly swept back wingspan but with straight line leading edges.

One source gives a maximum take-off weight in

the 20,000lb (9,000kg) class but this seems far too high. When the Dassault design team built their first delta in the early 1950s, the dimensions of the resulting MD.550 Mirage I were only marginally larger than those quoted for the XST. The fully-loaded weight was only 11,200lb (5,000kg).

To find a way of creating a delta closer to the 20,000lb (9,000kg) mark, one must look across the Atlantic to the US Air Force/NASA Lifting Body programme. The Martin Marietta X-24A flown in the late 1960s was only 24.5ft (7.47m) long and a mere 13.7ft (4.18m) in wingspan, much smaller than the XST, but weighed 11,000lb (5,000kg) gross. The later double-delta X-24B was close to the XST dimensions, weighing 13,000lb (5,900kg).

It may be no coincidence that one pilot who caught an air-to-air glimpse of the elusive XST while on a training mission at Nellis AFB described the shape as being like the X-24. A deep fuselage and wing would make the aircraft easy to build and provide the internal volume needed for the easy installation and removal of internally-mounted RAM during experimental tests.

Given the modest thrust of a pair of "dry" J85s, all-up weights of no more than 12,000lb (5,400kg) would seem likely but such a judgment reflects modern trends in fighter thrust/weight ratios of unity or higher. Stay subsonic, as did the XST, and a much lower ratio can be accepted.

A ratio of 0.4 would give the XST a maximum weight of around 14,000lb (6,350kg), but the figure of 19,000lb (8,620kg), which a ratio of 0.3 would yield, is definitely on the high side given the built-in headwind resulting from the aircraft's novel airframe. Most sources have described this as being smoothly blended but in practice it was almost certainly faceted, a configuration which would have done little for the XST's handling qualities or overall airframe drag.

CRASHES

One report in the early 1980s suggested that the XST airframe was built at least in part from Dow Chemicals' "Fibaloy", a composite material with glass fibres woven into a plastic base. Other sources give the designation "Fiberloy" and identify the fibres as boron.

The first XST was completed in the autumn of 1977, when it was flown by a C-5 Galaxy to the "Ranch" airstrip at the Tonopah test range near Nellis AFB. Here it made its first flight in November 1977. By the late summer of 1978, a second aircraft was reported to be under flight test.

Once the XST's flying characteristics had been explored, and to judge by the reputation of the later stealth fighter these could not have been good, the aircraft could be used for the critical tests of its invisibility to radar. During trials, it was flown against captured Soviet radar and missile systems to see just how elusive a target it presented.

Top: US research work with "lifting bodies" in the late 1960s and early 1970s may have given Lockheed the confidence to use a "hump backed" shape for the XST.

Above: Seen from this angle, the X-24B bears some resemblance to the F-117A, and presumably to the earlier XST stealth technology demonstrator.

Right: While the B-2 was still under wraps, several analysts attempted artist's impressions. This concept by Bill Gunston was more sensible than many rival "designs", and boldly predicted the absence of vertical surfaces. Those ventral inlets would have been a poor stealth feature in a high-level bomber which is the B-2's main rôle.

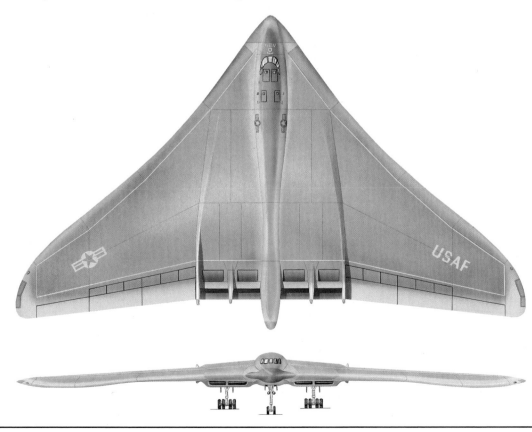

Accidents apart, the results of the flight test programme seem to have been excellent. By the autumn of 1980, several programmes had been launched. US government spending on the new technology rose by a further factor of 10, bringing it to 100 times its early-1977 level.

In the late 1970s and early 1980s, DARPA had conducted a series of cruise missile penetration evaluations. Intended to assess the weapon's ability to cope with Soviet defences, these tested the weapon's radar and IR signatures in the presence of background clutter and its ability to use terrain masking. The data gathered were used to predict the likely capability of future Soviet defence systems against small cruise missile targets.

In 1980, DARPA launched a programme known as "Teal Dawn". This was intended to develop technology for stealth cruise missiles. At least one company — General Dynamics — is known to have flown test hardware as part of this programme, while other data may have been provided by flight testing of the highly-classified Lockheed stealth cruise missile. By 1980, this is known to have been on flight test from B-52 aircraft based at Edwards AFB.

All of this development flying seems to have been conducted from the Groom Lake test facility at Nellis AFB, Nevada, although Eielson AFB, Alaska, was also linked to reports of stealth aircraft trials.

On 4 May 1978, an unidentified aircraft operating from Nellis AFB crashed but the USAF declined to make any statement beyond the straight admission that an accident had occured in which a pilot was slightly injured. A USAF spokesman would only add that "for security reasons that is all the information available". An injured pilot, 52 year old William Park, who claimed to work for Lockheed, was admitted to a Los Angeles hospital, treated for multiple fractures and concussion, then quickly discharged four days later.

At first, the aircraft was thought to be a TR-1 but by late in the month, sources were confirming that the incident involved a prototype stealth aircraft. The XST fleet had suffered its first casualty, probably the result of an in-flight break-up. This information led me to write a news story "Stealth Aircraft Lost in Nevada" in *Flight International*'s 27 May issue. A second less-publicised crash in 1982 which reduced the XST fleet to three is thought to have been due to an equipment failure.

Early "Stealth Bomber" Concept

SABRE PENETRATOR

By this time the B-1 seemed likely to emulate the XB-70 in being reduced to a museum piece. As recounted earlier, President Carter announced in June 1977 that he would not approve production of the new bomber. Although convinced that conventional bombers were too vulnerable to modern air defences, behind the scenes he gave the go-ahead for studies of possible bombers based on low-observable technology. These were carried out under a secret programme code-named "Saber Penetrator".

In the summer of 1980, a growing number of Executive and Congressional officials were briefed on the stealth bomber concept. At the same time, the political battle between President Carter and California Governor Ronald Reagan for the US Presidency began to hot up. Stealth was about to become a factor in the US election.

In its issue of 4 August 1980, *Aviation Week* quoted an unidentified Administration official as talking of "a growing perception that we have made a mistake in cancelling B-1" and reported that the House-Senate Authorization Conference Committee favoured the purchase of one or even two new types of bomber. Insistent that a new bomber be fielded by 1987, the committee suggested the bulding of 100 modified B-1s, followed by 100 new-technology bombers "using all new technology, particularly stealth technology to avoid radar detection".

A week later, the magazine carried an item headed "Bomber Biases". President Carter remained opposed to the B-1, the magazine reported, and was not convinced that the USAF was agreed on the need for a new bomber. Identifying one of the aircraft candidates as "the advanced stealth bomber", the story stated that "the White House intends to continue studies" of new bombers, adding that "Some Administration officials believe a delay in the studies will allow more time to perfect stealth technology".

LEAKS

In the September issue of *Armed Forces Journal International*, Bejamin F. Schemmer revealed that hundreds of millions of dollars were being spent on programmes to which only a few dozen US Government officials were privy to full details. "Several different types of aircraft have been built. Scores of flight test hours have been accumulated on several prototypes, although only a handful of pilots have flown the planes."

No one single technical trick was responsible for stealth, he explained, correctly identifying all the main techniques used for signature reduction — structural shaping, composites, IR shielding and surface treatment with RAM.

AFJI had known about "essential elements of the program for several years", claimed Schemmer, "but has not revealed them following a request by a senior Pentagon official in mid-1978 that AFJI not print, on national security grounds, a story...about the first stealth test prototypes".

Acting in response to the growing number of stories, on 22 August Defense Secretary Harold Brown released some limited information on the classified programme. The United States had built aircraft which could not be intercepted by existing or projected Soviet air defences,

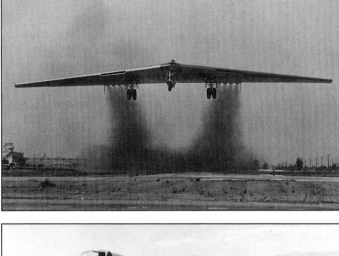

he explained. He denied that the existence of stealth technology had been a factor in President Carter's decision to cancel the B-1 bomber but suggested that "any new bomber will use some elements of this technology".

Background information was presented by Perry, who explained how stealth was a "complex synthesis" of many techniques which were now classified at the "highest security level". In the three years since 1977 the USA had made "remarkable advances" in the new technology and was beginning to develop practical applications. A degree of stealth technology could be applied to existing aircraft, he explained, but stealth would be most effective when applied to a new design. The cost of a stealth aircraft would not be substantially different from that of conventional designs.

Top: **Dense clouds of smoke from eight Allison J35 turbojets made the take-off of Northrop's YB-49 flying wing far from stealthy!**

Above: **The experience needed to design flying wing bombers was obtained from the private-venture Northrop N-1M, which flew in 1940.**

Below: **White nose markings on the B-1B may aid refuelling-boom operators but under some conditions may compromise camouflage.**

The Republican Party claimed that information of stealth technology has been improperly released by the Administration in order to boost its image on the sensitive topic of defence — Reagan was attacking the Democrats as being "soft" on defence issues. It was even suggested that the source of the leaks might have been none other than Defense Secretary Brown.

Two months later, Reagan won the Presidential election, bringing into power a new Administration determined to boost America's defence capability. The most obvious way of doing this was to exploit the new stealth technology.

FLYING WINGS

The year 1981 was to prove to be a key year for stealth.

In the summer of that year, Lockheed was given a secret contract to develop and manufacture a production aircraft based on the XST. The company also received the go-ahead to develop a stealthy cruise missile. In early 1981, Congress directed that a new bomber be developed for SAC but did not specify what form this aircraft should take, simply ordering an initial operating capability (IOC) by 1987. A total of $300 million in development money was added to the 1981 defence budget, along with $75 million for long-lead procurement.

The USAF was ordered to decide by 15 March 1981 on the type of aircraft to be ordered. The obvious candidate was an advanced derivative of the B-1 but the USAF was pushing a stretched derivative of the FB-111A known as the FB-111H, while behind the scenes lurked the possibility of an all-new aircraft based on stealth technology.

A Request for Proposals on what was then known as the Advanced Technology Bomber (ATB) was issued in 1981. To bid for the task of building the new aircraft, Lockheed linked up with Rockwell to create a team combining massive expertise in stealth and bomber technology. Lockheed based its design on the F-117A, so it probably used faceting as a means of reducing RCS.

In a little-reported programme in the late 1970s, Northrop invested large amounts of company money in a secret programme to develop expertise in low-observables technology. By

1981, it was ready to challenge Lockheed for the task of building the new bomber. Like Lockheed, the company teamed up with an established bomber design team, in this case Boeing.

In addition to its stealth expertise, Northrop also had extensive experience with flying wings, a configuration which potentially offered low RCS. The experimental N-1M had flown in 1940 and was followed by several examples of the NM-9 — one-third scale prototypes for the planned XB-35 bomber. The latter had a wing span of 172ft (52.4m) and was powered by four Pratt & Whitney Wasp Major engines driving contra-rotating propellers mounted at the trailing edge of the wing. The first flights were on 25 June 1946 but, even before they had flown, the decision had been taken to rebuild both prototypes as jet bombers, redesignating them XB-49. The first modified aircraft took to the air in October 1947, powered by eight 4,000lb (1,815kg) thrust Allison J-35-A-15 engines, and was followed in January 1948 by the second example. The latter aircraft crashed in June 1948 following an in-flight structural failure. Although some pre-production YB-49 and YRB-49 aircraft were subsequently built, the USAF abandoned the flying wing concept in the early 1950s and none of the Northop bombers saw operational service.

In its late 1970s bomber studies, Boeing had looked at tailed and tailless delta

designs. Like Northrop, Boeing wanted to exploit the fact that radar energy tends to diffract off flat horizontal surfaces, while long-chord wing sections of the type used in delta or flying wing designs are deep enough to allow the use of radar-absorbent structures, and internally-mounted RAM. Rockwell had also looked at flying wings during the same period, including a 77ft (23.5m) span design in the FB-111 performance class, but it is not clear whether a similar configuration was offered for the ATB competition.

ADVANCED BOMBER

Attractive though the ATB might be, there seemed little chance of its being developed or fielded by the 1987 deadline imposed by Congress. In July 1981 US Air Force Secretary Verne Orr stated that a stealth bomber might take ten to twelve years to develop. Any attempts to field it earlier would involve "tremendous cost". In the decade or more which development of a stealth bomber would take, the Soviet Union might be able to develop new types of sensor other than radar and IR which could be used to detect stealth aircraft, providing a partial or even total countermeasure. The Air Force would prefer a B-1 available in 1986 rather than a stealth bomber in 1992, he suggested.

Reagan solved the bomber dilemma on 2 October 1981 by announcing that the B-1 would be restored to production status allowing a

Above: **Heavy shadows and a dark matt finish hide the long wingspan of the B-2 as the first prototype rolls out from the hangar.**

batch of 100 to be built. While these aircraft provided a low-risk boost to SAC's strength, a new advanced technology stealth bomber aircraft could be developed in great secrecy for service in the early 1990s.

Later that month, Northrop was selected to develop the new bomber and its public relations department issued what was probably its shortest-ever press release. The entire text consisted of a mere 75 words:
"LOS ANGELES -- Oct. 20, 1981 -- Mr. Thomas V. Jones, Chairman of the board of Northrop Corporation, confirmed today that Northop has been notified by the Air Force of its selection as prime contractor to conduct initial research and development on advanced bomber concepts. This effort will have a material impact on Northrop. The key team members are Boeing, LTV/Vought and General Electric Aircraft Engine Group.
All details are classified, and no further comments will be made".

They meant what they said. In future press briefings for Northrop products, it was consistently made clear that this one subject would never be covered. With virtually all details of the new stealth fighter, stealth bomber and new cruise missile shrouded in a blanket of secrecy, the era of the "black" programme had arrived.

THE WORLD OF BLACK PROGRAMMES

One consequence of the build-up in US military strength during the eight-year Reagan Administration was a concentration on high-technology programmes such as the Strategic Defense Initiative ("Star Wars"). In parallel with this has been a growing tendency for much of the Pentagon's high-technology budget to disappear under a cloak of secrecy in what were dubbed "black" programmes.

"Black", that is to say, virtually invisible programmes are not new. The "Project Manhattan" effort to develop the atomic bomb during the Second World War was probably the first. Similar secret efforts saw the development of the U-2 spyplane and its A-12 successor, while the same category of high security has always shrouded the US reconnaissance satellite programme.

What few people realise is that the costs of these secret and largely unreported programmes exceeded that earmarked for the Strategic Defense Initiative. "Black" spending in the late 1980s and early 1990s is expected to be around $100 billion (US).

On the B-2 stealth bomber, the programme has been heavily compartmentalised in the interests of secrecy to a point which some observers claim must act as a barrier to the communications needed for efficient design and development work. Yet the DoD apparently considers the need for secrecy to be paramount, if the heavy US involvement in stealth technology is to pay off.

Watertight secrecy may be good for security but, as the "black" cloak fell over a greater portion of the Pentagon budget, some critics questioned whether such classified military programmes were spending money wisely. Denied special security clearance, most members of Congress cannot even review the budgets of "black" programmes.

For a nation so committed to openness, democracy and accountability as the United States, "black" programmes

have introduced a new way of working. Secrecy covering stealth projects has been so tight that the USAF is reported to have filed false flight plans with civilian agencies when stealth aircraft were being flown, according to *Washington Post* sources in 1987. In the same year *Aviation Week* reported that the DoD had even instructed some contractors to falsify their records in order to conceal the fact that they were running "black" programmes.

SECRECY

In some cases, excessive secrecy was hampering procurement decisions. In 1987, Congress learned that one US service had recently attempted to start a major "black" development programme, unaware that a similar programme had been under way for several years as a "black" programme by another service.

With US defence budgets shrinking in the final years of the Reagan Presidency, some members of Congress, and even some military leaders, have questioned the wisdom of concealing a growing share of the budget in ever more expensive "black" programmes. In the late 1980s, there were more than 200 such projects.

To this day, the best-known "black" programme is the Lockheed stealth fighter. The secret contract awarded in the summer of 1978 covered development of the aircraft and manufacture of a first batch of 20 production examples. In parallel with this work, General Electric was given a contract to develop a non-afterburning version of the F404 engine to power the new aircraft. The FY82 defence budget is thought to have contained as much as $1,000 million in "black" funding for the programme.

Although the stealth fighter was often referred to as the F-19 during the early 1980s, the USAF has always insisted that the designation F-19 has never been assigned. The ostensible reason of a risk of confusion with the MiG-19 is obvious nonsense; the designation F-21 was cheerfully assigned to the Kfir fighters leased from Israel for use in dissimilar combat training programmes. There were suggestions that the true designation might be RF-19 or even AR-19 (Attack/ Reconnaissance 19).

F-117A

The true designation "F-117A" first emerged in the winter of 1987/88 and may represent a novel form of disinformation. The USAF aircraft designation system abandoned in the early1960s had ended with the F-110 Spectre (the original designation of the USAF version of the Phantom) and the F-111. Had it been continued, with the incorporation of the designs developed for the US Navy, we would have had the F-112 Tomcat, F-113 Eagle, F-114 Fighting Falcon, Northrop YF-115 LWF prototype, and the F-116 Hornet. Next in line for the "F-19" would be F-117!

The official designation of the aircraft is "Senior Trend", a USAF two-word code-name similar to the "Have Blue" designation applied to early stealth prototypes. It is also known as the CSIRS (Covert Survivable In-weather Reconnaissance Strike) — pronounced "See-Sirs". Some reports suggested that the aircraft's popular name was "Ghost" or "Specter" but it now seems that the name "Nighthawk" was chosen. It is possible that the other names were applied to the XST prototypes.

Lockheed had probably been working on the new design since the late 1970s, so construction of the prototype was swift, leading to a first flight in 1981. Although based on experience gained with the XST, the F-117A was significantly larger. To reduce the RCS, the Skunk Works relied on fuselage faceting. Although this technique results in an ungainly-looking aircraft, it was probably the best way of creating a low-

RCS design using the RAM technology of the late 1970s. The F-117A is around 50ft (15.5m) in length, and 40ft (12m) in wingspan. These figures put it in the same size and weight class as the Dassault-Breguet Super Mirage 4000, and suggest a maximum loaded weight of around 45,000lb (20,400kg). Two non-afterburning F404 turbofans each give between 10,800 — 12,500lb (4,900 — 5,670kg) of installed thrust, bringing the thrust:weight ratio to an acceptable 0.5 — 0.55.

SHAPING

When the USAF released its first artist's impression of the B-2 in April 1988, many observers wondered why the older F-117A had not been the first stealth design to be publicly released. Air Force Chief of Staff General Larry D. Welch explained in May 1988 that the Air Force was more concerned about the Soviets seeing examples of early stealth technology than the B-2. The low RCS of the first stealth aircraft (he did not specifically describe this as the F-117A) depends almost exclusively on the aircraft's shape, he claimed, while the B-2 combines a variety of low-observable technologies. A good photograph of the F-117A would betray most of its secrets, thus explaining the extensive measures the USAF has taken to keep the type away from prying eyes.

The first F-117A squadron was formed in October 1983 at the Groom Lake facility at Nellis AFB, California. Early in its service career, the aircraft seems to have experienced problems — hardly surprising in such a revolutionary design. By 1987, most of these had been solved. Lengthy working-up trials had proved the aircraft's ability to cope with radar-based defences.

In August 1986, the *Washington Post* published an account of the Nellis operation with a headline proclaiming, "50 'Stealth' Fighters in Operation; Secret Squadrons Fly at Night From Bases in Nevada". Several squadrons of the new aircraft were based in the Nevada desert near Tonopah, southeast of Reno, the newspaper claimed. The aircraft spent the daylight hours hidden in hangars and flew at night under the control of Tactical Air Command. Pentagon spokesman Fred S. Hoffman declined to comment on the

Left: Given it's coat of "Iron Ball' paint in 1970, this was the last 100th Strategic Reconnaissance Wing U-2 to literally go "black".

Below: The first F-117A photo to be released had been carefully selected to give little away. Under-exposed so as to show little detail, then heavily airbrushed to hide the inlet configuration, it cleverly gave a false impression of the aircraft's sharp wing sweep angle.

report and a USAF spokesman would only say "We're wrapped in iron as far as commenting on low observables."

TONOPAH BASE

Following up on the story, the Associated Press stated that according to one source it had spoken to, only "a couple of dozen" aircraft had been built. It was almost certainly deliberate disinformation, a technique which Bill Sweetman claims was used in 1985/86 to help keep the programme under wraps. At least 50 were in service by the end of 1986 at what he identified as Tonopah Air Force Station, Nevada. A new base close to Tonopah in the northwest corner of the Nellis range, this outwardly resembles the SR-71 operating base at Beale AFB, California, in that its aircraft are stored in a large number of individual hangars. According to Bill Sweetman, who has published a photograph of the site taken from outside the base's security perimeter, the base has 42 "hangarettes" each large enough to hold two aircraft, plus five large hangars presumably used for maintenance.

According to some US newpaper reports, a klaxon horn is sounded at F-117A bases before the aircraft is exposed to view. All personnel not cleared to see the aircraft are said to be required to lie face down on the ground until the aircraft is out of sight! It all sounds more like legend than a realistic way of operating a mid-1980s military base. Such reports can almost certainly be dismissed.

One odd fact is that the Tonopah base is visible from a public road. "At the time the base was planned, nobody expected that the shape of the aircraft would not have been revealed by the time that it entered service", Sweetman suggested in early 1987.

For most of the time, the F-117A flies either over the Nellis range or in corridors between Nellis and Edwards AFB and George AFB in the Mojave Desert, California. Reports that the aircraft was being used outside the USA first appeared in the mid-1980s. In 1986, *Defense News* reported that the F-117A was being flight tested in Europe, probably from Mildenhall, Suffolk, England, but only under the cover of darkness or bad weather.

"The paper did not indicate what dangerous targets the newest spy plane was flying

over", reported the Soviet news agency Tass. "One cannot rule out the possibility that these planes are being used for spying missions in Europe."

LIMITED NUMBERS

The aircraft is unlikely to fly to its overseas deployment sites as, for one thing, the standard USAF in-flight refuelling receptacle has a high RCS. The normal deployment method is as cargo in a C-5 Galaxy. The F-117A is also reported to have been operating from airfields as far afield as Alaska and Japan.

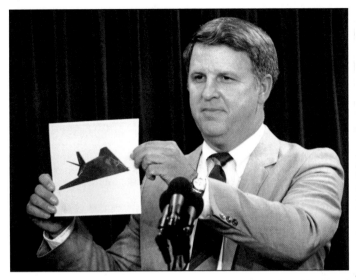

Above: **November 10th 1988 — Assistant Secretary of Defense for Public Affairs J. Daniel Howard releases the first F-117A photo.**

By 1987 Lockheed was reported to have built about 56 F-117As. A total run of 100 had been planned but the aircraft's high cost had forced a reduction. By this time, at least two squadrons were operational with Tactical Air Command.

The Air Force had planned to shut down Lockheed's production line, but the company lobbied Congress in the hope of receiving a follow-on order. Construction

of enough aircraft to equip a second wing would help offset the reduction in tactical nuclear power resulting from the withdrawal and destruction of land-based intermediate- and shorter-range nuclear weapons under the Intermediate-Range Nuclear Forces (INF) Treaty.

Late in 1987 Senate Armed Services Committee Chairman Sam Nunn persuaded his colleagues to include in the Fiscal Year 1988 defence budget the additional funds needed to keep the line open. This was not the deal for which Lockheed had hoped; the new batch was intended only as attrition replacements and was for less than half a dozen aircraft.

By the time that the F-1117A was declassified in November 1988, the US Air Force had received a total of 52 aircraft, and Lockheed was due to deliver a further 7 by the end of the decade. On completion, the line was due to close.

Although more F-117As would be useful as back-up and attrition aircraft for the Tonopah wing, there is little chance of a large follow-on order once the 59th example has been delivered in Fiscal Year 1990. The USAF budget is already stretched by unanticipated costs such as the B-1B "get well"

programme. It is also likely that the rapid pace of stealth technology has made the ten year old F-117A design obsolescent.

DECLASSIFICATION

Early in 1987, the USAF and the Pentagon seriously considered reducing the classification of the F-117A, a move which would make sense with the B-2 stealth bomber due to be rolled out in the following year, followed in the early 1990s by other stealthy designs such as the Navy's A-12 and the USAF's YF-22 and YF-23. If the Pentagon continues to try to hide stealth aircraft, "we're going to have to build a roof over the Air Force", one specialist told the *Washington Post* that year. Despite pressure from Congress, nothing was done.

Right: **The concept of the flying wing bomber was tested in 1947 by the jet-powered Northrop YB-49, a rebuilt version of the earlier turboprop powered YB-35. Both were rejected in favour of more conventionally shaped aircraft.**

Below: **The B-1B may have offered reduced RCS, but the performance of the aircraft and its EW suite have been sharply criticised.**

By early October 1988, the time finally seemed right to unveil the F-117A. With the B-2 due to be rolled out in the following month, continued high classification of an older design seemed illogical, while a court case in which some Lockheed employees were alleging damage to health from exposure to dangerous chemicals used in F-117A manufacture seemed likely to reveal more information.

On 4 October, all was ready for the big event. Press releases (complete with photo) were prepared and Senator Chic Hecht of Nevada was ready to speak to the press that afternoon. At the last moment the plan was scrubbed, apparently after intense debate at what one newspaper report described as the "highest levels of the Defense Department and on Capitol Hill". One theory behind the sudden clampdown was that the unveiling of the aircraft during a Presidential election campaign could be seen as a political ploy. "There was a bi-partisan view that this was not the most auspicious time for this", one DoD source told the

Associated Press, suggesting that the aircraft might be unveiled after the election.

Although the *Washington Times* had managed to obtain a draft copy of the press release, publishing this on the morning of 4 October, the photo stayed under wraps until 10 November. Under-exposed and heavily retouched, the picture finally released to the press was almost as uniformative as early 1960s photos of Soviet space exploits. It did, however, represent a landmark in the history of black programmes. No Western aircraft in aviation history had remained "under wraps" for so long.

B-2 BOMBER

The initial development contract for the larger and more sohisticated B-2 bomber was worth $7,300 million. The first five years of the programme were a technology-demonstration phase which may have been timed to end in early 1985 just about the same time as B-1B production was running down. Had problems emerged with the flying-wing aircraft, a follow-on order for the B-1B or the proposed B-1C could have been placed.

Work on the technology needed for the B-2 initially went faster than anticipated, proving more effective than planners had hoped when confronted by the technology used in current-generation Soviet radar systems and new threats still under development in Soviet laboratories.

The technology-demonstration phase of the programme may have included the airborne testing of a scaled-down prototype. Probably built to 1/2 scale and powered by four non-afterburning F404s, this would provide RCS data, information on stability and control of such an unconventional shape. Most sources agree that it flew sometime in 1982.

It is possible that this trials aircraft was rebuilt in the mid-1980s to become more representative of the proposed production configuration. One source told me in the spring of 1988 that the sub-scale aircraft had been flying for about 15 months, a date in complete disagreement with earlier accounts and which (if true) could only be explained by either a rebuilt, or even an all-new second test aircraft.

"From the outset, we stressed that the B-2 is on the leading edge of technology, and there were some very significant technical risks associated with the B-2", USAF Chief of Staff General Larry D. Welsh was to tell the British magazine *Defence* in early 1988. "We had some twelve risk areas we identified, and insisted on closure of each of those risk areas before we embarked on full-scale development. Since we closed out that risk reduction effort, we really haven't had any surprises. Since that time, development

has proceeded quite smoothly."

By 1983, the results obtained from early ATB development work were already better than had been anticiptated, giving the USAF the confidence needed to press ahead with the new aircraft at the expense of any follow-on B-1B procurement.

PUBLICITY

At the Farnborough Air Show held every two years in England, the world's aerospace companies rent chalets which face the runways and flying displays. Best-positioned of these is Chalet A1, a coveted location hired years ago by the Northrop Corporation of the USA, whose booking was promptly renewed for each

Below: **Released on 20th April 1988, this artist's impression of the B-2 gave the world its first view of a USAF stealth aircraft. Some**

subsequent show. However, 1988 saw a break in this long-running scheme. Not only was the US company not occupying its traditional site — it was not exhibiting at the show at all.

The reason for abandoning this prime piece of Farnborough real estate was not penny-pinching but the fact that the company was in the embarrassing position of being unable to discuss its latest products — all were highly-secret "black" programmes the end results of which would not be available for export in the foreseeable future.

Back in the days when Chalet A1 was Northrop territory, many aviation journalists — including the author — would *rendezvous* there on the first "press-only"

journalists were sceptical, but the drawing in fact proved reasonably accurate, apart from the missing engine exhausts.

day of the show. The object of this exercise was to meet the company's chief designer Lee Begin. Most companies are nervous about letting their head of advanced projects mix with journalists but Northrop allowed Begin to "hold court" with a small audience of experienced defence journalists with whom a mutual rapport had been established over the years.

At these sessions, Begin would talk about his company's projects — some times on the record and sometimes as unpublishable background — with a degree of freedom which would have induced apoplexy in the Public Relations departments of lesser corporations. That was the way he worked — the journalists he trusted were given extensive briefings but

Right: **Every line of those curves is dictated by stealth. The dark patches under the leading edge are for conformal radars.**

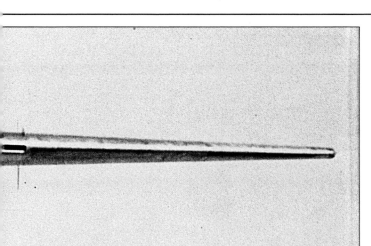

Left: **With a conventional fuselage eliminated, a flying wing offers little head-on visual or radar cross section, as this YB-49 clearly demonstrates.**

Specified to cruise at Mach 0.8 over ranges of up to 5,000nm (9,250km) — a distance equal to the Soviet aircraft's range — the ATB was to weigh 280,000lb (127,000kg) at take-off and carry a payload of 10,000lb (4,500kg). During the early 1980s, the design was scaled up several times until it was in the same general range and payload class as the B-1B. In early 1984, the B-2 was reported to weigh around 400,000lb (181,400kg) at take-off and to carry a maximum internal weapon load of approximately 40,000lb (18,100kg).

Work on the B-2 is carried out in a former Ford Motor Company automobile-assembly plant in Pico Rivera, California, probably the largest secret defence industrial site in the United States. Tight security is constantly maintained. An article on the installation in May 1987 in the *Los Angeles Times* reported that none of the more than 12,000 people employed there was prepared to be interviewed or even named. "The fact that security has been so good is a tribute to the people in the programme", an official said.

There was no doubt that the plant was known to Soviet Intelligence, the newspaper concluded. Apparently they had been helped by a novel lapse in security. Several years before, an employee had sneaked up onto the roof of the plant, the newspaper claimed, and painted "a vulgar Russian expression that was large enough to be detected by Soviet spy satellites".

CONSTRUCTION

By 1986, a full-scale engineering mock-up had been built at Pico Rivera. This allowed the basic design to be established, with the last significant changes being added in 1986. Early in the programme, the decision was made to build the prototypes using production tooling. This was probably done for the reasons that transition from prototype to production aircraft would be made easier and, less obvious, the fact that the use of production tooling would allow engineers to maintain close tolerances when assembling the aircraft's structure and skin.

At a meeting of Northrop shareholders held in May 1988, company chairman Thomas Jones described how the tooling "can be adjusted to accuracies of within one thousandth of an inch [0.0254mm]. The end result is a system that allows every major structural assembly of

they in turn accepted the restrictions which he sometimes imposed as the price of gaining access to a man who was helping shape the future of aviation. I do not know of any occasion where anyone let him down.

CONFIGURATION

At the 1983 Paris Air Show, Begin showed me sketches of some of his future concepts for jet fighters — concepts which still remain "under wraps" (and unreported by me) five years later. When I asked if I could have copies of his sketches, he laughed, but declined. "The public relations department would lose their lunch if they even knew you'd seen them! But I think you'll find this interesting." Reaching into his briefcase, he handed me a copy of a recent paper he had written on the history of Northrop "Flying Wing" aircraft.

I was puzzled. Lee knew that my interest in 1940s and early 1950s aviation history was minimal. Why did he think I would find his paper of interest? Not until several weeks later did the long-delayed penny finally drop — the only conceivable reason why Begin would be spending his valuable time dusting off Flying Wing History had to be that the same configuration was being used for the then highly-secret Northrop Advanced Technology Bomber.

When first planned, the Northop aircraft was designed to be an approximate match for the Soviet Tu-26 Backfire.

the B-2, regardless of complexity, to fit together exactly as designed." What Jones did not tell the assembly was that the reason for these exacting tolerances was related to the aircraft's stealth characteristics. The electrical discontinuity created by small gaps can scatter electro-magnetic energy. On the B-1B, small gaps in the skin were closed by sealing with conductive adhesive tape but a more sophisticated design solution was probably required for the less-observable B-2.

"The ATB is proceeding satisfactorily", General Welch said in January 1987. "We've got thousands of hours of wind-tunnel tests", he added, although it had not yet flown. So efficient was the aerodynamic design that the new aircraft would be an attractive proposition even if it hadn't been stealthy, he explained.

On 19 November 1987, the USAF awarded Northrop a $2,000 million production contract for the B-2, a move which was not cleared for public release until 26 January 1988. On that date, the Air Force confirmed that production funding would be granted to Northrop and to the main sub-contractors — Boeing, LTV and General Electric — but spokesman Captain Jay DeFrank would not identify the rôles of these companies, give the number of bombers which the money would buy nor even say whether at the firm, fixed-price contract or some other type had been awarded. Nor would the Air Force comment on reports that the date of the first flight had slipped.

NEW METHODS

For a long time, the date of the aircraft's roll-out and first flight remained classified. These were widely expected to take place in late 1987 but the date came and went. Delivery to Northrop's new final-assembly facility at Palmdale airport, California, of the first set of B-2 wings did not take place until August 1987 when they were flown in by a Lockheed C-5 Galaxy.

The USAF was not disturbed by the slippage to early 1988, having foreseen the

possibility of delays. General Thomas McMullen, then head of the USAF's Aeronautical Systems Division (ASD) had explained a year earlier that the new bomber had "met challenges, and there are more to come, but they are straightforward engineering issues. That is not to say that there are no risks; there is certainly a schedule risk, and some technical risks."

Early in January 1988 the *Los Angeles Times* quoted two unidentified Northrop employees involved in the programme and Wall Street

B-2 Advanced Technology Bomber

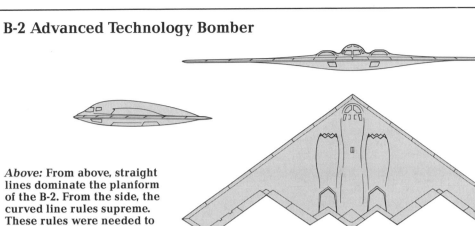

Above: **From above, straight lines dominate the planform of the B-2. From the side, the curved line rules supreme. These rules were needed to minimise RCS.**

Left: **Shrouded in white plastic and rubber mats, production B-2s take shape on the Northrop line. Black screens cover all inlets, plus the leading edges on the rear two aircraft.**

securities analysts as saying that the bomber's first test-flight had been delayed by four months and was not expected until August of that year. Northrop sources had declined to discuss the reasons for the slippage, the newspaper said. The *Washington Post* suggested that the slippage might delay initial operational capability (IOC) "perhaps more than a year" due to unspecified "technical and production problems".

It seems that one area of difficulty lay in the inlets. By April 1988, the prototype had not yet received its engines. Installation of the powerplant was reported not to be imminent. *Aviation Week* suggested that a "major redesign of the inlet and powerplant mounting structure" was likely and could be implemented on the fourth full-scale development aircraft.

Some of the difficulties may have sprung from the aircraft's massive use of composites, as engineering staff learned to adapt conventional tooling and metal-orientated production and assembly methods to the new materials. For this reason, "holes drilled in composite materials sometimes come out oblong-shaped", *Aviation Week* reported in early 1988. Despite the use of production-type tooling, installation of components on the prototype was largely a matter of labour-intensive hand fitting.

One unfortunate side effect of the high degree of compartmentalisation demanded for security reasons was that sub-contractors whose equipment had to work together were not

able to communicate with each other. Only after delivery did incompatibility problems emerge, forcing time consuming and expensive modification and redesign work. Technical drawings were in many cases being reworked rather than confirmed.

PROBLEMS

Problems were also reported with the aircraft's windscreen — part of the load-bearing structure — and with cracking of the composite leading edges. The B-2 is the first large and heavy aircraft to use large areas of composite honeycomb, so such problems were always a possibility as designers and assemblers learned how to handle and fabricate components made in the new material.

The short timescale may also have resulted in sub-assemblies being shipped to the Palmdale final-assembly plant before all testing had been completed, causing unplanned trouble-shooting and modification work on the assembled aircraft. "Ship One is literally crawling with people", an unidentified observer told *Aviation Week* in April 1988, "and most of them aren't Northrop people, because they can't even get on the airplane."

Despite highly-publicised programme-management problems at Northrop, Under Secretary of Defense for Strategic and Theater Nuclear Forces Dr Lawrence Woodruff told the House Armed Services Committee in the spring of 1988 that the programme was "progressing well" but insisted that, in response to Congressional concerns, the USAF has set up "an initiative for maintaining cost, contractor performance and management discipline within the B-2 program" and that Northrop was assessing "the condition of its own management system".

News that Boeing was hiring extra staff for the Palmdale final assembly plant, while Northrop was apparently laying off hundreds of staff from its Pico Rivera facility, led to speculation that Boeing had been secretly given an increased rôle in the management of the programme. This was strongly denied by Northrop which issued a USAF-approved statement emphasising at no changes in programme management had been made or were planned. Boeing's hiring of staff was directly due to that company's work as a sub-contractor to Northrop, the statement indicated.

REVEALED

On 20 April 1988, the USAF released an artist's impression of the B-2 and confirmed that the prototype would fly in the autumn. ''The first flight of the Advanced Technology Bomber, or B-2, is currently scheduled for this fall'', the service said. The bomber would take off from the final assembly facility at Air Force Plant 42 in Palmdale then land at the Air Force Flight Test Center at Edwards AFB, where flight testing would be carried out. ''The initial flight of the B-2 will highlight the return of the flying wing design to military aviation'', it was stated. No date was given for the maiden flight, however, and the service refused to give further details of the aircraft's size, crew number, weapons load, performance or cost.

The drawing which provided few details of its construction aside from its general shape was not totally accurate; the USAF admitted that several details had either been omitted or altered. The science-fiction shape created some scepticism but, during an interview with *Defence* magazine, USAF Chief of Staff General Larry Welch insisted that the drawing was generally accurate. ''There are a few details that are obscured for security reasons. You will note that there are no exhausts in the picture.''

According to the USAF, the shape of the new bomber had been declassified because the prototype would soon ''be outside doing things and people will see it''. Some saw the sudden de-classification as a public-relations ruse, an unexpected move designed to defuse growing Congressional demands for greater access to information on the growing number of major ''black'' programmes.

Left: Security breach or public relations ploy? A light aircraft overflew the B-2 rollout and revealed the novel shape of the exhausts.

Above: In the course of development, ALCM-B was modified to reduce its RCS, a move dictated by advances in Soviet air defences.

Below: As the B-2 lifts off the runway, the huge main undercarriage doors probably act as vertical stabilising surfaces.

guidance systems and better engines of the 1980s, coupling these with stealth technology.

The idea of a low-RCS cruise missile was not new. In testimony before the Senate Armed Services Committee in 1977 John B. Walsh, DoD Deputy Director of Space and Strategic Systems described how studies had been carried out into ways of reducing missile RCS.

A formal requirement for a new cruise missile was drawn up that same month and the programme was approved by President Reagan in August. A request for proposals was issued to industry in September. Technology for a new cruise missile was already in hand, thanks to programmes such as DARPA's little-publicised Teal Dawn. This had explored areas such as airframe shaping, RAM and advanced propulsion. All designs to be evaluated would use the same engine, the Williams International F112 turbofan which entered full-scale development in July 1982. The IOC date for the new missile was targeted for 1986, a goal which some saw as unrealistic even in 1982. It was in fact to prove hopelessly optimistic.

COMPETITION

Boeing, Lockheed and General Dynamics all competed for the task of building the new missile. Having developed the ALCM-A and -B, Boeing was obviously in a good position to win the new programme and, given the fact that ALCM production was being cut back, had the strongest incentive to do so. Unfortunately, Boeing faced severe competition. Lockheed had the useful experience gained from its own stealth cruise missile programme, while General Dynamics had worked on Teal Dawn and so was clearly in a good position to bid for the new weapon.

At the time, General Dynamics was somewhat under a cloud, the results of quality-control problems with the Tomahawk. Working in the company's favour was the fact that its Teal Dawn experience would give it the head start needed to match the ambitious timescale of the new missile. From the first, the company seems to have set the pace, while its rivals had to embark on redesigns of their submissions.

The initial Boeing submission was a development of the AGM-86 design but the company soon

Roll-out had been expected in September 1988, leading to a first flight in October or November, but these dates could not be met. On 12th November, the long-awaited roll-out finally took place. The audience was given only a frontal view of the new bomber, but a light aircraft which overflew the rollout ceremony provided *Aviation Week* with an unauthorised view of the hidden rear section.

For the next eight months, the B-2 became the world's best known and most criticised "hangar queen". Technical problems delayed the maiden flight until 17 July 1989.

CRUISE MISSILES

The B-2 may have been developed in near-total secrecy, but the security blackout around America's stealth cruise missile work has been even tighter. Despite late-1970s claims that existing cruise missiles such as the

ALCM and Tomahawk were virtually unstoppable, by the early 1980s Pentagon planners feared that growing Soviet EW expertise might allow them to interfere with the radar elements of the TERCOM guidance system and that cruise missiles — particularly the GLCM — were becoming vulnerable to SA-10 attack.

During the development of Tomahawk and the ALCM, tests had been carried out to measure the weapons' radar, IR and visual signatures. As a result of this work, RCS, IR output and luminosity were all reduced. It was now clear that this was not enough. In the short term, the USAF hoped to counter the SA-10 and interceptor threats by modifying its cruise missile fleet, adding an on-board active ECM system based on work carried out in an extensive programme codenamed "Have Rust".

A three-year development programme was envisaged, allowing deployment in the

mid-1980s. ALCMs would have to be modified but GLCM rounds would be delivered complete with the EW sub-system when these weapons were deployed in the early 1980s. The status of the cruise missile EW programme remains highly classified. One source told me in 1988 that the scheme had not gone ahead in the form originally planned but confirmed that some improvements had been made to the weapons.

In July 1982 the USAF completed a study of possible next-generation cruise missiles and concluded that development of an improved model using the latest technologies could counter the sort of air defence system which the Soviet Union was expected to field in the 1990s. Just as the AGM-86 and BGM-109 had exploited mid-1970s breakthroughs in technology such as miniature electronics and small low-consumption turbofan engines, the new weapon would use the improved realised that this could not provide the performance needed to gain the new contract. By late 1982, the company was reported to be frantically working on a higher-risk concept able to take greater advantage of the latest stealth developments. Boeing was "scrambling to come up with a new aeronautical design", a DoD official told *Aviation Week* in November of that year.

Like Boeing, Lockheed redesigned its entry. The first design offered was stealthy but proved aerodynamically unstable. It also required external carriage, a feature not desirable in a world of low-RCS warplanes.

Progress was swift enough to allow the USAF to scale down its ALCM procurement. The Air Force had planned to buy 3,418 ALCMs but, in February 1983, announced that production of the ALCM-B would end after the FY83 buy, bringing the total number of rounds delivered to only 1,499. The planned ALCM-C would not be built.

AGM-129

On 15 April 1983, General Dynamics was announced winner of the Advanced Cruise Missile (ACM) competition. It was given a fixed-price contract which covered full-scale development of the AGM-129 and contained options on the first two production lots. Such was the new programme's high classification that the Air Force would not release details of the total value of the contract, the number of rounds to be procured or the programme schedule. Unofficial estimates suggested that the unit cost of the new missile would be about $3 million, with the entire ACM programme costing about $7,000 million.

The targets set for the ACM were ambitious. In addition to being stealthier than the current ALCM, it was required to have better guidance, a lower terrain-following altitude and a longer range, probably around 2,300 miles (3,700km). After launch, the new missile was expected to fly up to 1,000 miles (1,600km) farther than current cruise missiles, travelling around, rather than through, Soviet air defences.

As in the case of manned stealth aircraft, reducing the RCS involved careful shaping. At one time, the design was reported to have no vertical tail, information which must have caused some amusement

at the company's plant where the ACM's vertical surfaces are built. The engine installation is designed for minimum IR output, reducing the tiny engine's ability to attract heat-seeking missiles.

On 6 January 1987, the US Defense Secretary Caspar W. Weinberger claimed that the AGM-129 was making "good progress" and announced that its first deployment would be at K. I. Sawyer AFB, Michigan. First deliveries of the missile to the base would begin by 1989, said Pentagon spokesman Robert Sims, and preparations for deployment would be under way by the end of the year.

K.I. Sawyer was a B-52 base which had been in the headlines two months before when the USAF deployed its 131st ALCM-armed B-52 there. This exceeded the limits on cruise-missile-equipped bombers set out in the unratified SALT II treaty, demonstrating President Reagan's decision to stop complying with its conditions. Some members of Congress had criticised the deployment, claiming that it would undermine then-current efforts to secure a new arms treaty, a fear which was to

prove groundless. On the day of Weinberger's speech, the Pentagon said the 132nd ALCM-armed B-52 had been delivered to K.I. Sawyer on 22 December and that the 133rd would follow in January.

DELAYS

Weinberger told reporters in January 1987 that ACM was enjoying "very good progress" but, behind the scenes, trouble was brewing. Four months later, Lt.Gen Bernard P. Randolph, Assistant Secretary for Acquisition, told a closed hearing of the House Appropriations Committee that General Dynamics had done "less than a perfect job in managing their sub-contractors" on the ACM programme. It became increasingly obvious that the programme was suffering serious delays and cost over-runs. Late the same year, General Randolph, by then promoted to head of Air Force Systems Command, confirmed that the programme was a year behind schedule. "We are a year behind, and we will stay behind." Flight trials were behind schedule, he admitted.

Above: **Much of the technology needed for the USAF's new ATF was tested on the Advanced Fighter Technology Integration (AFTI) F-16.**

Below: General Dynamics AGM-129 Advanced Cruise Missile (seen here being carried by a B-52 trials aircraft) is stealthy with more range than ALCM.

In November 1987, the USAF announced that McDonnell Douglas, the company which had second-sourced the Tomahawk cruise missile, had been awarded a $1.2 million contract "for technology transfer leading to a second-source production capability of the advanced cruise missile". General Dynamics would provide the technical specifications and other manufacturing documents for the AGM-129 to McDonnell Douglas. Once the latter had set up its own

Below: The USAF's F-15 STOL demonstrator tested other ATF-applicable technology, including two-dimensional thrust-vectoring nozzles.

ACM line, the USAF would be able to award subsequent production contracts on a competitive basis. No reason was given for the decision but it was widely seen as a move intended to counter growing Congressional criticism and one which would allow competitive bidding for future contracts to drive down the weapon's cost.

By April 1988, the programme was reported to be at least three years behind schedule and likely to cost an additional $2,000 million. A report issued by House Armed Services Committee Chairman Les Aspin described the ACM programme as a "procurement disaster", citing deficiencies in quality control and inept supervision by the Air Force and the manufacturer. Aspin blamed the delays and cost over-runs on what he described as mismanagement by General Dynamics and the USAF. "The highly classified Advanced Cruise Missile is the worst system I reviewed", he stated. The report was vague as to the exact nature of the ACM's problems, noting simply that the project was "protected in nearly all interesting details by high classification".

More bad news was to come. To date the programme had produced only three missiles, the *Washington Post* claimed on 21 April, while the USAF had not met a 1986 Congressional demand that at least six successful test flights be carried out before production was begun. Missiles had failed and crashed "randomly" during recent test flights, the newspaper reported, adding that the defects appeared to be in components produced

by sub-contractors rather than by General Dynamics.

Problems seem to have arisen in several areas. Quality control problems at General Dynamics had been responsible for the initial one-year slippage. In 1987 a total of 44 critical components in the missile were singled out for quality control checks, while the company accepted Air Force recommendations for ground testing the missile prior to beginning flight tests. In the spring of 1988 General Welch spoke of unspecified "design and manufacturing concerns" which would require further testing.

DEPLOYMENT

Early flight trials seem to have high-lighted other problems. The weapon's low-RCS shape seems to have had an adverse effect on its flying characteristics, while other problems emerged with the missile's computer software. In June 1988, SAC commander General John Chain told an Air Force Association symposium that the programme "...is not coming along as quickly or as well as I would like". Deputy Chief of Staff, Plans and Operations, Lt.Gen. Michael Dugan expained that the results of early flight trials had been erratic, having included "a couple of flights that didn't do especially well". Work was under way to identify and correct the problems, he stated, but "testing has not been completed yet, so how it will all sort out, I just don't know".

IOC is still expected to take place on the B-52H bombers of the 410th Bomb Wing at Sawyer AFB, Michigan, but no date has been revealed. The

missile will then be supplied to the four B-1B wings. By the early 1990s, the USAF expects to deploy 1,500 ACMs which will make up about half of the service's cruise missile strength.

NEW FIGHTERS

In parallel with these 1983 cruise missile decisions, the USAF seems to have decided to incorporate a significant degree of stealth technology into its planned Advanced Tactical Fighter (ATF). Designed to handle air-to-air and air-to-ground missions, the aircraft is intended to have the performance needed to evade Soviet air defences, allowing it to penetrate deeply in order to attack Warsaw Pact fighters and air bases.

Concept-definition studies of the new fighter and an associated advanced technology engine started in September 1983 when the USAF awarded study contracts — each worth around $900,000 — to Boeing, General Dynamics, Grumman, Lockheed, McDonnell Douglas, Northrop and Rockwell.

In October 1985 the USAF asked contractors to submit proposals for a fighter able to enter service in the mid-1990s as the eventual replacement for its F-15 Eagle and F-16 Fighting Falcon. Bids were to be submitted by December of that year and would lead to between two and four companies, or teams of companies, being selected to take part in a three-year study intended to balance the performance and cost of the new fighter against its operational requirements. Choice of a contractor to develop, flight-test and produce ATF would be made in early 1989, with the aircraft making its first flight in late 1991 and eventually entering Air Force service in the mid-1990s.

The USAF intends to take advantage of the latest developments in aerodynamics, propulsion, avionics, materials and manufacturing techniques. Much of the required technology will be drawn from current programmes such as the AFTI/F-16, Grumman X-29 forward-swept wing demonstrator and the

F-117A stealth fighter. Likely features of the new fighter will be vectored-thrust (for STOL performance or even in-flight agility), "stealth" technology, integrated fire/flight control systems with high-technology cockpit displays and large-scale use of built-in test equipment.

PROTOTYPES

Late in 1986, the USAF decided to restructure the programme. Instead of flying a single selected design in late 1991, it would now select two rival concepts to be flown as competitive prototypes, an arrangement which the service last used in the mid-1970s competition for the YF-16/YF-17 Lightweight Fighter. In April 1987, the USAF Systems Command awarded two industrial teams contracts worth $691 million covering a 50-month development programme. A target date of October 1989 was set for the first flights.

In the past, the US DoD has fully funded the costs which industry has faced when developing advanced weapons but this is no longer the case

Above: **The forward-swept wing Grumman X-29 pioneered new areas of flight control, and better methods of building composite wings.**

in the late 1980s. On ATF, the USAF's investment will be more than matched by the money which the industry will provide. Lockheed announced that its team expected to spend around $700 million, with its partners providing a further $300 million. Similar cost-sharing arrangements exist in the rival team.

The impact of this level of investment on the companies involved will be massive, particularly for the team which loses. The winners will have at least gained the Western world's biggest fighter deal between now and the end of the century. However, the DoD is adamant that this massive investment will not be repaid by the US Government either directly by special funding or indirectly through increased profit margins. Companies on the losing team will see literally hundreds of millions of dollars of company

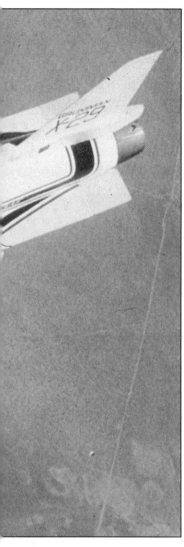

investment written off for no return.

Even the winners will not find things easy. General Dynamics took only two years of F-16 production to move the programme into profit; the equivalent break point for the ATF will be 12 or even 15 years. Malcolm Currie, the Chairman of Hughes Aircraft, has even gone so far as to predict that on a discounted cash flow basis, the successful ATF team may never break even. Spending 1988 dollars today would simply result in a return in further devalued mid-1990s dollars.

SELF REPAIRING

One of the first activities carried out by both teams was a study of possible methods of risk reduction and alternative technologies. This was ordered as part of a larger Systems Requirement Review carried out by the Air Force.

Powerplant development is running ahead of that of the airframe, a wise policy in any aircraft programme. In October 1983, General Electric and Pratt & Whitney were given $200 million contracts covering the

development and ground testing of rival designs of a Joint Advanced Fighter Engine (JAFE).

Likely features of these new engines include a low by-pass ratio, advanced powder-metal alloy turbine discs, ceramic seals, FADEC, 50 per cent fewer parts than on current engines, reduced number of stages, higher rotational speeds, better high-temperature blade capabilities and lower crack propagation rates, two-dimensional thrust vectoring (including reverse thrust) and shingle-liner combustors.

In current engines most of the air from the compressor by-passes the combustor, in order to cool the latter. Only a small portion enters the combustor to be mixed with the incoming fuel and burned. This technique works well under steady state conditions such as take-off and cruise but is less efficient in air combat — a régime which requires frequent and rapid changes of throttle setting. The end result is thermal fatigue of the engine. In an attempt to reduce this problem, the USAF Aeronautical Systems Division has developed the

shingle-liner combustor, a configuration whose inner section "floats" within the outer, reducing thermal stress. The resulting combustor is heavier and more expensive than conventional designs but the USAF believes the trade-off to be worthwhile.

Pratt & Whitney's engine is the PW5000, designated XF119 by the US DoD. This ran for the first time in late 1986. The rival design from General Electric is the GE37. Designated XF120, this variable by-pass design began bench tests in mid-1987.

Both engines are being put through about 850 hours of core and engine tests, plus about 250 hours of accelerated mission testing, including short-cycle mission profiles. In early 1988, both teams received contracts worth close to $342 million for the development of flightworthy "YF" engines. One YF-22 and one YF-23 will be powered by the YF119, the other example of each prototype by the YF120.

AVIONICS

Full-scale development of the avionics systems of the ATF is expected to cost $2,800 million. Much of the equipment specified for the aircraft is expected to be common to the two competing designs. ATF will make major use of VHSIC technology, probably a mixture of Phase I and the newer and more advanced Phase II. This will provide integrated circuits (ICs) containing 50 — 100 times more components than current types and able to operate ten times faster. As a result, the number of ICs used in the aircraft will be about a hundredth of that of today's most advanced fighters, so fewer black boxes and less electrical cabling will be required.

ATF uses the USAF's new Pave Pillar avionics architecture. Intended for incorporation in future US military aircraft, this specifies that the avionics take the form of three main sub-systems dedicated to mission management, sensor management and vehicle management.

The mission-management system (MMS) is made up of the terrain following/avoidance, navigation, fire-control, stores management and EW systems, while the sensor-management system (SMS) combines the aircraft's radar, IRST, integrated signal processing, encrypted data

Right: Wing/body blending, outward-canted tail fins, and inlets under the wing were low-RCS features of this Rockwell ATF proposal.

Below: The wing camber on the Mission Adaptive Wing F-111 can change to match flight conditions, a low-RCS alternative to slats/flaps.

communications and JTIDS interface, allocating processor power to the sensor sub-systems as required. Functions such as cockpit controls and displays, flight controls and engine and electrical-power controls are combined in the integrated vehicle-management systems (VMS).

These three main systems are interconnected by a 50MHz high-speed fibre-optic bus, while the VMS also has its own bus. A separate video bus connects the aircrew displays with the stores-management system.

All sub-systems are made up from combinations of common modules. Manufactured in line-replaceable unit (LRU) form, these in turn use a series of ultra-high density ICs developed under the very-high-speed integrated circuit (VHSIC) programme. This level of integration will make it easy for information to be passed from one avionics system to another. It may allow two systems to share a single radome, minimising the degradation of RCS due to the latter.

ATF will have avionics whose complexity dwarfs that of earlier warplanes, a complexity which could spell lower reliability and a reduced mean time between failures (MTBF). On existing aircraft, reliability of vital systems is provided by duplication or even triplication. In the long run, such measures only provide

"get you home" capability, although the crew can of course opt to press on and complete the combat task rather than abort immediately. The aircraft keeps flying but to embark on another mission without curing the original failure would be unwise except in a military emergency.

SELF REPAIRING

The USAF decided that the best way of raising avionics reliability would be to devise systems able to "heal" themselves, a concept first mooted for possible use of deep-space probes and now adopted as part of Pave Pillar. Nobody is suggesting that the aircraft carry an R2D2-style "droid" complete with soldering gun and test meter — that sort of self-healing capability is closer to Star Wars than to tomorrow's USAF. The goal of Pave Pillar is to create electronic systems so complex that they can automatically by-pass or compensate for individual failures of any element.

Self-repairing technology is likely to be applied to the ATF flight-control systems. In early 1984 the USAF's Aeronautical Systems Division (ASD) issued its first request for proposals on a programme intended to explore the technology required for such systems, then to develop an operational system suitable for use in an advanced fighter aircraft.

The traditional method of providing redundancy in a flight-control system involves providing additional components so as to ensure that a control surface will always move in response to the pilot's demands. For example, a surface may be moved by several actuators, so that failure of one does not result in loss of control of that surface.

A self-repairing system will take a different approach. If a control surface fails, the flight-control system will automatically reconfigure itself, distributing the control functions among the surviving surfaces. To take a very simple example, if an aileron fails or is shot away in combat, roll control can be maintained by differential movement of the horizontal stabilisers.

The first task faced by ASD is that of proving the concept using laboratory simulations and flying testbeds. The latter will almost certainly be a modified light aircraft fitted with digital fly-by-wire (FBW) controls. This will provide the operating experience needed to create future operational systems and the data required in order to simulate accurately aircraft on which some of the flying controls have failed or are only partially operative.

The goal of a definitive system would be to provide the pilot of a damaged or defective aircraft with the maximum possible amount of

Above: **This futuristic shape formed the basis of several "stealth fighter" construction kits, but was only an advertising artwork used by EW manufacturer Loral.**

Below: **Not much stealth technology is visible in this Grumman advanced fighter proposal of the early 1980s. The inlets would be good radar targets.**

Left: **McDonnell Douglas' "Big Picture" cockpit would bring Macintosh-style computer graphics and user-friendliness to the fighter cockpit, but was probably conceived too late for ATF.**

control. At best, he would be able to continue with his mission or switch to a less demanding alternative mission so that the sortie is not wasted. In cases of more critical damage or failure, the pilot would expect to be able to abort the mission and return to base or, in the worst case, fly out of hostile airspace in a controlled manner with the crippled aircraft remaining stable enough to permit safe ejection once over friendly territory.

One potential problem with FBW systems and other electronic controls is that electromagnetic interference (EMI) which manages to get into the system can cause spurious commands or other erroneous behaviour. At least one Tornado crash has been blamed on signals from a powerful radio transmitter close to the aircraft's flight path, while the US Army modified its UH-60 fleet last year to reduce vulnerability of its controls to interference from radar or radio signals.

FLY-BY-LIGHT

Fly-by-light control systems based on fibre optics offer a more EMI-resistant form of flight controls than today's fly-by-wire systems. Such a system was proposed for the US Navy's Sentinel 5000 airship. Both of the USAF's Advanced Tactical fighter (ATF) designs — the YF-22 and YF-23 — are expected to have fly-by-light controls, while a similar feature is being considered as a preferred option for the multinational Tonal attack helicopter.

Hercules has announced that it is developing a fly-by-light system for an unidentified application but the use of artwork based on the Lockheed ATF drawings in company advertisements leaves the reader in no doubt as to the identity of the application. Fibre optics will be an essential component of "smart skins" with built-in facilities for monitoring structural integrity and battle damage of composite structure, says Hercules.

RADAR

The ATF radar is being developed by Westinghouse, teamed with Texas Instruments (TI). In April 1987, the team won this vital contract for both the YF-22A and the YF-23A, a blow to rival radar giant Hughes Aircraft, which had teamed up with General Electric to bid for the ATF radar. Factors which influenced the decision include, both companies work on the USAF's Ultra-Reliable Radar (URR) programme, while Westinghouse has applied VHSIC technology to the new signal processor introduced by the F-16C/D upgrade programme.

Size, weight and power requirements of the ATF radar are expected to be around 10 per cent of those of current sets, while maintenance man-hours could be similarly reduced. Despite this, data through-put could be up to 100 times that of current radars.

Technology for the ATF radar was proven under the USAF's Ultra-Reliable Radar (URR) programme. As part of this, Westinghouse developed a circular solid-state phased array antenna consisting of approximately 2,000 active transmit/receive modules based on gallium arsenide (GaAs) technology. Each module transmits power of about 2 watts.

The beam is steered by adjusting the phase of the signal transmitted by each individual module, while the phase of the signal received by each will indicate the angle of arrival of the echo. Use of this technology eliminates the high voltages and high-power transmitting tubes used in current-generation radars using mechanical scanning or phase shifters. On the receive side, the use of modules removes the losses associated with the waveguides traditionally used to link the antenna to the radar's receiver.

Failure of a single module will have little effect on the

overall performance of the entire system, argues TI, the failure of several allowing performance to degrade progressively. Defining "failure" as the point at which 5 per cent of the modules have failed, TI anticipates an MTBF of between 4,000 and 5,000 hours for the antenna and about 2,000 hours for an entire radar. This compares with the 40 to 50 hours typical of many current-generation radars.

According to TI, the size of the antenna sidelobes is reduced, a useful electronic counter-countermeasures (ECCM) feature, and the radar can operate in up to 26 modes simultaneously, shaping the beams to suit specific purposes. Inevitably, there are penalties. Complexity, weight and cost all rise (although life cycle costs may be reduced thanks to increased reliability), while performance is reduced as beam angle increases in deflection away from the boresight.

For the URR test radar, the assembly of individual modules required large amounts of hand labour, a technique which would be uneconomical for a production radar, but monolithic GaAs technology holds the promise of allowing automated assembly techniques. The definitive ATF radar will use 3,000 transmit/receive modules, each consisting of four MMIC (monolithic microwave integrated circuit) chips — a drive amplifier, digital phase shifter and low-noise amplifier (all by Texas Instruments) and a Westinghouse RF power amplifier.

Instead of assigning the processing task to computers contained within the radar, on the ATF processing is handled by external signal processors made by Hughes (YF-22A) and AT&T (YF-23A). Both will use the same software, however.

The aircraft will use the computing power of its avionics suite to filter the information being passed to the pilot, presenting him with the data needed for the phase of the mission which he is flying. This will prevent information overload.

SYSTEMS

ATF is likely to have voice command, artificial intelligence, helmet sights, improved sensor trackers — true head-up capability and a reduction of pilot workload of up to 80 per cent. The systems may present the pilot with a

virtual image of the enemy terrain ahead, complete with a recommended flight path. The aircraft's data banks include analysis of similar missions — either laboratory-simulated, flown in training or even in recent combat — the ATF's processing power could be used to draw on the lessons to be gained from these analyses, then apply them when compiling its recommendations for the mission being flown.

The ATF will be fitted with the integrated electronic-

warfare system (INEWS) which has been described as "the most ambitious and expensive program in electronic warfare history". Phase one demonstration and validation contracts have been awarded to two teams — Sanders Associates, teamed with General Electric, and TRW, teamed with Westinghouse.

The aircraft's Integrated Communication Navigation Identification Avionics (ICNIA) will combine the functions of current

Above: **The Wright-Patterson AFB MAGIC (Microprocessor Application of Graphics and Interactive Communications) simulator is used to test the integration of voice-control and pictorial-format cockpit technology.**

Below: **Computer graphics could reduce ATF pilot workload. On this USAF artwork, a white "highway in the sky" shows the pilot a route past an enemy SAM envelope and jet fighter (both shown in red).**

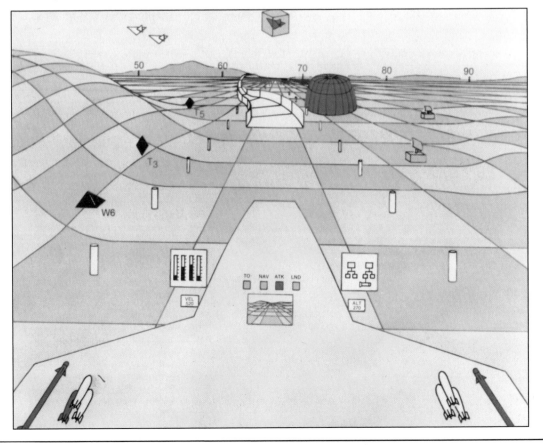

communications equipment such as HF SSB, VHF, SINCGARS, UHF, Have Quick, EJS and JTIDS; navaids such as VOR/ILS, MLS, Tacan and GPS, plus transponder and interrogator facilities compatible with the Mk XII and Mk XV IFF systems. ICNIA will be based on common digital and RF processing modules using advanced VLSI circuits and will be about half the size of the systems it will replace.

Like the F-15 Eagle, ATF will have an internal gun but this will not be the current 20mm M61A1 six-barrel gun. Eight years of technology investigation by the Armament Division at Eglin AFB led to General Electric's Armament and Electrical Systems Division at Burlington, Vermont, and ARES Inc of Fort Clinton, Iowa, being assigned the task of developing a new advanced-technology gun for future fighters.

In 1984 both companies selected ammunition developed by Ford Aerospace for use in their designs. This surrounds the projectile with a high-density moulded propellant charge and encloses the resulting assembly in a cylindrical steel case. When the round is fired, a small charge located immediately behind the projectile accelerates it into the barrel before the main charge ignites.

Early in 1985 both companies were awarded contracts worth $3.1 million to develop a gun suitable for use on the ATF. The muzzle velocity of the M61 is about 3,500ft/sec (1,000ms) but the performance goal of the new gun is 5,000ft/sec (1,500ms). A two- year development phase is expected to end in a shoot-off at Eglin AFB when the USAF will select a winner to develop the definitive 20mm or 30mm calibre weapon over the following two years.

NAVAL STEALTH

Much less information is available on the other US "stealthy" aircraft programme — the US Navy's A-12 Advanced Tactical Aircraft (ATA). First reported in 1985, this will be a subsonic all-weather aircraft able to carry out all-weather or night deep interdiction missions.

Work had been under way in secret for some time. The USN had, for example, been a partner of the USAF in the Joint Advanced Fighter Engine (JAFE) programme,

Top: **Another computer graphic shows a route exploiting a gap in the low-level coverage between two SA-2 Guideline SAM sites.**

which resulted in the rival GE and P&W engines for the ATF prototypes, but withdrew in 1984 when it became obvious that the resulting engines would not be suitable for the ATA programme.

In April 1985 Congress was asked to re-allocate $5 million of FY85 money to cover initial work on technology for the ATA, such as radar, FLIR and IRST, and for work involving NASA's oblique- wing technology demonstrator aircraft. Right from the start it became obvious that the ATA would use stealth technology developed by the USAF. In this way, the USN hoped to move into this USAF-pioneered field without spending large sums of its own research and development money.

Only two industrial teams responded to the Navy's Request For Proposals — General Dynamics, teamed with McDonnell Douglas, and

Above: **No-one expects the ATF or A-12 to use a pivoted wing, but some see the technique as being valuable in future stealth designs.**

Northrop, teamed with Grumman and LTV. With the collapse of the T- 46 programme, Fairchild was out of the military aircraft business, while Boeing, Lockheed and Rockwell seem to have declined to bid.

By late 1987 it became obvious that the USN could not support both the A-12 (at that time still known simply as the ATA) and the new F404-engined Grumman A-6F Intruder. Work on the A-6F was stopped. This decision has probably increased the urgency of the A-12 programme. The basic Intruder has been in service since the 1960s and the planned fielding of the A-6F in 1989 would have modernised the Navy's strike power pending the later arrival of the A-12.

The Long Island company might have hoped to recoup its losses on the A-6F

(unofficially estimated to be at least $150 million) by winning a share of the ATA work. This was not to happen. In a surprise move in late December, the Northrop/Grumman/LTV team (widely tipped to win the ATA competition) declined to submit "best and final" bids for the task of developing the new aircraft.

On 24 December 1987, a mere four days after Northrop's virtual withdrawal from the competition, the Navy pronounced the General Dynamics/McDonnell Douglas team winners of the contract to develop the new aircraft. Although the ATA programme was thought to be worth an estimated $35,000 million, the initial contract was worth only $241,000.

The A-12 is due to replace the US Navy's A-6E fleet in the mid to late 1990s and a total buy of around 450 seems likely. The USMC hopes to obtain 60 A-12 aircraft as replacements for the A-6E. Should no money be available, the Corps could be forced to switch to the F-18D Plus version of the Hornet. Like the proposed Hornet 2000, this was shelved in 1988 before even reaching the status of a formal proposal. According to the USMC Deputy Chief of Staff for Aviation, Gen. Charles C. Pitman, it remains a "fallback option" in the event of A-12 proving too expensive.

Under a MoU signed in April 1986 between the USAF and USN, the Air Force will consider the A-12 as a potential replacement for the F-111 and, in the longer term, for the F-15E. Initial A-12 deliveries will be to the USN, with the USAF getting its first A-12s around 1998. Like earlier USN types adopted by the USAF, the A-12 will be modified by the USAF to match Air Force requirements and make it better suited to land- based operations. By 1988, discussions between the two services had not thrown up any problems in this area.

PROJECT AURORA

In February 1985 a Pentagon budget document accidentally disclosed the existence of another "black" programme. Valued at $2,300 million, this USAF project was code-named "Aurora". Reporting the incident, the *Washington Post* quoted unidentified Pentagon sources as saying Aurora might have something to do with the new stealth bomber or at least with stealth technology. Air Force officials declined to discuss Aurora, beyond confirming the accuracy of the numbers listed in the budget documents. "That is a classified program and we can't talk about it", said Maj. Richard Ziegler, an Air Force spokesman.

For almost three years, no more was known about this "black" programme but in January 1988 the *New York Times* reported that the USAF was developing a replacement for the ageing SR-71 Blackbird. This was described as a long-range reconnaissance jet which used "special equipment" to avoid radar detection. The performance claimed was a major step over that of the SR-71 — a cruising speed of more than 3,800 mph (6,100 km/h), plus a ceiling of more than 100,000ft (33,000m). This Mach 5 stealth design is widely reported to be the mysterious Aurora.

GRASSBLADE

Even less is known about another "black" programme code-named "Grassblade". This is known to be a stealth helicopter under development for the US Army. Given the presence of a whirling rotor, the idea of a stealth helicopter might seem bizarre but a degree of stealth technology has also been applied to the US Army's planned LHX helicopter. Artists' impressions of the rival LHX designs revealed at the 1988 Farnborough Air Show showed that both incorporated some signature reduction technology. The Army specification insisted that the undercarriage be retractable and that weapons be carried internally. The Boeing/Sikorsky design mounts ordnance on upward-swinging gull-wing doors in the fuselage sides, while the McDonnell Douglas/Bell team favoured carriage within a combined wing/sponson. The two designs also took different approaches to the tail area. Boeing/Sikorsky offer a "V" tail and a Gazelle-style fenestron rotor, while McDonnell Douglas/Bell use a NOTAR (NO TAil Rotor) ducted exhaust system.

Other nations are looking at stealthy helicopters. The Japan Ground Self-Defence Force needs a replacement for its current fleet of McDonnell Douglas/Kawasaki OH-6D light observation helicopters and is considering the development of a new design. This would be powered by a

new 800-1,000shp turboshaft engine being developed by a team of Japanese companies including Ishikawajima-Harima, Kawasaki and Mitsubishi. Stealth technology would be incorporated to some degree in this small combat helicopter.

EMPLOYMENT

In the two years prior to the unveiling of the first US stealth aircraft, the entire topic of low-observables gradually crept into the open as aerospace companies began to feature stealth in their recruiting advertisements. Most vociferous would-be employer was Northrop, whose advertisements took a dramatic line. One advert for the B-2 plant at Pico Rivera featured a newly hired man telling his old colleagues how he would now be working in a

building with "no windows, restricted access on all doors. They only let me see the employment lobby". Another asked engineers to "Work on a project so advanced, that's all we can tell you". Another claimed that, "It will be the most important plane built during your career . . . whether you work here or not". In all cases, the division placing the advert was Pico Rivera. Skills in demand were "RCS model designers and builders", "RCS analysis" and engineers to work on "Visual/IR/Acoustic signature reduction". An earlier 1987 advertisement linked to the company's ATF work had sought engineers able to perform "RCS analysis in support of signature reduction concepts, including shaping and RAM/RAS applications". In August 1988, a Northrop advert invited people with modem-equipped

home computers to make a telephone call to one of the company's computers. Given the log-in password "CAREER ACCESS", the machine would provide an up to date listing of current vacancies.

McDonnell Douglas at St Louis advertised for engineers with two or even five years directly applicable experience in "low observables", while McDonnell Douglas Helicopters at Mesa, Arizona, simply wanted "RCS engineers". General Dynamics' Fort Worth division sought engineers with at least three years experience in "antenna low observables" or one year's experience in "research, design and processing of aerospace structural composite materials". At the Boeing plant in Seattle, "low-observable engineers" were needed to work on "analytical and experimental studies to

reduce the electro-optical signatures of advanced aircraft''.

OTHER PROGRAMMES

Not all the companies looking for stealth expertise have identifiable programmes and clues to the existence of other ''black'' stealth programmes could be found by watching the recruiting patterns. If anybody in the Kremlin was reading the job ads with the same zeal that I was, they would have been equally intrigued by LTV's announcement in an October 1988 advertisement that in addition to having been selected in 1982 as a major team member on the B-2, in 1985 it had won a ''competition to become a major team member for research and development on another high-technology aircraft''.

The company was now looking for ''RCS engineers'' with ''three or more years' experience in design of low observable structures and components and the construction and testing of scaled models''. It was also looking for engineers with experience of ''RCS prediction techniques and the translation of vehicle geometry into mathematical terms for computer input and the development of computer codes to predict signatures''. Vacancies also existed for ''RAM engineers'' with ''four or more years' experience including formulation and fabrication of RAM materials and structures''. It all pointed to a new stealth programme, particularly the references to modelling work.

In a January 1988 advertisement headed ''Create an Illusion'', Rockwell International, builders of the

B-1, boasted of their involvement in the development of radar-absorbing structure (RAS) materials in the 1960s and 1970s. The list of skills for which it was now recruiting were a veritable catalogue of stealth technology and included ''Engineers skilled in radar cross-section reduction using RAM/RAS technology, aperture-reduction techniques and techniques of specular and non-specular scattering reduction from vehicle scatterers. Experience with actual vehicle radar and IR reduction, including model testing over a broad frequency spectrum . . . engineers who are skilled in the design of low radar cross-section vehicles''.

The airframe manufacturers were not the only recruiters. Textron Aerostructures advertised for a ''low observables R&D engineer'' to ''establish and expand (a) low observables technology program''. Engine builder Pratt & Whitney required degreed engineers with directly-related experience in ''observables technology'', while a Swedlow advert for engineers to work on cockpit transparencies mentioned RCS. TRW's ballistic missiles division looked for ''Radar Signature Analysts'' and ''Optics Analysts'' able to work on ''RCS/signature predications, descrimination algorithms, sensor performance evaluation''.

From known contracts and these job advertisements, it is possible to draw up a list of the main aerospace companies and their involvement in various programmes. This shows the convoluted patterns of stealth-related ''alliances''. For example, Boeing and Northrop are partners on the B-2 but rivals on the ATF, while General Dynamics and McDonnell Douglas are partners on the A-12 but rivals on the ATF. Several companies are working on unidentified oprogrammes, while Grumman has no apparent stakes in stealth.

In parallel with these all-new ''black'' programmes, other research efforts are investigating ways of adding stealth technology to current US combat aircraft. Rumours of a stealthy version of the F-16 seem to have first surfaced in 1988, describing how some aircraft had been treated with ferrite paint and had light sources for active visual camouflage installed in their intakes. Three squadrons had been deployed, one

Above: **The ATA wil be powered by the General Electric F404/F5D2 turbofan, a derivative of the non-afterburning F404-400.**

Below: **This Bell Helicopter artwork of a possible LHX helicopter configuration features internally-stowed missile armament.**

Above: **On the McDonnell Douglas/Bell LHX design, the armament is stowed out of sight of enemy radar in a combined wing/sponson.**

US Aerospace and Stealth Programmes

Company	Programme						
	F-117A	YF-22	YF-23	A-12	B-2	Aurora	?
Boeing		▨			▨		
General Dynamics		▨					
General Electric							
Lockheed						▨	
LTV							
McDonnell Douglas				▨	▨		
McDD Helicopter							▨
Northrop					▨		
Pratt & Whitney	▨						
Rockwell							▨

programmes being under way. The technique has been used before. In the latter part of the 1970s, US intelligence mounted such an exercise to watch for the first signs that the technology needed to create a Warsaw Pact equivalent of the Boeing E-3 AWACS was emerging from Soviet laboratories.

INTELLIGENCE

Most positive clues to the existence of Soviet stealth aircraft would probably come from human agents working within design laboratories and aircraft factories. To take an example, in the late 1970s news that the first prototype of the Tupolev Blackjack bomber was under assembly "leaked" from the US intelligence community a year ahead of the anticipated roll-out date.

In the case of stealth, the US enjoyed the advantage of having an agent working undetected by the KGB within one of the Moscow laboratories tasked with stealth research. It was a massive stroke of luck but one which was to be lost thanks to an inept blunder by the CIA.

In February 1985 the Soviets arrested Paul M. Stambaugh, a second

source told me in 1988, and had been deployed in Alaska, Spain and mainland USA.

Stealth technology is also one of the features which Grumman is proposing under its "Tomcat 21" project. Aimed at keeping the F-14 effective into the next century, this would give the aircraft an extra 2,600lb (1,180kg) of internal fuel, uprated General Electric F110-429 engines and new avionics. The latter would include an air-to-ground FLIR, a laser ranger/tracker and an improved version of the Hughes APC-71 radar incorporating high-resolution synthetic-aperture modes for the 24 hour all-weather delivery of air-to-ground ordnance. The moveable vanes currently fitted to the aircraft wing gloves would be removed and the glove extended to provide the equivalent area and volume needed for the extra internal fuel. No details of the proposed RCS-reduction measures have been released.

The greatest mystery in the world of low-observables is the status of Soviet stealth technology. Having read a draft of one of the first magazine articles ever written about stealth aircraft, Nancy Biglin, then circulation manager of *Armed Forces Journal,* asked one of the magazine's editors "Do the Russians have one of these airplanes?" Told that this was unlikely, she countered by asking "But how would we know, if they can't be seen?" A long silence followed, as the impact of her comment sunk home.

Detecting the undetectable is in theory an intelligence officer's nightmare. It is likely

that the CIA and DIA have sunk considerable effort into keeping tabs on Soviet stealth work. This has almost certainly involved at least three parallel efforts. Most obvious of these is the regular scrutiny of known Soviet aircraft plants for signs of a new aircraft being rolled out and to watch for its entering flight test at the Ramenskoye test centre. It would in theory be possible to assemble prototypes at an airfield not normally involved in aircraft manufacture and not to send these first examples to Ramenskoye but the logistic problems would be

severe. The CIA probably maintains a regular satellite watch on all Soviet airfields capable of operating combat aircraft. Movement of major sub-assemblies either by road or air stands a good chance of being detected.

Long-range warning of a Soviet stealth programme has probably been obtained by carefully monitoring selected areas of Soviet military research and development. By watching for developments in these vital technologies needed to create a Soviet stealth aircraft, intelligence analysts would be able to judge the likelihood of such

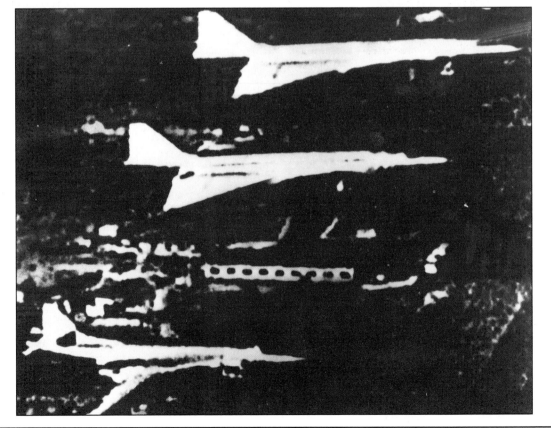

secretary in the Moscow embassy. The arrest was carried out as he was meeting Adolf G. Tolkachev, a Soviet national who was working as a CIA agent. Stambaugh had been caught in the act of receiving secrets "of a defence nature" from his contact, the Soviets announced. He was declared *persona non grata* and expelled from the Soviet Union.

Official announcements identified Tolkachev simply as "a staff worker of a Moscow research institute". This colourless description concealed from the soviet public the fact that the man was by profession an aviation engineer and worked at a Moscow research institute tasked with developing the most advanced forms of military aircraft technology. Tolkachev had been in a position to keep his US employers informed of the latest Soviet advances in highly-classified areas of airborne electronics systems such as radars and electronic countermeasures.

Even more importantly, he could report on Soviet work in the field of stealth technology. At a time when the US was making great advances in stealth technology, flying its

Above: **Soviet air attache Col Vladimir Izmaylov was expelled from the USA in 1986, accused of gathering intelligence on stealth.**

Left: **Taken by a US spy satellite, this photograph was "leaked" in 1983 to give the world its first look at the Blackjack bomber (bottom).**

own F-117A stealth fighter and designing the exotic B-2 bomber and Advanced Cruise Missile as formidable challenges to future Soviet air defences, Tolkachev had allowed the US to monitor Soviet attempts to create similar stealth technology for its own use.

An investigation showed that Tolkachev had been betrayed to the KGB by Edward L. Howard, an ex-CIA officer who had been trained in the early 1980s for duty in Moscow as an agent handler but who had been fired before ever being posted to the Soviet capital.

SOVIET ESPIONAGE

Like all US "black" programmes, stealth technology was a natural target for Soviet espionage. On Tuesday 18 December 1984, FBI agents went to an apartment in Downey, a suburb 10 miles (16km) southeast of Los Angeles, and arrested Thomas Patrick Cavanagh, a 40 year old employee of Northrop's Advanced Systems Division at Pico Rivera, California. He was charged with attempting to transmit classified US defence information regarding an advanced military project that used low observable technology.

Cavanagh had been a Northrop employee since 1981. According to the FBI, he had stolen classified technical manuals, blueprints, drawings and a list of sub-contractors from his employer and had then tried to contact and meet officials of the Soviet Union in the hopes of selling the material for $25,000. At this point, his scheme went wrong.

The "Soviet officials" with whom he became involved turned out to be FBI agents. "To our knowledge, he never actually contacted Soviet officials", Assistant FBI Director Bill Baker told reporters following Cavanagh's arrest.

ARRESTED

In October 1984 Colonel Vladimir Makarovich Izmaylov of the Soviet Air Force had been posted to the USA as Air Attaché. Formerly a squadron navigator and staff officer in the Soviet Air Force, he had already served a four-year tour of duty in the USA during the late 1970s. His new posting was to end in a more spectacular fashion than the first. On the night of Friday 20 June 1986, the 43 year old Soviet colonel went by night to a wooded area on a secluded road in Fort Washington, Maryland, where he dug up a package, then buried a milk carton containing cash and instructions written in invisible ink. Minutes later, a short scuffle with waiting FBI agents resulted in his arrest, ending another attempt to steal stealth secrets.

The operation which led to his arrest had been another FBI entrapment scheme. In this case, the Soviet official had been only too real — it was the "traitor" who had proved to be a phoney. Working for the Soviet military intelligence organisation GRU (military equivalent to the better-known KGB), Izmaylov, who lived at Wildwood Towers in Arlington, had tried late in 1985 to recruit a USAF officer. The target was carefully

selected. Posted to the Washington area, he was a man likely to have access to high-level classified information.

This officer, whose identity was not released, reported Izmaylov's overtures to his superiors and a scheme to exploit the situation was drawn up. The US officer agreed to play the rôle of traitor, while working undercover with the FBI and the US Air Force's Office of Special Investigations. The aim of the operation was to find out what specific types of information the Soviets were trying to get and to gather useful data on Soviet espionage methods.

For more than a year the FBI and the Air Force Office of Special Investigations kept track of Izmaylov's clandestine meetings with the US officer, often using hidden cameras to record the proceedings.

As the relationship proceeded, the US officer periodically handed over Air Force documents to Izmaylov in exchange for cash payments. The first of these was received in January 1986.

EXPULSION

By June, the FBI had all the information it needed. It had obtained a valuable insight into soviet espionage "trade-craft" and had learned the prime targets of Izmaylov's operation — the Strategic Defense Initiative (SDI), the Trans-atmospheric Vehicle Program, a US cruise missile programme (probably the AGM-129 Advanced Cruise Missile) and stealth technology. It was time to wind the operation up.

In early June, a meeting was scheduled for the 20th of the month. When that night came, Izmaylov went to Fort Foote Road, near Oxon Hill Road, Fort Washington, and buried another milk carton close to a telephone pole. He then headed for a wooded area about a mile away near Riverview Road and the Federal Communications Center. The FBI agents closed in, arresting him at 10.10pm. There was a brief struggle as Izmaylov swung a blow at agents taking him into custody, the latter announced, and the attaché was subsequently handcuffed. A search showed that he was carrying a switchblade knife with a four-inch (10cm) blade but at no time did the arrested man attempt to use it as a weapon. Izmaylov explained that he was lost and had been looking for a fishing spot but the FBI stated that there were no fishing sites in the immediate area and that no fishing tackle had been found in the attaché's car.

When examined, the milk carton was found to contain $8,000 in cash, the latest instalment in a series of payments totalling $41,000, and instructions written in invisible ink on cellophane. In it, Izmaylov thanked his American contact for the latest batch of documents but registered "some

disappointment that it was not all grade 'A'". Izmaylov said that he hoped "that you'll make an extra effort in getting info I specified in previous messages" but warned his contact against attracting attention to himself when spending the money.

At a press conference to announce the arrest, the FBI told reporters that the United States had foiled "an aggressive Soviet Military Intelligence operation" and warned that the GRU had been "very, very aggressive" in trying to recruit military personnel based in the Washington area. They praised the unidentified Air Force officer for helping "to thwart a significant loss of highly classified weapons to the Soviets". Had Izmaylov found a genuine traitor, the United States would have suffered "significant loss of highly classified weapons and programs systems materials to the Soviets". Instead, the USA had obtained what was described as "significant insights relevant to Soviet intelligence . . . and Soviet knowledge of US classified programs . . . It was a very profitable venture".

The unfortunate Izmaylov was released into the custody of Soviet embassy officials after his status as a displomat had been confirmed. Soviet minister-councillor Victor F.

Above: The SS-N-21 cruise missile probably relies on small size for low RCS, but later designs are expected to use stealth technology.

Below: The Su-27 Flanker is not a stealth fighter, but its radar and weapons will probably be upgraded for use against stealthy targets.

Isakov was summoned to the State Department and told that Izmaylov would be expelled as *persona non grata*.

SOVIET STEALTH

In May 1986, *International Defense Review* quoted the USAF Aeronautical Systems Division commander as saying that the US was "ten to 15 years ahead" of the Soviet Union in stealth technology and "we may be further ahead than that".

It is a lead which seems to be holding. During a 1988 Aerospace Education Foundation meeting, USAF Assistant Secretary for Acquisition John F. Welch was asked if the US held a lead in stealth technology over the Soviet Union and if so whether that lead could be maintained. He replied "The answer has to be — yes, and hush up". His humorous response was followed by the statement that the US did have a commanding lead and that given suitable exploitation and security "it can be an enduring one".

In 1985 the US Navy predicted that Soviet aircraft and missiles incorporating stealth technology would enter service by the end of the decade. The need to cope with these had been a driving force in the decision to fit the

Grumman F-14D version of Tomcat with an infra-red search and track (IRST) system.

A 1986 prediction by Bill Sweetman that the first Soviet stealth application would be a naval cruise missile seems to have been correct. Some low-observable features are thought to be incorporated in the SS-N-24 cruise missile. Around 40ft (12m) long, 4.1ft (1.25m) in diameter and with a wingspan of 19.5ft (5.94m), this is being deployed in submarine-launched and land-based forms. A US DoD drawing shows the weapon rising to the surface in wingless form, deploying highly-swept wing and tail surfaces and igniting its rocket motor.

A possibly early candidate for stealth technology is likely to be the new Soviet reconnaissance aircraft first reported under the designation "Ram-M". Very little is known about this twin-tailed high-altitude reconnaissance aircraft.

The Soviet Union is known to be working on at least two new models of fighter aircraft and these will be logical candidates for some degree of stealth. There is as yet no reported Soviet equivalent of the Lockheeed F-117A — the mid-1980s Testor/Italeri model kit of the "MiG-37 Ferret E" is pure speculation.

Following the appearance of the MiG-29 Fulcrum at the 1988 Farnborough Air Show, Soviet TV commentator Vladimir Tsvestov showed viewers the Testor/Italeri

"MiG-37 Ferret" model which he had bought in a toy shop in Tokyo. "In our country it is still shrouded in a thick and heavy veil of secrecy but in Japan children are already playing with this plane . . . If we really have not managed to keep it secret and we are guarding what has long been no secret to the whole world, why not in fact offer for sale the MiG-37, or the Soviet stealth . . . a plane invisible to radar?"

Tupolev's giant Tu-160 Blackjack has little or no stealth technology but little is known concerning a second reported new Tupolev design. First stated to be a bomber version of the Tu-144 Charger supersonic airliner, it now seems more likely to be a super cruise bomber derived from the abandoned SST and designed to fly for long periods of time at supersonic speeds. Like the Tu-160, it is likely to carry the new AS-X-19 supersonic cruise missile.

JAPAN

Other than by the Super Powers, very little effort is being put into stealth technology. One notable exception is Japan. In its search for a suitable aircraft to replace the Mitsubishi F-1 fighter-bomber during the mid-1980s, Japan looked at several approaches. The most obvious was a new indigenously-developed aircraft based on stealth technology. Some work in this area was already under way. In January 1982, the Japan

Self Defence Agency had admitted that it was carrying out research into stealth.

To draw up plans for a new stealthy fighter, an industrial team known as the FS-X (Fighter, Support, eXperimental) Joint Study Team was set up. Headed by Mitsubishi Heavy Industries, this included Kawasaki, Fuji Heavy Industries, engine maker Ishisawajima-Harima and the Mitsubishi Electric company.

Working at Mitsubishi Heavy Industries' Nagoya Works under chief engineer Irtsuro Masuda, a team of 31 engineers took as their starting point a 1983 experimental conversion of a Mitsubishi T-2 trainer. The design which took shape on their drawing boards was intended to have a low-altitude combat radius of up to 450nm (833km) at mach 0.9 while carrying a payload of four Type 80 ASM-1 anti-ship missiles.

As the new design took shape, the various companies involved began to explore some of the key technologies needed for the new aircraft. Mitsibishi joined forces with its partners to research the stealth technology needed for the FS-X. New types of RAM were developed and tested in the anechoic chamber at Mitsubishi's Komaki South factory, while software

***Below:* Although the Tu-160 Blackjack is similar in appearance to the B-1, its simpler shape will make it a better radar target.**

engineers tackled the task of creating computer programmes for the design of RAM and the prediction of aircraft RCS.

The company also carried out tests of new metal-working techniques such as super-plastic forming and diffusion bonding. Other efforts explored the use of advanced composite materials, fabricating major FS-X components for structural testing.

The avionics suite would be developed by Mitsubishi Electric, Fujitsu and NEC. Like the T-2 research aircraft on which the Mitsubishi design was based, the latter would have a CCV-type (control-configured vehicle) flight control system offering fully-decoupled flight modes, including the ability to fly with its nose angled to the line of flight.

EXPORT PROBLEMS

By 1987 the team was convinced that its FS-X would have a higher performance and lower cost than rival designs, all of which were being offered by foreign companies. Unfortunately, their design faced political headwinds.

One of the problems which Japan faces when developing military hardware is that the Government prohibits the export of military equipment. If the FS-X was to go ahead, the team had to persuade the Government that the new aircraft would be economical to produce in the 80 to 100 production run being envisaged. At the same time, Japanese Prime Minister Yasuhiro Nakasone was under pressure to award at least part of the contract to a foreign company, a means of helping current balance of trade disagreements between Japan, the USA and Western Europe.

In March 1987, unidentified officials of the Japan Self Defence Agency told the Asahi News Service that there was a good chance that FS-X would be a joint development by Japan and a US manufacturer. If such an international solution is chosen, it was explained, Japanese industry would carry out between 60 and 70 per cent of the work, the remainder being placed overseas.

Four aircraft were seen as alternatives to the indigenous design: developed versions of one of the existing Western fighters — the F-16 Fighting Falcon, F-18 Hornet, F-15

Above: **Experience with the T-2 CCV research aircraft gave Mitsubishi engineers the confidence to propose an all-Japanese FS-X fighter.**

Eagle and the Panavia Tornado. The European aircraft was probably dismissed quite quickly but the US aircraft looked attractive, particularly since the manufacturers of the F-16 and F-18 were already proposing upgraded export versions.

US PROPOSALS

McDonnell Douglas offered a modified version of the F-18 Hornet, incorporating increased wing sweep and improved range and air-to-air capability. The FS-X requirement favoured a twin-engined design, so General Dynamics proposed a new version of the F-16 Fighting Falcon. Known as the FX-4, this was powered by two engines in the 20,000lb (9,000kg) thrust class — either GE F404s or P&W PW1120s.

Final proposals for the new aircraft were presented in April 1987, so that the Government would make a decision in the summer, allowing funding for the programme to be included in the next year's defence budget. The programme could

Right: **The latest configuration of Mirage 2000 cockpit narrows the technology gap between the French fighter and its US**

involve up to 250 fighters.

Early in October 1987, Japan announced that the FS-X would be a derivative of an existing US aircraft, the choice of the basic airframe being either the F-16 or the F-15. Defence Minister Yuko Kurihara announced that the chosen airframe would be fitted with selected items of Japanese technology, such as a phased-array radar and a new fire-control system, and would also incorporate stealth technology.

The main problem with the F-18 was cost. Studies had shown that this was the US aircraft best-suited to be the basis for the planned FS-X but that the likely cost of modifying the F-18 would have been about 30 per cent more expensive than the JASDF had budgeted for the FS-X programme.

At this stage, it seemed likely that an F-15 derivative would be selected — the Eagle was already in JASDF service in the interceptor rôle and being licence-built by Mitsubishi. Development costs of around $715 million were predicted. The F-16 was seen as a less likely candidate,

rivals. **One feature not found on US fighters is the novel 'head-level' CRT display mounted directly under the main HUD.**

since early discussions between the Japanese and General Dynamics had bogged down over the relative merits of single- versus twin-engined aircraft.

SX-3

By the autumn of 1987, however, discussions had focussed on a design the reported designation of which was SX-3 (perhaps a mis-spelling of "FX-3"). A stage beyond the "big-winged" Agile Falcon being proposed to Western Europe, SX-3 was intended to incorporate advanced technology composite materials in the forward and aft fuselage sections and in the increased-span wings. It would also incorporate the stealth measures planned for the indigenous design.

This F-16 derivative was selected by the Japan Self Defence Agency, a decision which received the formal endorsement of the Japanese National Security Council in October 1987. The decision was not popular in Japan. Both local industry and the JASDF had backed the

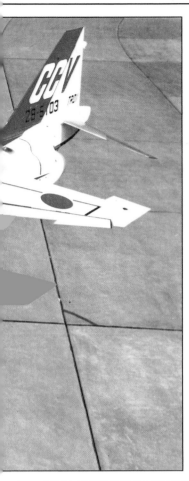

indigenous design and now criticised the deal as having been forced upon their country for political reasons, a result of the US trade deficit with Japan.

It also aroused controversy in the USA, with critics charging that one of America's largest commercial opponents was being given access to US technology, while virtually all of the changes being made to the basic design would fall into the category of Japanese-developed technology which the USA might one day have to purchase. An *Aviation Week* editorial stated bluntly that "a significant part of the technological lead that has been won by the exertions of thousands of American aerospace engineers over 40-50 years should not have been squandered at the stroke of a pen" and called for the agreement to be revised or even cancelled.

Other critics suggested that F-16 technology would find its way to the Soviet Union under the sort of illicit deal which had seen Toshiba provide the Soviets with milling technology which may have enabled the Soviet Navy to deploy acoustically "steathier" submarines.

In 1988 the two Governments signed a MoU which would give Japanese industry access to many advanced US technologies. It specified that any Japanese refinements to existing technologies must be made available to the USA free of charge, while technology developed entirely by Japan had to be requested (and paid for) by the USA.

OTHER COUNTRIES

China is also working on stealth technology. On 26 January 1987, Hangzhou radio reported that "practicable stealth technologies and theories" had been mastered and claimed that a "considerable quantity" of experimental data had been collected by Chinese scientists and engineers. "It will not be long before our country can make our own stealth aircraft", listeners were told.

Very little stealth-related work has been reported in Western Europe. RAM treated aircraft were tested at Farnborough in the 1950s, while a pair of Canberra light bombers belonging to 51 Sqn RAF were treated with RAM during the late 1950s and early 1960s and tested at Wyton, home of the Royal Air Force's small ELINT fleet.

The latest generation of European military aircraft — EFA and Rafale — incorporate some degree of RCS reduction but probably not enough to be militarily significant. In this respect, they are likely to be inferior to the US ATF and ATA and represent a transitional pattern between aircraft of the F-15/16 generation and the newer YF-22/23. It all seems rather reminiscent of the efforts by some design teams in the mid-1930s to avoid going the whole way in the transition from open-cockpit fabric-covered biplanes with fix undercarriages to the era of all-metal monoplanes with closed cockpits and retractable undercarriages.

Some would argue that Western Europe simply cannot afford to adopt stealth technology on a large scale. Accountants have probably used such arguments since the days when iron weapons replaced those of bronze.

History dismisses such claims. The iron wielding but otherwise primitive Dorians consigned the bronze-age Mycenaean civilisation of ancient Greece to the history book, ushering in a dark age which would last until the birth of Classical Greece. Similarly, by launching the battleship *Dreadnought* in 1906, the Royal Navy condemned the entire fleets of its rivals and even its own fleet to near-instant obsolescence. When the Battle of Jutland was fought little more than a decade later, only a handful of pre-*Dreadnought* vessels were involved. Most had been scrapped as hopelessly obsolete.

West Germany and Italy are known to be working on stealth technology, both individually and in collaboration. In 1986 the UK magazine *Flight International* published a drawing of the Dornier LA-2000, a proposed subsonic ground-attack aircraft. The original drawing on which the magazine's sketch was based had not been released by the company but seems to have "leaked" from the German defence ministry.

The drawing showed a small delta-winged aircraft, the pure triangular shape of which was marred only by a raised section on the centreline. This incorporated a small canopy close to the apex of the delta. The aircraft's two engines were located in a propulsion bay mounted under the wing. The inlet was between a quarter and a third of the way back from the nose. The two low-by-pass-ratio turbofans — each with a thrust of 5,600lb (2,550kg) — feed a single two-dimensional vectoring nozzle at the trailing edge of the wing. Two large elevons, mounted on either side of the wing trailing edge, would presumably share the task of controlling the aircraft. An internal weapons bay of about 200 cubic feet (6 m³) capacity contains a retractable weapons platform.

LIGHT STEALTH

Dornier declines to discuss the LA-2000 project but, given the financial demands of the Eurofighter programme, the little delta is unlikely to take wing in its current form. It could be scaled down to form the basis of a proposed German/Italian stealth anti-radar drone. Equipped with an RCS-enhancing Luneburg lens which could be activated and de-activated by command or

Left: The dazzling flight performance of Rafale A has not blinded France to the need for RCS reduction.

Below: The inlet and cockpit of Rafale were potential RCS weaknesses which required careful design.

went. The company did have a tiny stand at the 1988 Farnborough Air Show but this was not manned on any of the five occasions when I stopped by in the hopes of discussing the programme with Company officials.

Most of the other "low-signature" designs on offer are light observation aircraft. Their reduced RCS is mostly the result of modest dimensions. These sailplane-like aircraft are thus mid-1980s equivalents of the Vietnam-era YO-3A. A handful of examples will illustrate these modest designs.

Schweizer Aircraft's single-engined SA-2-37A is largely intended for police or customs use, having been designed to have a low acoustic signature. It can carry a two-man crew in its side- by-side cockpit, plus up to 750lb (340kg) of palletised mission equipment (such as cameras, FLIR, LLTV and a data link) in a payload bay, access to which is obtained via a large rear hatch door and removeable belly skin panels.

Low radar, IR and acoustic signatures are claimed for the two- seat *HB Flugzeugbau* HB-32 Scanliner. Powered by a 96hp VW-2400G piston engine, this Austrian design can carry pod mounted equipment such as a side-looking airborne radar (SLAR) or mini-FLIR on underwing hardpoints. The maximum take-off weight is only 1,873lb (850kg) and a maximum payload of 282lb (128kg) can only be carried when the aircraft is being flown by a single pilot.

by a pre-set programme, such an RPV could present defences with an appearing and disappearing target.

Little is being done in other countries to exploit stealth technology in the design of aircraft or missiles. At the 1987 Paris Air Show a new company, Venga Aircraft, claimed a low radar signature for their proposed TG-10 twin-engined trainer. Built largely from composites, this could be powered by a pair of GE J85 or CJ610, Rolls-Royce Viper 632 or 680 or the P&W Canada JT15D-4C. Externally, the TG-10 resembles the Northrop F-5 but has Hornet-style twin verticals mounted ahead of the horizontal stabiliser. The aircraft is suitable for advanced training and ground attack.

It is hard to take the concept seriously. Composite construction is not really suited to the needs of developing nations — the aircraft's professed target market. It may be corrosion free but it is not as easy to repair as aluminium. Any reduction in RCS could only come from the use of non-metallic constructional materials and the outward-canted vertical fins.

Moulds for the aircraft's composite structure — carbon fibre sandwiched with a divincel foam core — were reported to be under construction in Scottsdale, Arizona, in the summer of 1987 but the planned roll-out date of late 1987 came and

Above: The British Aerospace EAP prototype has rectangular inlets of the type first planned for EFA.

Below: **The curved inlets shown on the EFA mockup were a modification which reduced the aircraft's RCS.**

LOCKHEED U-2 and TR-1

Rôle: high-altitude reconnaissance
Length: 63ft 0in (19.20m)
Wingspan: 103ft 0in (31.39m)
Height: 16ft 0in (4.88m)
Max. take-off weight: 40,000lb (18,140kg)
Max. speed: More than 373kts (691km/h)
Ceiling: 90,000ft (27,400m)
Range: More than 2,600nm (4,800km)
Armament: None
Powerplant: One Pratt & Whitney J75-P-13B turbojet of 17,000lb (7,710kg) dry thrust

In March 1953 the USAF drew up a specification for a reconnaissance aircraft able to fly at heights far above those obtainable from existing types and interceptors. It proposed the creation of a subsonic single-seat aircraft with a radius of 1,500 miles (2,400km) and the ability to fly over its target at a height of 70,000ft (21,000km) or more while carrying a sensor payload weighing between 100 and 700lb (45 and 300kg). The resulting design was expected to combine the latest in turbojet engine technology with an airframe whose light construction and high aspect-ratio wings would be more reminiscent of sailplanes than combat aircraft.

The aircraft would be unarmed, so it had to be difficult to detect and hard to intercept. Both qualities were obtained largely by giving the aircraft a cruising height well above that of contemporary interceptors. The formal specification recognised that "the enemy will have limited methods of detection and/or interception of a vehicle of the required performance. The greatest opposition to the operation of this aircraft can be expected to be encountered from guided missiles."

To minimise the chances of detection, paragraph 2 (g) of the specification demanded that "Consideration will be given in the design of the vehicle to minimising the detectability by enemy radar." The need to avoid emitting signals which an enemy might detect was also appreciated. Navigation was to be by

means of "a non-emanating system" while the sole item of communications equipment would be a simple short-range UHF radio. "No emanations from the aircraft will be permitted over enemy territory."

Although not invited to bid for the programme, Lockheed had learned of the new requirement. In May 1954, the company proposed a J73-engined CL-282 variant of its F-104 Starfighter. This was rejected in favour of the Bell Model 67 and Martin 294 designs. In November of the same year, an evaluation of updated Lockheed proposals led to a contract being placed for a small batch of aircraft. The Bell Model 67 (designated X-16) was cancelled, while the Martin design was to emerge as the long-span RB-57D.

Working in conditions of unparalleled secrecy, Lockheed designer Kelly Johnson and his "Skunk Works" team built the first prototype in only eight months, rolling it out at the

then-new Groom Lake AFB, Nevada, in mid July 1955. A brief but unplanned hop during taxing trials on 29 July was followed by a first flight on 1 August. This first aircraft was designated U-2, with the early production examples being U-2A.

As originally fielded, the U-2 flew with an all-black paint scheme designed to minimise its visibility at high altitudes. Contributing to its avoidance of radar detection were its small size — not much larger than a jet fighter — and its clean lines. At first sight, its long-span wings might seem like ideal radar reflectors but in practice their vast span is so great than they resonate in the HF band rather than at radar frequencies.

When further developing the aircraft to create new versions in the late 1960s and early 1970s, Lockheed is reported to have looked at ways of making it stealthier. None left the drawing board. Optimised as it was for

ultimate high-altitude performance, the basic design was so specialised that it left the design team with little leeway for large-scale modifications. Most of the changes which followed were aerodynamic. The only move which made the type stealthier was the introduction of a new paint scheme containing radar-absorbing "iron-ball" ferrite pigment.

The initial production run was of about 55 aircraft. At least seven U-2As were reworked as U-2Bs, receiving structural strengthening and the more powerful Pratt & Whitney J75-P-13 turbojet. The follow-on U-2C (a mixture of reworked and new-build aircraft) introduced a slightly extended nose, a long dorsal equipment fairing, increased fuel capacity, enlarged intakes and the J75-P-13B engine.

The U-2D has a modified Q bay (fuselage equipment bay) able to house specialised sensors or a second crew member, while the U-2E was a

Above: The main anti-radar feature of the TR-1 is its skin of "Iron Ball" paint. As its nickname suggests, this material consists of tiny particles of magnetic material (known as ferrite) suspended in a non-magnetic binder. When a radar wave strikes the aircraft, some of its energy is absorbed by this paint. The individual ferrite particles are magnetised then remagnetised in the opposite polarity billions of times each second by the cycles in the wave's magnetic field.

CIA version with advanced ECM systems. At least four U-2As were modified to U-2F designation by the addition of a USAF-style refuelling receptacle.

The aircraft returned to production in 1968 in its U-2R form, a variant which had first flown in prototype form on 28 August 1967. Powered by the same J75-P-13B engine as the earlier U-2C, this was intended to overcome the airframe imposed performance limitations of the older aircraft, improve handling characteristics, increase the range and payload and provide a less cramped cockpit.

The result may have resembled the earlier U-2 models but it was essentially an all-new design. The wingspan was increased by 23ft (7m) with the outboard 5.9ft (1.8m) of each wing folding inwards for storage. Its maximum ceiling altitude is reported to be 75,000ft (22,860m), slightly below that of the earlier models. Most obvious new features of the U-2R are the underwing equipment pods which supplement the volume of the fuselage bays. In 1978 these were replaced by still larger underwing fairings known as "superpods".

A set of 25 serial numbers was assigned to the initial batch of U-2Rs but the number actually built in this initial production run was at least 14, but probably 17. Aircraft were initially assigned to both the USAF and the CIA, rapidly supplanting the older models, but the surviving CIA examples were passed to the USAF in 1974.

The final version of the U-2 family was the TR-1. Externally near-identical to the U-2R, it was ordered in 1979 to act as a source of "day or night, high-altitude, all weather stand-off surveillance of a battle area in direct support of US and allied ground and air forces". Currently the most important production variant of an aircraft the Soviets once dubbed "the black lady of espionage", the TR-1 will serve into the 1990s, ensuring that the final member of this series of pioneering stealth aircraft will remain in service well after the last example of its supersonic SR-71 replacement has been retired.

Right: Originally built for the CIA as a U-2A, 66701 was later assigned to the USAF. Rebuilt as a U-2B, then as a U-2C, it was painted for the first time in 1970.

97

LOCKHEED SR-71 BLACKBIRD

Rôle: Strategic reconnaissance
Length: 107ft 5in (32.74m)
Wingspan: 55ft 7in (16.94m)
Height: 18ft 6in (5.64m)
Max. take-off weight: 170,000lb (77,000kg)
Max. speed: Mach 3 +
Service ceiling: approx. 86,000ft (26,000m)
Range: 2,600nm (4,800km)
Armament: none
Powerplant: two Pratt & Whitney J58 each of 32,500lb (14,700kg) thrust with afterburner.

Despite their age, the small fleet of SR-71 Blackbird aircraft represented a unique intelligence-gathering asset right up to their moment of final retirement in late 1989. More than a quarter of a century after the type's first flight, this sinister-looking aircraft could still operate with impunity in the face of most defence systems. The Soviet Union was probably the only nation able to defend itself against Blackbirds. Others have tried — firing off SA-2 Guidelines against SR-71s has become a regular event for the North Korean air defences — but to date the exercise has proved fruitless. In 1986 Blackbirds operated in the face of the threat posed by Libyan SA-5 Gammon long-range/high-altitude missile

batteries in order to record the results of US air strikes against targets in both Tripoli and Benghazi.

Like the XB-70 bomber programme, the A-12 project required a long series of technological developments to make Mach 3 flight possible. Materials, lubricants, powerplants, fuels and subsystems all had to be custom-developed. When the aircraft cruises for prolonged periods at Mach 3, the external skin temperature rises to at least 450 degrees Celsius and to more than 1,000 degrees in areas where the thermal effects are severest. To cope with this level of thermal stress, most of the airframe is made from Beta B-120 titanium alloy.

When designing the U-2, Lockheed had been able to take only limited RCS-reduction measures but the A-12 took the entire art a massive step forward. As North American designers working on the XB-70 bomber and the F-108 Rapier fighter had discovered, creating an aircraft able to cruise at Mach 3 was difficult enough but, in creating the A-12, the Skunk Works tackled the tasks of combining this level of performance with stealth.

Comparison of the A-12 with the similar-sized F-108 is

instructive. The fighter had an angular appearance, which bordered on ugliness, with a slab-sided forward fuselage, box-shaped rear fuselage and wedge inlets — features which were highly radar reflective. The A-12 had rounded lines with extensive use being made of wing/body blending, while its engines were fed by inlets whose conical centrebodies would help shield the compressor face from radar observation. The twin fins were canted inwards to reduce their radar reflectivity, while the long chines on the forward fuselage presented highly-inclined surfaces to incoming radar energy.

Invisible to the untrained eye was another breakthrough in stealth technology — the use of plastic materials in areas such as the wing leading edges, chines and elevons. Developed by Lockheed, this took the form of a radar-absorbent plastic honeycomb designed to cope with temperatures of up to 600°F (315°C). On the A-12, it accounted for 20 per cent of the total wing area. It was not strong enough be used structurally in a Mach 3 design, so it was added to the leading and trailing edge in the form of V-shaped sections.

The Skunk Works is also reported to have flown experimental components such as all-plastic vertical fins.

The dark paint finish used to help radiate heat away from the aircraft gave rise to the unofficial designation "Blackbird". It was designed with two qualities in mind. It offered high heat emissivity, so helping to radiate friction-generated heat when the aircraft was cruising at Mach 3. It also incorporated the radar-absorbing "iron ball" ferrite-based pigment used on the U-2 and TR-1.

The first A-12 prototype was completed in the winter of 1961/62 and made its maiden flight (with interim J75 turbojet engines) on 26 April 1962; deliveries to the CIA started towards the end of that year. By that time a second variant existed — the YF-12A interceptor. The first of three prototype fighters flew in August 1963 but, although extensively tested, the type was never adopted for service. Fifteen A-12s were built, all but one of which were single seat aircraft.

Existence of the aircraft was revealed by President Johnson on 29 February 1964, although he gave the designation incorrectly as "A-11". Four months later, he revealed that a definitive

Left: **The SR-71 gave the world its first example of wing-body blending, a significant method of reducing RCS taken to extreme in the B-2.**

Above: **Most of the SR-71's sensor payload is packed into equipment bays within the long chines. Built from metal,** **these incorporate RAM and are carefully blended with the fuselage, measures aimed at reducing overall RCS.**

operational version was under development but once more gave a wrong designation, referring to the new aircraft as the SR-71. It was to have been designated RS-71 (Reconnaissance-Strike) rather than SR (Strategic reconnaissance). To this day it remains unclear whether this was due to a slip of the Presidential tongue or an attempt to divert attention from a possible secondary nuclear-strike rôle. A dedicated R-12 nuclear strike derivative of the A-12 is known to have been proposed but rejected.

The SR-71 had been ordered at the end of 1962. Like the U-2, the A-12 had been a single-seat aircraft (although several two-seat trainer versions of the latter were completed). The SR-71 had a two-seat cockpit, a configuration first tested on the YF-12A. It was also slightly larger and heavier than the A-12. The chines were made from metal and used to house the aircraft's reconnaissance sensors.

First flight of the SR-71 took place on 22 December 1964,

the aircraft being one of an initial batch of six. Production deliveries started in January 1966 with the delivery to the USAF of the first SR-71B two-seater. The first SR-71A was delivered in May of the same year. In total, 32 SR-71s were built, all but two of which were two-seaters.

Just how well the aircraft's RCS-reduction measures worked remain debatable but classified. Not all of the components flight-tested in plastic found their way into the production aircraft. In his book *Stealth Aircraft*, Bill Sweetman recalls with amusement how when the USAF flew an SR-71 to the 1974 Farnborough Air Show, Plessey Radar announced that its AR-5D civil air-surveillance radar had detected the plane at a range of more than 200 miles (320km).

To some extent, the degree of radar-invisibility achieved did not really matter. Blackbird's sheer speed and high-altitude capability has made it invulnerable to interception from the day of its first flight to the day of its eventual final retirement.

Above: Despite being the first Western aircraft to incorporate significant RCS-reduction features, the SR-71 also offered Mach 3 performance and an undeniable beauty. The aircraft made extensive use of RAM in all the sharp horizontal edges which might be seen by an enemy radar — the chines, wing leading edges, and elevons. Further RCS reduction was provided by the use of "Iron Ball" paint. So sophisticated is the aircraft, that it is hard to remember that the first production delivery was in 1966. Over twenty years later, the high cost of keeping the aircraft operational has led to the final eight or so examples being retired.

LOCKHEED YO-3A AND E-SYSTEMS/GROB EGRETT-1

LOCKHEED YO-3
Rôle: Tactical night reconnaissance
Length: c.30ft (9m)
Wingspan: 57ft 1in (17.4m)
Weight loaded: More than 3,000lb (1,360kg)
Armament: None
Powerplant: One 210hp (157kW) Continental IO-360 piston engine

EGRETT 1
Rôle: Signals intelligence (SIGINT) gathering
Length: c.26ft (8m)
Wingspan: c.70ft (22m)
Operating altitude: 50,000 — 60,000ft (15 — 18km)
Powerplant: One Garrett TPE331-14 turboprop engine with a maximum output of 1,600hp (1,200kW)

For most readers, the phrase "stealth aircraft" probably summons up images of fighters and bombers, yet the two propeller-driven surveillance aircraft shown here illustrate alternative approaches to covert flight. Lockheed's YO-3 was developed during the Vietnam War and was the end result of a programme which had started in 1966. Realising that the Vietcong guerillas often moved by night, the US Department of Defense asked Lockheed to develop an aircraft able to observe such activity in a clandestine manner.

Since the Vietcong had no radars, radar signature could be disregarded, while night operation allowed the visual signature to be reduced to acceptable levels by camouflage. The enemy had no passive IR systems, so the only signature which needed to be reduced was the noise created by the powerplant and propeller.

The first aircraft to be tested was the QT-2 (Quiet Thruster, 2-place). Based on a civilian Schweizer 2-32 sailplane, this flew for the first time in July 1967. It was powered by a single heavily-muffled 100hp (75kW) Continental piston engine driving a slow-turning propeller via a two-stage belt-drive with a reduction ratio of 5.34:1. Tests results were promising enough to warrant sending two black-painted QT-2PC — the modified QT-2 plus a second new-build aircraft — to Vietnam for operational testing.

During its night sorties, the aircraft was able to detect and monitor a wide range of hitherto unobserved Vietcong activities, giving the Army the confidence to order the development of the custom-designed YO-3 aircraft. As an interim step, Lockheed built and flew the Q-Star, another rebuilt Schweizer 2-32. Its wing was strengthened and given an extended inner-section trailing edge. Like the QT-2 and -2PC, the Q-Star had a single muffled engine, mounted above and behind the cockpit, driving the slow-turning propeller via a long drive shaft which ran forward and over the cockpit canopy. This aircraft was extensively used in tests of low-noise propellers.

The first Lockheed YO-3A flew in the spring of 1969, less than a year after the Army signed the development contract. This retained the Q-Star wing (modified to accept a retractable undercarriage) low-mounted on a new fuselage which incorporated a tandem cockpit with a large clear-view canopy, plus a nose-mounted engine bay. Powerplant was a muffled 210hp (157kW) Continental IO-360 piston engine whose exhaust gases were led away into a long fairing running aft along the starboard side of the fuselage. Placed in limited production and fitted with specialised sensors, the YO-3A was deployed to Vietnam in 1970. Fourteen were built and all seem to have been withdrawn from service when the Vietnam War ended.

The E-Systems/Grob Egrett 1 is a more recent design which started flight tests on 24 June 1987 at the *Luftwaffe's* Manching flight-test centre. Officially, the Egrett is simply a "multi-purpose all-composite turboprop aircraft" but a SIGINT rôle was apparently intended from the start. Its designation is reported to reflect the names of the companies involved — E-Systems, Burkhart GRob Flugzeugbau and GarrETT. German designation is thought to be D-500.

According to E-Systems, Egrett is aimed at providing a reasonably priced platform for applications such as geographical survey, environmental protection and communications, these ostensibly civil tasks are thought to be cover for a US/German project to develop a small electronics platform with low radar and IR signatures.

The aircraft includes features which would hardly appeal to the traditional Grob customer as the cockpit is mounted over the wing roots, a location which gives a poor view sideways and downwards, and which caused one aviation magazine to speculate that the type might be a piloted prototype for a future RPV.

Egrett's deep bellied fuselage has the volume needed to carry its payload of electronic equipment, while a substantial portion of the output power from the 1,600hp (1,200kW) Garrett TPE331-14 turboprop engine is probably being used to drive electrical generators rather than the four-blade propeller. The remainder is used to lift this small aircraft to an operating altitude thought to be between 50,000 and 60,000ft (15 and 18km).

Above: Developed for use during the Vietnam War, the Lockheed YO-3A was based on experience gained with the earlier QT-2 and Q-Star. Design goal was acoustic stealth, so that the aircraft could be used at night to detect and monitor Vietcong movements. Exhaust gases from the engine were ducted through a long silencer mounted on the starboard side of the fuselage. The emerging gases would also have been a poor IR target for any Vietcong SA-7 shoulder-fired SAMs.

Involvement of E-Systems — a US company well known for its EW, SIGINT and command and control expertise — as prime contractor may indicate that the aircraft is intended to serve as a remotely-controlled reconnaissance platform monitoring over-the-horizon VHF and UHF communications links and microwave radar signals. A formation of two would be able to measure the relative bearing of all signals detected, allowing the location of the emitter to be deduced.

Conventional high-flying platforms such as the Lockheed TR-1 probably offer a large enough radar target to be engageable by long-range SAMs such as the SA-5 Gammon. Egrett will have a much smaller radar signature, so would be a more difficult target. If operated as an RPV, it would not put aircrew lives at risk.

If committed to production, the aircraft could be operational by the mid-1990s. In German service, Egrett would be integrated into that nation's current ELINT system, a network of ground sites positioned along the East/West border.

Above: **This YO-3A is being flown from the rear cockpit. The front seat may have been for the systems operator.**

Left: Development and flight testing of the Egrett has been shrouded in secrecy, but some clues as to its performance have been released. On 1 September 1988, an Egrett flown by test pilot Einar Enevoldson climbed to an altitude of 49,212ft (15,000m) in 42 minutes 37 seconds, reached a height of 53,786ft (16,394m), and maintained a height of 53,236ft (16,226m). All were new records for a land-based turboprop-powered aircraft with a minimum weight of 6,800lb (3,048kg). Production aircraft could enter *Luftwaffe* service in the mid-1990s.

ROCKWELL INTERNATIONAL B-1B

Rôle: strategic bomber
Length: 147ft 0in (44.81m)
Height: 34ft 0in (10.36m)
Wingspan: 78ft 2in (23.83m) swept, 136ft 8in (41.66m) unswept
Max. take-off weight: 477,000lb (216,370kg)
Max. speed: Mach 1.25
Range: c.6,475nm (12,000km)
Armament: up to 75,000lb (34,000kg) of ordnance in three international weapons bays
Powerplant: four General Electric F101-GE-102 turbofans, each of c.30,000lb (13,600kg) with after-burning

When President Reagan entered office in 1981, he was determined to improve America's defences. One of the biggest problems he faced, after the controversial MX ICBM, was the so-called "bomber gap". The B-52 had been designed in the early 1950s, entered service in 1955 and been phased out of production in the early 1960s. President Carter had ordered development of the stealthy Advanced Technology Bomber (ATB) but this was still in the earliest stages of development and not due to fly until the late 1980s.

The only aircraft available to fill the gap was the B-1 but this existed only as a handful of B-1A prototypes. Reagan ordered a batch of 100 improved B-1B production models, giving the USAF and Rockwell the problem of getting it into production, then into service early enough to make a useful contribution to SAC's strength before the ATB arrived. That timescale called for a five-year programme rather than the seven to ten years normally needed to field a major weapons system.

The B-1A had already been designed to have a much lower RCS than the B-52 it would replace. By the early 1980s, Soviet development of improved defence systems intended to cope with ALCM and Tomahawk cruise missiles — weapons such as the SA-10 and SA-N-6 — made the Rockwell bomber seem increasingly vulnerable, so steps were taken to lower its overall RCS.

In 1983 Rockwell was reported to have teamed with Lockheed to apply stealth technology tested in the F-117A "Senior Trend" stealth fighter programme to the larger aircraft. There was a limit to what could be done, given the fact that the B-1 already existed, so could not be extensively redesigned to incorporate the latest stealth principles. Research soon showed that the RCS of the B-1B could be reduced to less than 1 square metre.

The inlets were redesigned, eliminating the variable ramps needed for Mach 2 flight. The revised design has inlet sides and splitter plates, swept slightly backwards from the vertical, and incorporates curved ducts and streamwise radar-absorbent baffles. RAM was also added as a duct lining material.

A major move towards reducing the aircraft's RCS was the removal of the fuselage dorsal spine. This had originally been fitted to house electrical cabling associated with the aircraft's Westinghouse ALQ-153 tail-warning system. When the USAF opted to integrate the tail-warning task directly into the ALQ-161, this reflective spine could be removed.

New absorbent seals for the B-1B wing were developed by the British company Woodville Polymers. These replaced an earlier less-absorbent design in part of an exercise which saw the inboard wing redesigned.

Among the measures taken under later 1985 contracts for RCS-reduction were a series of modifications to the nose radome cavity and to cavities in the fuselage side fairings. A special adhesive tape was also applied to all seams in the skin once system testing had been completed and prior to painting. This tape was probably electrically conductive and thus linked all the skin panels together into a common conducting surface, thus eliminating surface discontinuities which would re-radiate energy.

The B-1B's RCS is one hundredth of that of the B-52 and a seventh of that of the FB-111. In May 1986, *International Defense Review* quoted the USAF Aeronautical Systems Division commander as saying that when the B-1 flew into the 1985 Paris Air Show, the French were surprised by its small radar cross-section.

Left: **Careful engineering has given the B-1B a head-on RCS of less than 1 sq m, making it a more difficult radar target than a small fighter.**

Below: The rounded shape of the B-1A fuselage had played a significant part in getting the RCS an order of magnitude better than that of the B-52. Reducing the B-1B RCS by as much again involved painstaking attention to detail, with RAM being applied to key areas of the fuselage and wings to damp out radar hot spots.

"They didn't believe we could do it." The bomber has half the RCS of the Cessna 172 light aircraft which German pilot Mathias Rust used to make his unauthorised 1987 landing in Red Square.

The aircraft has also proved to be an elusive target for defending fighters during Red Flag exercises. "In order for the monitoring radar to get our position, we either have to climb or put our transponders on", the commander of SAC's 337th Bombardment Squadron told *Aviation Week* in 1987.

In October 1986, well ahead of the Congressional 1987 deadline, the first B-1B squadron was declared fully operational at Dyess AFB, Texas. The base had 15 aircraft, 12 of which had enough defensive avionics to allow them to be declared operational.

By the winter of 1983/4, a faction within the USAF had tried to have a follow-on order placed for the Rockwell B-1. They argued that a further 100 aircraft could be built for a sum of around $10 billion (US). Another argument in favour of the Rockwell bomber was that it was running under cost and ahead of schedule. If a follow-on batch were planned, funding for long lead-time production hardware would have been needed in the Fiscal Year 1986 budget proposals.

As an alternative to the B-2, Rockwell proposed a developed B-1 under the unofficial designation B-1C. Most of the proposed changes were intended to further reduce the aircraft's RCS. Details of the proposed design were never revealed but it seems likely that the amount of RAM in the aircraft would have been sharply increased. Logical locations for redesign with radar-absorbent structural material would have been the fuselage sides, empennage and parts of the wing. A more extensive redesign of the inlet system might have also reduced RCS. Even with such redesign, it is unlikely that RCS could have been reduced to less than $0.1m^2$.

With delivery of the 100th and final B-1B due in April 1988 and no prospect of a follow-on order, Rockwell began to lay off staff, with more than 10,000 leaving the B-1 operation in the first half of 1987 alone. In the spring of 1988, Rockwell announced that its long-established North American Aircraft division at Columbus, Ohio, would cease operations over the next 15 months. The final B-1B was delivered on schedule. The

Above: The engine nacelles (seen below in cross section) had to be redesigned on the B-1B to add anti-radar baffles and a curved duct. These moves had a drastic effect on top speed, making the aircraft subsonic under most flight conditions, but the price was worth paying. Radar signals could no longer enter the inlet and pass down to reflect from the front face of the engine. This reduces RCS, and also prevents advanced radar signal-processing algorithms being used to observe the modulation effects of the rotating fan stages, a phenomenon which can allow radars to identify the type of aircraft being tracked.

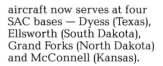

aircraft now serves at four SAC bases — Dyess (Texas), Ellsworth (South Dakota), Grand Forks (North Dakota) and McConnell (Kansas).

TUPOLEV TU-160 BLACKJACK

Rôle: Strategic bomber
Length: 177ft (53.9m)
Wingspan: 182ft (55.5m) max
Max. take-off weight:
590,000lb (267,600kg)
Tactical radius: 3,930nm
(7,300km)
Max. speed: Mach 2.3 at
altitude
Armament: Up to 36,000lb
(16,300kg) of bombs and
missiles
Powerplant: Four turbofans,
each of 50,000lb (22,700kg)
thrust with afterburner

In the late 1970s, US intelligence learned that the Soviet Union was building a large variable-geometry strategic bomber. Exactly how this information was obtained remains a mystery but it does not seem to have been by reconnaissance satellite. At the time when I wrote my first story on the aircraft for *Flight International,* the first prototype of the new bomber had not yet been rolled out of the assembly plant. Was it a successful COMINT intercept or even the work of an agent? Perhaps the CIA and KGB files on the affair of the Soviet scientist Adolf Tolkachev (betrayed by ex-CIA man Edward Howard and executed in 1986) hold the key to this minor mystery.

Work on the new bomber probably started in the early 1970s, soon after the first flight of the Tu-26 Backfire. Operational testing of the latter aircraft between 1970 and 1975 probably gave the Soviet Air Force confidence that the manned penetrating bomber was still a viable strategic option for the late 1980s and early 1990s.

Full-scale development may have started around 1977, with the first prototype flying in 1981. Development was to be protracted. By mid-1988 the aircraft had been in flight test for seven years. Some observers have suggested that this was due to problems with avionics, but judgment must

be reserved. The gestation time of all recent soviet combat types has been lengthy, probably a reflection on their high complexity compared with earlier types, rather than to specific development problems.

US intelligence had expected the new bomber to enter service in 1986 but, in practice, the first regiment did not form until 1988 at Dolon air base in the south-central Soviet Union. On 2 August of that year, one example was shown to US Defense Secretary Frank Carlucci, during his visit to Kubinka air base near Moscow, and two more were flown overhead. At that time, Colonel-General Boris Korolkov, First Deputy Commander-in-Chief of the Soviet Air Forces explained that the bomber had only recently become operational. The example inspection by

Carlucci carried the tail number "12". At least eleven were thought to have been built by that time and production was continuing.

Blackjack is built at Kazan. Large-scale production is expected in the early 1990s. US intelligence expects a production run of about 100 but the projected peak annual production rate of 30 seems high for such a modest run. Rockwell management was able to lay off staff when the high-range short production run of B-1 bombers ended but Soviet planning is unlikely to find a similar move acceptable.

The new Soviet bomber is about 20 per cent larger than the B-1B. It is also faster and has a longer range. The aircraft has a four-man crew, all of whom are equipped with ejector seats. As on the B-1, the pilots have fighter-style control sticks instead of the traditional control yokes normally used on heavy bombers and transports.

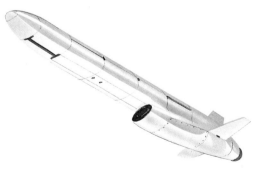

Above: Like the US AGM-86 ALCM and BGM-109 Tomahawk, the Soviet AS-15 air-launched cruise missile relies on small size rather than stealth technology to keep RCS to a minimum. This drawing shows a ventral air inlet, a configuration which would keep the engine fan hidden from the look-down radars on US fighters.

Blackjack has a nose radome and is equipped for terrain-following flight. Aft of the radome is a chin-mounted EO fairing, presumably for a low-level navaid which may allow the aircraft to fly covertly at low level without running its radar.

A powerful EW suite is carried, much of whose equipment may be located in a 10 to 15ft (3 to 4.5m) long avionics bay located just aft of the crew stations for the offensive and defensive systems operators, through which a narrow passageway runs, connecting the cockpit with a belly-mounted crew entry hatch just ahead of the forward weapons bay.

The aircraft can carry a total of 36,000lb (16,300kg) of ordnance it two weapon bays. This can be a mix of free-falling bombs and AS-15 Kent cruise missiles. The latter weapon is subsonic and first entered service in 1984 on the Tupolev Bear-H bomber. On the older bomber the

AS-15 is carried externally but on Blackjack cruise missiles are carried on a rotary launcher which takes up two-thirds of the length of each weapon bay. Similar to the rotary launcher used on US bombers, it can carry six AS-15 missiles or 12 smaller missiles which apparently serve a similar rôle to Strategic Air Command's Boeing AGM-69 SRAM defence suppression missile. In the longer term, Blackjack will be armed with the new AS-X-19 supersonic cruise missile.

Just how stealthy the Tu-160 has proved to be in practice is an item of data buried deep in highly-classified files of both East and West. In theory at least, Blackjack could have been as stealthy as the B-1A, since this feature of the latter aircraft had been publicised before work started on the Tu-160. The aircraft is much cleaner than previous Soviet bombers but lacks the rounded and

sculptured appearance of the B-1. There seems to be no provision for external weapons carriage. Stowing all weapons internally is a move which will help minimise aircraft RCS.

Wing sweep is manual and can be varied from 20 to 65 degrees. RCS with the wing swept forward will be higher than in high-speed flight. As the wing moves to the fully forward position, a triangular section of the middle portion rises, creating a stubby fence around 3ft (0.9m) long and 3ft (0.9m) high. Being at right angles to the wing, this would tend to trap and return radar energy. It is unlikely to prove an operational problem, however, being raised only for take-off and landing.

The inlets which feed air to the four huge turbofan engines are shielded by the wing, so are not visible to look-down radars. The engine inlets have splitter plates incorporating variable ramps which allow supersonic flight

at speeds greater than Mach 2. Similar variable ramps were deleted from the B-1 as a cost saving measure during the redesign which resulted in the B-1B. The inlets do not seem to incorporate the RCS-reducing baffling used on the B-1B. According to Maj. Gen. Gordon Fornell, a USAF aide who accompanied Carlucci into the Blackjack shown at Kubinka, the inlets resembled those used on the North American XB-70.

Given that the Blackjack is physically larger than the B-1 and seems to have less built-in stealth technology, a realistic assessment would suggest an RCS of around 15 square metres — about a sixth of that of the B-52. Bearing in mind that it is early days in the evolution of this big bomber, future stealth-enhancing modifications similar to those applied to the B-1A to create the B-1B could cut RCS to about 2 square metres. A stealthier Blackjack could just be a matter of time.

Left: Bigger than the Rockwell B-1B, the Tupolev Blackjack is also faster, thanks to its variable-geometry inlets. By the standard of the late 1980s, the aircraft is relatively unstealthy, but having invested large amounts of money in the design, it is likely that the Soviet Union will put the new bomber through an improvement programme similar to that which created the B-1B. Modifications such as smoothing its external surfaces, revising the inlets, and treating radar "hot spots" with RAM, might reduce its RCS by an order of magnitude.

RECONNAISSANCE RPVs

Soon after the combat début of the Ryan Model 147B RPV in the autumn of 1964, drones were returning to base with photos of fighters flying between 5,000 and 10,000ft (1,500 and 3,000m) below them. Although SAM sites could do nothing against these tiny targets, manned fighters were soon scoring kills. The first drone to be shot down was 147B No. B-19 which was lost over southern China on 15 November. Later reports suggest that it was attacked by 15 to 20 fighters which made a large number of passes before scoring the kill. Similar mass attack tactics were adopted by the North Vietnamese Air Force, leading to further drone losses.

The 147B model fielded in the late 1960s had a cruise altitude of 65,000 — 70,000ft (19,800 — 21,300m) and incorporated some measures intended to reduce vulnerability to interception. A RAM installation known as HIDE (High-absorbency Integrated Defense) was fitted to the inlet to reduce RCS, while the HEMP (H model Evasive Maneuver Program) system used a RWR tuned to Vietnamese fighter radar frequencies to initiate programmed turns if a MiG closed in for a firing pass. A later HAT-RAC (High Altitude Threat Recognition and Countermeasures) system took the concept a stage further, responding to SAM and fighter radars by initiating flight manoeuvres.

Contrails were to remain the Firebee's weak link. The 1962 test interceptions had shown how trails could betray a drone. Work on a "no-con" version started in that year. This involved two QC-2Cs equipped with a system which injected a chemical agent into the exhaust. It was not very successful. Some H models carried an anti-contrail system known as CRL. Developed by Cambridge Research Laboratories, it was intended to suppress the contrail at specific altitudes. A history of the drone programme describes this as "quite successful".

Successor to the 147H was the 147T. This had a more powerful Continental J100-CA-100 engine offering 45 per cent more thrust, boosting cruise height to between 66,300 and 75,000ft (20,200 and 22,850m). The 147T retained the HIDE system. Other RCS-reduction measures included greater use of built-in RAM in areas such as the nose, wings, dorsal spine and tail surfaces. A

Above: Lockheed's YMQM-105 Aquila started life as a simple RPV which would offer many advantages over mid-1970s piston-engined designs, while having a lower RCS. As the requirement grew more ambitious, high-technology systems were added and the total cost of the system skyrocketted.

wing-root fillet which blended the wing into the fuselage also helped reduce RCS. Operations with the 147T started in 1969. This basic design led to the follow-on ELINT model used in the early-1970s "Combat Dawn" programme, the TE and the improved TF.

The limited degree of stealth technology built into the Firebee was extended in the later Teledyne Ryan AQM-91A Model 154. Development of this large RPV was ordered in 1966, under the USAF's "Compass Arrow" programme. In the summer of 1969, the emergency descent of one example onto a road at the Los Alamos Scientific Laboratory gave a first glimpse of the first custom-designed stealth aircraft to enter service. Almost half as long again as the Fibrebee and weighing up to 5,245lb (2,379kg), the Model 154 had many features first proposed in the unbuilt 1960-vintage Model 136 "Red Wagon" RPV. These included a dorsal engine installation and inward canted twin fins. The 48ft (14.6m) span wing was swept and was low-mounted on the flat-bottomed fuselage, a configuration intended to reduce overall RCS when seen from below.

Another stealth RPV programme had been started in 1961 but was to remain under wraps until the mid-1970s. Lockheed's D-21 drone was a slender delta-winged Mach 3 + design which obviously borrowed some technology from the A-12 and SR-71, including

wing-body blending for minimum RCS. The RPV was built around a single Marquardt RJ43-MA-11 ramjet, the jetpipe of which was extended to minimise the drone's IR signature. Designed for flight at speeds of more than 2,000mph (3,200km/h), the D-21 followed the lead set by the Lockheed A-12 in making large-scale use of titanium but also incorporated large amounts of composite materials, including RAM. It was 43ft 2in (13.16m) long,

about 19ft (5.8m) in wingspan and weighed about 20,000lb (9,000kg) at launch. After returning from hostile airspace, the drone would eject a data capsule and then be destroyed, presumably by built-in explosive charges. The capsule descended by parachute and was snatched in mid-air by a C-130.

Photographs of the D-21 clearly show a dark grey area extending across the centre of the wing and fuselage and, apparently, over a similar area of the underside. A close-up photo of a D-21 published in Jay Millar's monograph *Lockheed SR-71/YF-12/D-21* clearly shows that this section is slightly raised, indicating the possibility that it was added as a modification. Millar suggests that this feature is " . . . apparently a thermal blanket" but other observers have identified this as being a form of RAM blanket similar to that applied to early models of reconnaissance Firebee.

Left: The full story of Lockheed's D-21 RPV remains shrouded in mystery. Capable of a top speed of more than Mach 4 after release from SR-71 or B-52 launch aircraft, the D-21 was (and probably still is) the United States' fastest air-breathing vehicle. The ramjet-powered aircraft also improved upon the stealth technology used in the SR-71, particularly in the use of composites and RAM. Only a handful of operational missions were flown.

In its original form, the D-21 was mounted above the rear fuselage of a modified A-12 and then released at high altitude and high speed (reportedly Mach 3.15). From this point it could reach a top speed of Mach 4 and a ceiling of more than 100,000ft (30,500m). Maximum range is reported to have been 1,250 miles (2,010km).

On 30 July 1966, a newly-released D-21 struck the parent aircraft's tail section, causing the A-12 to crash. Although a second A-12 launch aircraft had been built, the D-21 was redesigned for subsonic launch from underwing pylons on two modified B-52H aircraft, with rocket boosters taking the D-21 to ramjet operating speeds. At the same time a fixed inlet centrebody replaced the earlier moving design, a modification which resulted in the designation being changed to GTD-21B. Several missions were flown in the Far East, (presumably over China) under the USAF's "Senior Bowl" programme, but were stopped in 1972. The

17 surviving examples of the 38 built between 1964 and 1967 were placed in storage.

A much lower level of technology was used in the Lockheed YMQM-105 Aquila. Intended for target acquisition, this 330lb (150kg) piston-engined flying wing first flew as a prototype air vehicle in 1975. Results seemed promising enough to allow full-scale development to be ordered in 1979. As the requirements grew more ambitious, costs soared. The programme came under repeated attack and the Fiscal Year 1988 defence budget submitted to Congress in November 1987 finally killed the Aquila programme, with no funding being authorised. Aquila used much less body-wing blending than the B-2 and relied for its low RCS on a combination of small size, careful shaping and the wide-spread use of composites. Some of these techniques have since been applied to the GEC Avionics Phoenix, a twin-boom piston engined spotting RPV developed for the British Army.

Right: In developing the Model 147T long-wing version of the Firebee reconnaissance drone, Teledyne engineers applied RAM to the nose, wings, dorsal spine and tail, and added a degree of wing-body blending. By 1969

it was ready for service, flying into the face of Chinese and North Vietnamese air defences. Despite all the aid which the Soviet Union could give, they never fully mastered the art of downing these tricky radar targets.

Left: The use of RAM and shaping on the Model 147T gave Teledyne the confidence to tackle the custom-designed Model 154 stealth RPV. The flat underside reduced radar reflectivity from below, while the sloped fuselage sides and tail surfaces cut RCS at higher aspect angles. The Model 154 (also known as the AQM-91A Compass Arrow) flew at high altitude, so the dorsal engine bay screened the engine inlet and exhaust from upward-looking radars.

EUROPEAN FIGHTER AIRCRAFT (EFA)

Rôle: multi-rôle fighter
Length: 47ft 7in (14.5m)
Wingspan: 34ft 5in (10.5m)
Max. take-off weight:
37,480lb (17,000kg)
Max. speed: greater than
mach 1.8
Tactical radius: 250—300nm
(460—550km)
Armament: six air-to-air
missiles plus an internal
cannon
Powerplant: two Eurojet
EJ200 turbofans each of
20,000lb (9,070kg) with after-
burning

The most important new
military aircraft
programme in Western
Europe is the planned
European Fighter Aircraft
(EFA) being developed by
Britain, West Germany, Italy
and Spain. Under a
memorandum of
understanding signed in May
1988, this twin-engined
canard-delta will be built by
British Aerospace (UK), MBB
(West Germany), Aeritalia
(Italy) and CASA (Spain).
Initial prototypes will be
powered by two Turbo-Union
RB.199-122 turbofans but later
prototypes will have the
production engine. Known as
the EJ200.200, this twin-shaft
turbofan is being developed

by the Eurojet consortium, a
collaborative venture by Rolls-
Royce (UK), MTU (West
Germany), Fiat (Italy) and
Sener (Spain).

In its basic single-seat
version, EFA is optimised for
the air-to-air rôle but will
have a secondary attack
capability. A two-seater will
be available for training.

The first prototype
(designated P.01) is due to fly
at Manching in West
Germany late in 1991. It will
be followed three months
later by the British-built P.02.
Both will be powered by
Turbo-Union engines. BAe
Warton will also build P.03 —
the first two-seater and the
first EFA to be powered by the
EJ200 engine — and P0.5, the
first aircraft to have a full
avionics fit. P.04 will fly in
Italy in 1992. Full avionics
will also be carried by P.06,
P.07 (the second two-seater)
and P.08. Production aircraft

are due to enter service in
mid-1996.

Largest operators will be the
UK and West Germany, each
of whom hopes to order 250.
Italy is likely to buy some
170, with Spain taking 110.
Fly-away unit cost will be
about £10—12 million ($17—
20 million) in current prices.

Much of the technology
needed for EFA was proven
using the BAe EAP
(Experimental Aircraft
Programme) technology
demonstrator. When this
experimental aircraft was
rolled out in April 1986, a
BAe statement that the
aircraft embodied stealth
technology was received with
some scepticism by some
defence journalists and by
some RCS experts in the USA.
EAP and the follow-on EFA
were clearly not stealth
aircraft in the class of the
Lockheed F-117A or the
Advanced Tactical Fighter, so

the BAe statement was seen as
largely a matter of public
relations.

EFA is not a low-RCS design
but is designed for reduced
RCS, a more modest goal
which does not require the
specialised and costly
technology used in the F-117A
and B-2. Much can be
accomplished even by simple
measures such as keeping size
and weight to a minimum and
using rounded shapes and
profiles.

A good (if unplanned)
example of this is the BAe
Hawk, whose tiny RCS
apparently surprised its
creators. When the ventral
gun pack is fitted — not
exactly a bulky item of kit —
the aircraft's RCS is close to
doubled. Redesign the braking
chute housing, to substitute
rounded surfaces for the
current angular shape, treat
the air inlets with RAM and
then gold-flash the canopy to

Below: From this angle, the most prominent feature of the EFA is the ''smiling'' radar inlet. At first, the aircraft was to have an EAP-style rectangular inlet (see photo at bottom left), but tests showed that the curved configuration is stealthier. Since this drawing was prepared, the aircraft has gained another stealthy feature — a pod-mounted FLIR high on the port fuselage side above the canard.

This will act as a passive substitute for radar. Also added in mid-1989 were small strakes aft of and above the canards.

keep radar energy out and the single-seat Hawk 200 could prove to be a surprisingly elusive radar target.

Several factors help minimise EFA's RCS. It is a small aircraft and much of its profile is rounded. The main straight areas, such as the wing and fin leading edges, are highly swept, so will reflect radar energy in main lobes well away from the frontal sector. Extensive use is also made of carbon-fibre composites.

RCS is also reduced by careful attention to detail. At the 1987 Paris Air Show, a revised full-scale mock-up

Left: **Given the risks associated with test flying, building only a single EAP prototype was a gamble, but one which paid off.**

showed some of the refinements made to the design in the final stages of project definition work. The most obvious was a redesigned ventral intake. On the EAP and the original EFA design, this had been of rectangular shape but the final configuration is a slightly curved ''smiling'' design. This has less drag and less radar cross-section.

The RCS of the EFA will certainly be better than the 4m² typical of earlier fighters in this general weight class. No figure has been released but Bill Sweetman has estimated a value of around 2m², a figure which seems reasonable given the 2—3m² RCS of latest-generation Soviet types.

The rival teams offering radars for the aircraft were

also aware of the need to avoid betraying the aircraft's presence by a powerful radar signal. The MSD-200 designation of the GEC Avionics/AEG candidate stood for ''Multi-mode Silent Discrete 2000'', while the Ferranti-led team, offering the ECR-90, emphasised the LPI qualitites of their candidate.

The important question must be — is EFA's signature low enough to allow it to operate until the end of this century and beyond, or will the programme simply create a modern-day equivalent to the Gloster Gladiator? In 1983, towards the end of an interview with one of the United States' best-known aircraft designers, our conversation turned to the EFA programme. What, he wondered, was the purpose of

the programme? If it was largely intended to provide follow-on work for the factories currently building Tornado, that goal was obviously realisable. If it was seriously intended to match the air combat threats of the 1990s, that was another matter. ''I've seen the threat'', he assured me (presumably he meant that he had seen the DoD's assessment of what next-generation threats would be), '' . . . and that aircraft won't meet it.''

US attacks on European aircraft programmes are not uncommon, particularly when the European programme represents a sales threat, but such views are not confined to the United States. Writing in the January 1988 issue of *Air Force* magazine, John Taylor, editor of *Jane's All The World's Aircraft* stated bluntly that ''EFA re-invents the F-16, with refinements'' and went on to question its relevance to the 1990s. ''There is nothing wrong with the EFA by the standards of the late 1980s . . . but a new decade — still more a new century — requries new concepts.''

Some ATF-type capabilities might be added to EFA as part of its mid-life updating programme, a possibility foreseen by the RAF and *Luftwaffe* before the programme was launched. These could include three-dimensional thrust-vectoring, through angles of up to 10 degrees, and off-boresight weapon aiming by decoupling the fuselage by means of CCV flying surfaces and vectored thrust. Technology for such an up-date could be drawn from the results of flight testing of the advanced Rockwell/MBB X-31A.

DASSAULT-BREGUET RAFALE D & M

Rôle: multi-rôle fighter
Length: 49ft 2in (14.99m)
Height: 16ft 9in (5.1m)
Wingspan: 35ft 2in (10.72m)
Max. take-off weight:
40,000lb (18,200kg)
Max. speed: Mach 2
Tactical radius: 300 — 500nm
(556 — 926km)
Armament: up to 14,300lb
(6,500kg) of ordnance, plus
internal cannon
Powerplant: two SNECMA
M88-15 turbofans, each
16,530lb (7,500kg) with after-
burning.

At the 1983 Paris Air
Show, Dassault showed a
mock-up of a technology
demonstrator for a next-
generation fighter. Two
features of this ACX
(Advanced Combat
eXperimental) design proved
striking — the huge vertical
fin and the novel inlets. The
size of the fin had been
dictated by the need for

directional stability but the
inlets, which incorporated the
moveable conical centre-
bodies found in all Mirages
since the IIIC, were mounted
under the leading-edge root
extensions of a carefully
sculptured forward fuselage.

I assumed that this
configuration had been
adopted to ensure a good
airflow at high angles of
attack but Northrop's Lee
Begin had an alternative
theory. ''Take another look'',
he urged me, ''they're shaped
that way because of stealth.''
As the design was refined to
create today's Rafale, the tail

fin shrank in size, the lower
fuselage assumed a V-shaped
cross-section and the inlets
were changed for a simpler
pattern without centre-bodies
or other moving parts. There
was no loss of stealth,
however. The revised inlets
remained tucked under the
fuselage and largely screened
from the attention of look-
down radars.

Like the Eurofighter
consortium members, France
apparently concluded that the
cost of developing a truly
stealthy fighter was politically
and economically
unacceptable. Like EFA, the

Dassault-Breguet Rafale is a
reduced-RCS design.

In France, the task of
developing RCS-prediction
software was tackled by
Thomson-CSF. In order to
allow a start to be made on
the task of eliminating ''hot
spots'' from the design,
Thomson-CSF adapted
existing software and used
this to study the radar cross-
section of the aircraft. Three
areas are quickly identified as
major contributions to RCS —
the radar, the inlets and the
engine face.

A parallel effort involved
developing software for the

Above: **Although not a true
stealth fighter, Rafale will
have a lower radar cross
section than today's Mirage
F1 or Mirage 2000.**

Below: Seen visually, Rafale's rounded inlets seem very conspicuous. Yet they're one of the aircraft's stealthier features. Today's air combat is at low level, and major threats include AEW radar and interceptors equipped with look-down radars.

From most observation angles above the aircraft, the inlets — a prime radar target in any aircraft — are concealed by the forward fuselage. They're barely visible in the photo at the bottom of the opposite page, for example. The aircraft shown here is on an

interception mission, and carries two Matra R530F radar-guided missiles, plus two wingtip-mounted Magics. If tasked with an air-superiority mission into unfriendly skies, it would probably carry the new MICA medium-range missile.

Cray XMP 18 supercomputer which will allow the design of large metallic structures of up to 10 square metres in area. This would initially be used to carry out studies of aircraft inlet geometry.

The Rafale A prototype flew for the first time on 4 July 1986, just ahead of the rival BAe EAP. Like the British aircraft, it was a technology demonstrator rather than a true fighter prototype. About 1,000lb (450kg) heavier than the planned Rafale D production version, it was powered by two GE F404 turbofans.

Like the UK, France had hoped that a flying demonstrator might act as the catalyst for an international programme but the path to any agreement was made

difficult by conflicting views over aircraft weight. Given the close relationship between aircraft weight and cost, and the need to attract large-scale export orders to make programmes commercially viable, Dassault has always favoured light-weight designs. French determination that the cost (and thus the weight) of a next-generation fighter had to reflect the need for maximum export potential was one factor which prevented that nation joining the EFA programme.

The UK, West Germany, Italy and Spain chose to go their own way with the EFA, leaving France to continue with Rafale as a national venture. The Rafale D production aircraft will be

slightly smaller and lighter than EFA. It will thus meet French marketing requirements and be able to use SNECMA's new M-88 twin-shaft turbofan, a less powerful engine than EFA's Eurojet EJ200.

The prototype Rafale D is due to fly in 1990. It should enter service six years later in single and two-seat versions, replacing older aircraft such as the Mirage IIIE and Jaguar. France's *Aéronavale* plans its own Rafale M version, a replacement for the ageing Vought F-8 Crusaders and subsonic Dassault-Breguet Super Etendards currently deployed aboard French aircraft carriers.

In the spring of 1988, Thomson-CSF gave an unclassified glimpse of French progress on stealth research when it released details of the work being done on the radar reflectivity of jet engines. Since the individual blades on the first fan stage are identical in shape, it is only necessary to model a single blade in the computer. The software is designed to predict the levels of electrical current which would be induced in a compressor blade by incoming radar energy. If the aircraft's radar cross-section is to be kept small, the magnitude of these currents (and that of the re-radiated energy which makes up the radar echo) must be kept to a minimum.

Treating a compressor to reduce these currents, and thus the amount of radar energy reflected, is a difficult

task. Radar-absorbent material (RAM) is not robust enough to cope with the stresses present in the rapidly-spinning blades. An alternative approach to minimising engine radar signature involves using dielectric material to re-direct the energy reflected by the blades, thus preventing it from escaping via the engine inlet. In early 1988, the available software could only simulate a metal blade but the modelling of dielectrically-treated blades was anticipated within another two years.

In parallel with this theoretical work, a series of test flights were made in the winter of 1987/88 to measure the RCS and the IR signature of the Rafale A demonstrator. A series of 13 missions were flown, allowing the radar signature to be assessed with different external loads and under several combat conditions. These includes an air-combat sortie, with the aircraft carrying two Matra Magic 2 heat-seeking missiles, and a low-level flight, with two 530 gallon (2,000 litre) external tanks.

The future of the Rafale project is already under attack, with suggestions that the programme could prove an "abyss for billions". All attempts to find possible partners willing to share the cost have failed but France seems determined to press on with Rafale as a national venture. The end product could be a more exportable, and marginally stealthier, aircraft than the rival EFA.

Originally designated FS-X (Fighter, Support, eXperimental), this planned replacement for the Mitsubishi F-1 fighter-bomber is a developed version of the General Dynamics F-16. Japan had hoped to build an indigenous design drawn up by a team headed by Mitsubishi. Based on the experimental CCV adaption of the T-2 supersonic trainer, this would have incorporated Japanese-developed stealth technology. In October 1987, the Japanese Defence Agency rejected this national design in favour of an F-16 derivative, a controversial decision which promptly received the formal endorsement of the Japanese National Security Council.

A factor which may have helped Japan select the F-16, rather than the F-15 or F-18 (designs which were also evaluated), is that stealth technology was apparently easier to incorporate within the GD aircraft. This was seen as more significant than the type's main disadvantage — its relatively limited internal volume available for new avionics. The final decision was taken after studies of the trade-offs between aircraft weight, internal volume and likely cost.

Development of the SX-3 is being handled by Mitsubishi Heavy Industries and involves a massive re-design of the Fighting Falcon airframe, a task which will leave only some 20 to 30 per cent unchanged. Mitsubishi Heavy Industries is prime contractor, responsible for overall design and integration. It will also build the forward fuselage. Kawasaki will build the centre and aft fuselage, while Fuji is expected to built the all-composite flying surfaces. The USA will participate in the development and production programme, receiving between 35 and 45 per cent of the work.

A stage beyond the "big-winged" Agile Falcon offered to Western Europe in the mid-1980s, SX-3 has a stretched aft fuselage, longer-span wings, vertical canards beneath the inlet and an improved engine. Advanced technology composite materials will be used in the new wings, tail surfaces and forward and aft fuselage sections. Other changes include a recontoured nose and a strengthened canopy.

A less obvious change is the incorporation of stealth technology. Fighting Falcon clearly has potential for significant RCS reduction. The cranked-wing F-16F (F-16XL) derivative flown by GD in 1982 has a lower RCS than the basic aircraft. This is due to its longer engine inlet, higher and compound leading edge sweep, involving higher angles than those of the standard wing, and deletion of the ventral surfaces.

Japanese work on stealth was first revealed in 1982. The work carried out in the mid-1980s on the indigenous FS-X project involved the development and testing of RAM materials and the creation of computer programmes for RCS prediction and RAM design. These Japanese-developed RAM materials are now to be applied to the SX-3 to reduce its radar signature. The entire leading edge will incorporate RAM, a move presumably intended to reduce front-sector RCS.

The avionics suite being developed by Mitsubishi Electric, Fujitsu and NECA will probably be based on a

Below: **Japan's ASM-1 anti-ship missile has metal wings, but a project to reduce its radar cross section, by fitting plastic wings incorporating RAM, was reported in 1983.**

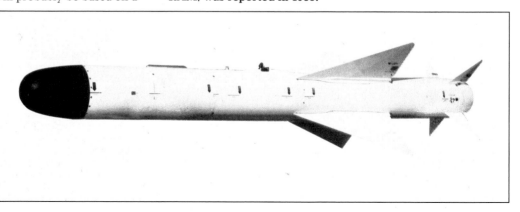

fibre-optical data bus. Mitsubishi has already demonstrated a star-coupled system conforming to MIL-STD-1773. Like the proposed Mitsubishi FS-X design, the SX-3 will have a CCV-type flight control system offering fully-decoupled flight modes, including the ability to fly with its nose angled to the line of flight.

The new radar in the SX-3 will have an active phased-array and will be able to switch rapidly between air-to-air and air-to-ground modes. It will also have a new INS (perhaps combined with a GPS satnav [satellite navigation] receiver), integrated EW system and mission computer. The computer system planned for

the FS-X would have been about one-third the size and one-fifth the weight of that used in the F-15J Eagle. Cockpit technologies planned for the FS-X, and thus possible features of the SX-3, include an instrument panel consisting of six digital displays and voice recognition/control.

The prototype SX-3 is expected to fly in 1993, beginning a three-year test programme. Production deliveries to the JASDF will begin in 1997. Under present plans, a total of 130 SX-3 aircraft will be built by the year 2001. Total cost of developing the SX-3 is likely to be more than $1,100 million. Unit cost of the aircraft has been predicted at

$35 million, while the total bill for the entire programme has been estimated at $7,000 million.

Armament will include several types of Japanese-developed missile. One of the primary strike weapons will be the Mitsubishi Type 80 ASM-1 anti-ship missile, a weapon which itself may incorporate some stealth measures. In June 1983, the Japanese newspaper *Asahi Shimbun* reported that the Defence Agency's Technical Research and Development Institute had placed an order with Mitsubishi Heavy Industries for RCS-reduction modifications to the ASM-1. This apparently involved replacing the missile's existing light metal-alloy wings with

new plastic surfaces incorporating ferrite-based RAM. Officials of the Institute were quoted as saying that the new wings would delay the detection of incoming ASM-1s by enemy vessels, reducing the time available for the activation and effective use of point-defence systems or electronic countermeasures such as jamming or chaff.

For air combat, the SX-3 will be able to carry the new Mitsubishi AAM-3, a dogfight weapon being developed for service on the F-15J and F-4J. Very little information is available on this missile, whose development is due to end in 1990. Japanese munition manufacturer Komatsu is known to be developing the warhead.

LOCKHEED F-117A SENIOR TREND

Rôle: reconnaissance/strike fighter
Length: c.50ft (15.5m)
Wingspan: c.40ft (12m)
Max. take-off weight: 45,000lb (20,400kg)
Max. speed: high subsonic
Tactical radius: 800–1,200nm (1,500–2,200km)
Armament: c.4,000lb (1,800kg) of stores carried internally
Powerplant: two non-afterburning General Electric F404 turbofans, each of 10,800–12,500lb (4,900–5,670kg)

As a result of the successful flight testing of the XST technology demonstrators starting in 1977, President Carter was able to authorise the development of a production stealth fighter in the following year. The project was codenamed "Senior Trend".

Although probably based on the general configuration of the XST, the F-117A was scaled up in size. This would have given a militarily useful range and allowed the carriage of operational sensors and stores. The XST had been powered by a pair of General Electric (GE) J85 turbojets and was probably short of thrust. The new fighter's increased size and weight required a more powerful engine, so GE was given a contract to develop a non-afterburning version of the F404.

This may have involved refanning the engine to increase its by-pass ratio, raising the dry thrust from the 10,800lb (4,900kg) typical of the basic engine to about 12,500lb (5,670kg). A similar refanning carried out to create the RM12 derivative of

the engine for Sweden's Gripen light fighter added 5 per cent to the airflow, boosting afterburning thrust from 16,000lb (7,260kg) to 18,000lb (8,160kg).

The engine developed for the Lockheed aircraft may also have provided some of the technology for the late 1980s Growth II F404, a more powerful variant offered for the proposed Hornet 2000. A 1988 GE press release describes how the latter 20,000lb (9,000kg) thrust class engine uses "components developed by other F404 derivative programs".

The first flight of an F-117A took place in June 1981 and the type was ready for operational service by the autumn of 1983. The first (and probably the sole) operator was the 4450th Tactical Group which became operational in October 1983.

The aircraft which project head Ben Rich and his Skunk Works team created was of very different shape to the widely-projected "F-19" seen in mid-1980s books and magazines and owes something to the Horten IX flying wing aircraft tested in Germany during 1944.

To keep RCS to a minimum, extensive use was made of faceting. Straight lines rather than curves dominate the aircraft's configuration. Its angular lines make one wonder, half-seriously, whether Ben Rich had impounded every set of French curves owned by Skunk works personnel.

According to reports circulating prior to the unveiling of the F-117A, part of the structure, such as spars, ribs and longerons, are made from Fiberloy. Some sources suggested that the same material is used for the aircraft skin and coated with RAM to reduce its reflectivity. The F-117A was probably developed too soon to take large-scale advantage of radar-absorbent structural (RAS) materials, although it has

been suggested that radar-absorbent reinforced carbon fibre (often referred to as carbon-carbon) is used for the leading edges, engine bays and forward fuselage. The entire skin is probably painted with ferrite, along with some of the internal components. Other probable RCS-reduction measures include keeping the use of metal fasteners to a minimum and the careful electrical bonding of all structural elements to eliminate small gaps which might re-radiate incoming hostile RF energy.

Approaching F-117As emit a distinctive high-pitched whine, while rearward noise is a muffled rumble. To keep noise to a minimum, the efflux from the twin F404s is passed through a system of baffles. The final nozzles are wide but shallow, spreading the exhaust gases into a fishtail-shaped plume of minimal IR signature. One published account claims that extensive sound lagging is provided within the engine bay to minimise the acoustic signature. This material was described as having inward pointing pyramids, suggesting confusion with RAM.

If fitted with conventional flying controls, the F-117A might prove tricky to fly, given its odd shape and tiny tail surfaces. To get around the problem, it is fitted with an advanced digital fly-by-wire flight control system developed by Lear Siegler. One indication of the type's restricted manoeuvrability is its wide traffic pattern. This suggests that an unusual degree of care is needed at low speeds. F-117A crews have apparently dubbed the aircraft the "Wobbly Goblin".

Very little is known about its sensor suite. The aircraft had been reported to carry a "quiet" (low-LPI) radar but there is no sign of a radome. The initial F-117A photo released by the Pentagon shows a heavily-retouched cavity just below the front of the canopy. This contains a spherical object about 12 inches (30cm) in diameter. Some observers claim that this is a flight-refuelling receptacle but it is more likely to be an electro-optical sensor, probably combining a laser ranger with a FLIR and/or low-light TV system.

The designation "stealth fighter" is partly a misnomer; the aircraft is essentially a strike aircraft designed to fly close to a target at slow speed, take reconnaissance imagery or launch a guided missile or "smart" bomb, then turn away. In terms of speed and agility it is no match for a traditional fighter. Distinctly subsonic, it could be a vulerable target if caught by an enemy fighter. To avoid this, it normally operates at night or in cloudy weather, conditions under which it is virtually undetectable.

It has been described as the most effective manned penetrator in the world for special reconnaissance or strike missions. In terms of radar penetration, the F-117A has met its specifications but at a price of restricted speed and manoeuvrability. Its successors such as the Advanced Tactical Fighter will combine stealth with improved speed, altitude and manoeuvrability.

Initial flight operations were conducted under cover of darkness. When the shape of the aircraft was declassified late in 1988, the USAF was finally able to operate the aircraft by day. Initial sightings were of aircraft flying close to their home base at Tonopah in Nevada, but by the summer of 1989, F-117As were openly flying over cities such as Reno in Nevada, and Palmdale California. Reports that the aircraft was being used outside the USA first appeared in the mid-1980s. In 1986, *Defense News* reported that the F-117A was being flight tested in Europe, probably from Mildenhall, Suffolk, England, but only under the cover of darkness or bad weather.

Left: So important was faceting to the stealth qualities of the F-117A, that the USAF kept the aircraft's appearance classified until November 1988. The "butterfly tail" has not been used on a military aircraft since the days of the Fouga Magister trainer. It eliminates one of the three traditional tail surfaces and avoids a radar reflective vertical fin, but control authority is limited at high speed. The F-117A has a fly-by-wire control system and is reported to be tricky to fly.

Left: The side view of the F-117A reveals what must surely be the strangest shape to fly since the 1930s. The steeply-sloped fuselage sides and the highly swept wing leading and trailing edges ensure that radar energy is deflected harmlessly, rather than being reflected back to the enemy radar. RCS is greatly reduced, but a penalty must be paid in terms of airframe drag and internal volume. According to early reports, the F-117A's payload is carried in two small weapon bays.

NORTHROP B-2 ADVANCED TECHNOLOGY BOMBER (ATB)

Rôle: strategic bomber
Length: 69ft (21.0m)
Height: 17ft (5.18m)
Wingspan: 172ft (52.43m)
Weights — empty: c.100,000lb (45,400kg)
loaded: c.330,000lb (149,700kg)
Max. speed: high subsonic (Mach 0.85?)
Ceiling: c.50,000ft (15,000m)
Tactical radius: c.4,500nm (8,330km) without airborne refuelling
Armament: c.40,000lb (18,000kg) of ordnance in internal bays
Powerplant: four General Electric F118-GE-100 turbofans each of 19,000lb (8,620kg).

Like the Lockheed F-117A stealth fighter, the B-2 bomber has the simplest possible front profile — two straight moderately-swept leading edges which meet at the nose. This layout ensures that the main RCS sidelobes in the forward sector are well away from the direction of flight. The massive saw-tooth trailing edge is made up from 10 straight edges, aligned at one of two fixed angles, a layout which will direct radar energy reflected from the trailing edges into two directions well away from the immediate rear of the aircraft. The inboard sections of the saw-tooth trailing edge are shorter than those further outboard, giving the aircraft a longer-chord centre section similar to that on the Lockheed F-117A.

Each wing side has a drag rudder and elevon on the outboard trailing edge, plus two more elevons on the next-inboard section. The central "beaver tail" forms another moving surface. Roll rate is similar to that of the F-111. The aircraft has no vertical stabiliser, a feature which helps reduce overall RCS. The aircraft has a quadruplex

digital flight control system. Developed by General Electric, this incorporates fly-by-wire (or even fly-by-light) controls, plus a sophisticated stability-augmentation system.

Segmented inlets on the upper wing feed air to the engines buried within the fuselage. A secondary inlet mounted just ahead of the main inlet and offset slightly outboard also draws in air, perhaps for engine bay and efflux cooling. The inlets make a significant contribution to total RCS. A redesign was needed to get these right and to solve the tough manufacturing problems associated with their complex shape.

The engine efflux is discharged via recessed cut-outs in the wing upper surface. Lined with heat-resistant carbon-carbon

Above: **The complex shape of the B-2 intakes and centre fuselage must be a manufacturing nightmare, but the shape and smoothness must be accurately controlled to minimise RCS.**

Above: Despite its novel lines and stealthy characteristics, the B-2 is a fuel-efficient aircraft. "The aerodynamic design of the ATB is markedly more efficient than its predecessors," says SAC commander Welsh. "It requires far fewer tankers, for example, to do its job than do current bombers because of the aerodynamic efficiency. It carries a very healthy bomb load and has very good range and would be a superb bomber even if it weren't stealthy."

material, these open-topped ducts are probably intended to spread the exhaust laterally to reduce its IR signature. Two doors on the upper surface of each nacelle are opened when the aircraft is taxying and flying at low speed. These are auxiliary inlets used to supply extra air to the engines.

A contrail-suppressing system is apparently carried. This may involve the injection of a chemical into the efflux, either by spraying it into the exhaust ducts or using it as an additive to the fuel. One chemical known to have anti-contrail properties is chloro-fluoro-sulphonic acid but, as its name suggests, this substance is highly corrosive.

The B-2 is the largest aircraft made mostly or even completely from composite materials. While the F-117A relies on external RAM, much of the surface of the B-2 is skinned in honeycomb-type RAS supplied by Hexcel

(continued over)

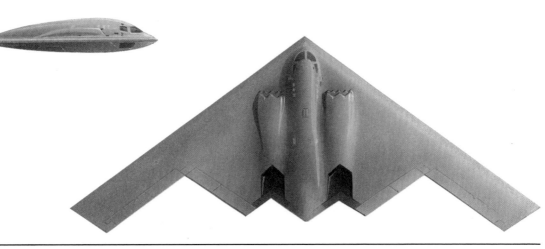

Right: Despite the complexity of the B-2 planform, it is composed of straight edges which are all aligned at one of two fixed angles. This ensures much of the incoming radar energy is "dumped" at angles well away from the front and rear sectors. By making large scale use of RAM and composites, the Northrop designers were able to use rounded lines rather than faceting, an essential step in providing the fuselage volume required.

Corporation's Advanced
Products Division. When first
shown, the prototype had
leading edges made from
shiny black plastic material.
These concealed the shape of
aircraft's radar-absorbent
leading edge surfaces.

As a manufacturing aid,
Northrop created a 3D
computer graphics system to
which the USAF and major
B-2 contractors have access.
This replaced many
conventional paper drawings
and allowed the fit of newly-
designed components to be
checked prior to manufacture.
The prototype aircraft was
largely assembled on
production tooling, with
computer-driven optical
theodolites being used to
check the positioning and
accuracy of the jigs. Such
high accuracies are needed to
maintain the planned RCS.

For a long time, the crew
size remained undecided. SAC
finally settled for two-man
operation by a pilot and a
dual-action pilot/navigator
but the cockpit has room for a
third crew member. Ordnance
is carried in weapons bays
located aft of the cockpit.
These are fitted with Boeing-
designed Advanced
Applications Rotary
launchers. The B-2 is
equipped for inflight
refuelling but this is not
required on the aircraft's
intended mission.

The aircraft was originally
intended to be a high-altitude
bomber but in 1984 the
programme was restructured
to allow a redesign of the
wing carry-through structure.
This cost about $1,000 million

Above: From the side it may
be ugly, but from the front
it's beautiful. Strategic Air
Command wants a fleet of 132
B-2 bombers, but the
price tag is giving the US
Congress second thoughts.
The full-scale production
order could be trimmed to
between 70 and 110.

Below: With an F-16 chase
plane close at hand to check
airspeed, the B-2 makes its
first flight at a maximum
speed of only 190kts.

Reconstruction began in 1989 and provided training facilities, new hangars and covered alert shelters. When not taking part in flight operations, the fleet will remain under cover. This is due at least in part to the need for security, although it has also been suggested that sheltering the aircraft will protect what has been described as the "easily marred skin".

Faced with the high cost of the 132-aircraft fleet, Congress decided to delay large-scale production until flight testing had confirmed that the B-2 would meet the USAF's requirements. Likely date for IOC is around 1993. The Northrop bomber will replace the B-1B in the penetration rôle, maintaining SAC's ability to penetrate Soviet air defences into the 21st Century. It is expected to remain in USAF service for about 30 years.

and delayed the programme by eight months but it achieved two major goals. The increased structural efficiency of the revised design gave greater strength for less weight, curing an identified weight-growth problem, and provided enough strength for terrain-following flight at low altitude. It also reduced RCS.

The design goal was probably for a RCS of at least an order of magnitude below that of the B-1B. The latter aircraft had already taken bomber RCS to less than 1 square metre, suggesting that the likely target figure for the Northrop aircraft was at least below $0.1m^2$, and could even be as little as $0.05m^2$.

Little is known about the aircraft's avionics and other systems. Dark patches visible under the wing leading edge on the prototype on either side of the nose gear are thought to be for a high-resolution Hughes LPI radar system able to detect and classify ground targets. On the prototype, the undercarriage was made from modified Boeing 757/767 landing gear components but later aircraft will have custom-designed replacements.

Following the first flight on 17 July 1989, work continued on a batch of four production aircraft. In the first stages of the programme, the number of aircraft to be built was reported as anything from 110 to 150 but a total of 132 was finally announced. Of these, 120 will be assigned to SAC as penetrating bombers. All but one of the remaining

examples will be delivered to the USAF, presumably to be used for training.

In 1992 the first production aircraft is expected to be ready for delivery to Whiteman AFB, some 65 miles (105km) south-east of Kansas City, Missouri. Currently the home of a Minuteman ICBM wing, Whiteman had not operated aircraft since the 1960s, so its runways and facilities needed extensive work.

Right: **Within months of this rollout ceremony for the first prototype, the new Bush administration announced a one year delay in the development programme.**

Below: **The cockpit transparencies form part of the load-bearing structure, and conform to the same complex shaping rules as the smoothly curved airframe.**

LOCKHEED AURORA

In February 1985, a budget document issued by the Pentagon accidentally disclosed the existence of a secret multi-billion-dollar USAF programme code-named "Aurora". According to the unclassified "P1" weapons procurement document, spending on the secret project would start in fiscal year 1986 (October 1985) with a funding of $80 million, rising to $2,270 million in the following year. Faced with press enquiries, embarrassed USAF officials refused to say any more about the programme, although unidentified Pentagon sources told the *Washington Post* that the programme might involve stealth technology or be linked in some way with the B-2 stealth bomber (then known simply as the Advanced Technology Bomber).

The designation "Aurora" was already in use, having been applied to the then recently-delivered CP-140 derivative of the Lockheed P-3 maritime-patrol aircraft. Essentially a P-3 airframe with S-3 Viking avionics, this had been developed for the Canadian Armed Forces. It was thus a good choice for a new covert programme. Any leaks of information or unauthorised glimpses of Aurora documentation could easily be explained away as being references to the Canadian aircraft.

Speculation soon centred around the possibility that the new project was a replacement for the ageing SR-71 Blackbird. The most obvious approach would be to develop an aircraft capable of still higher speeds, and heights. Rumours that an aircraft of this type was being developed, or had flown, had already begun to emerge.

Several artists' impression of high-speed aircraft had been released by the US aerospace industry during the early to mid-1980s. Most of the really "way-out" concepts had been developed by Lockheed and they include a huge 300,000lb (136,000kg) tailed delta design powered by four variable-cycle turbo-ramjet engines burning liquid methane. This ambitious design would have been able to fly at Mach 5. The company released some impressive artwork showing the aircraft in flight with its nose, wing/tail leading edges and engine inlets glowing red-hot as a result of fearsome kinetic heating.

In January 1988, the *New York Times* published an article claiming that the USAF was working on an SR-71 replacement — a long-range stealth aircraft able to fly at more than 3,800mph (6,100km/h), five times the speed of sound, and with a cruising altitude of more than 100,000ft (33,500m). "With the SR-71, they know we're there but they can't touch us", said one official quoted by the by the newspaper. "With the new technology, they won't even know we're there." No details of the project's status, costs or planned in-service date were available.

Further evidence for the new aircraft came the same month when *Armed Forces Journal International* revealed how reports by Sanford C. Bernstein & Co had suggested that Lockheed sales associated with stealth programmes would peak that year, at about $1,120 million, then settle down to around $752 million through the early 1990s. *AFJI* suggested that these large figures seemed "consistent with a major programme such as an SR-71 replacement".

A few months after the *New York Times* story, Air Force Secretary Edward C. Aldridge, commenting on the decision to begin retiring the SR-71 Blackbird fleet, remarked that although the Air Force would have to rely in the short term on satellites for all its strategic reconnaissance, the service would like to develop a new manned aircraft system, perhaps based on low-observable technology.

Left: Could this be the shape of the mysterious Project Aurora? The USAF would like a replacement for the SR-71 Blackbird, and talks as if no such aircraft were under development. But, as the F-117A programme has shown, the very existence of a black programme can be officially denied for a decade or more. One thing is sure, a major undisclosed stealth programme must exist if Lockheed's stealth-related earnings in the late 1980s and early 1990s are to match the figures which some observers predict.

Above: Like the SR-71, a replacement aircraft would probably not need a nose-mounted radar, making this area available for sensors. Other equipment would be packed into the chines (see below). Although some of the "black boxes" shown here look like conventional cameras, they use electro-optical technology to capture the image. As a result, the digitised images can be transmitted back for analysis in near real time, perhaps via a comsat link.

Little other hard information is available. In August 1988, *Aviation Week* reported that Boeing, General Dynamics, Lockheed, McDonnell Douglas, Garrett, General Electric and Pratt & Whiney had all been consulted by the USAF in a series of studies which had investigated the design of high-Mach aircraft.

Our artwork combines features taken from several Lockheed proposals and shows a low-RCS design able to cruise at speeds well above Mach 3.0. Operating at extreme heights, it would need to present a low radar signature only in a downward direction. Its inlets use a sharply-raked inverted configuration first seen on a proposed Lockheed hypersonic design. Its long lower edge would screen the intake and engine from ground-based radars. The jetpipes are extended to confine the IR emissions to the rearward sector.

Like the SR-71, such a design would be optimised for high-speed cruise and would have low manoeuvrability. The single vertical tail with no horizontal stabliser is a feature of a 1982 Lockheed design for an advanced fighter but recent advances in fly-by-wire technology would allow it to be reduced in size to the vestigial form shown here.

Combining high speed and stealth in a single design may seem odd but that is exactly what Kelly Johnson and his Skunk Works set out to do when they designed the A-12/SR-71. Sheer speed was a major factor in keeping the Blackbird effective until its retirement. However, the designers of the Aurora can neither assume that this philosophy will always hold good, nor can they assume that stealth technology will grant total invulnerability to a subsonic aircraft until the year 2010 and beyond. The shooting down of a bomber during a war is just another kill — the combat losses of B-52s over North Vietnam did not end the perceived useful life of the aircraft in its strategic rôle. Shooting down a reconnaissance aircraft can result in a major political crisis. The Aurora must be able to go "in harm's way" and return unscathed.

In the autumn of 1987, the US plastic model manufacturer Testor, creator of the first commercially released "F-19" construction kit launched its model of the "MiG-37B Ferret E" — a Soviet equivalent to the Lockheed stealth fighter. Its appearance must have caused a few smiles around the Mikoyan design bureau. As its manufacturer admitted, the kit illustrated a possible configuration for a stealthy MiG rather than an actual aircraft currently under development or flying.

Its reception in the Pentagon must have been less amusing. Here in widely-distributed form was the first model to illustrate the use of faceting as a RCS reduction technique. At a time when the Lockheed F-117A was still highly-classified, the basic technology it used was being openly illustrated. By the autumn of 1988, it was no secret in the aerospace world that the F-117A was closer in appearance to the "Mig-37B Ferret E" model than any of the "Lockheed F-19" kits on the market. "If you want to see what the F-117 looks like, look at that MiG-37 model", I was told by one source.

Evidence that the kit's faceted appearance was not the result of pure guesswork came in the choice of designation. At the time, the highest number issued in the MiG series of designations was MiG-31. In calling their new model the MiG-37, Testor had jumped not one designation but two.

That choice seems to have been a wise one. There is good evidence that the MiG-33 and -35 designations have already been earmarked (if not assigned) to a new air-superiority fighter and a lightweight dogfighter respectively. If the task of producing a Soviet stealth fighter is assigned to the Mikoyan bureau, the result could well be designated MiG-37. Testor had either been very lucky in their guesswork or had been talking to the right people when researching their new plastic kit.

Perhaps the most detailed unclassified look at the likely shape of future Soviet fighters has been that taken by Richard Ward of General Dynamics. In a technical paper *Mig-2000*, he has tried to predict the technology which might appear in a Soviet fighter fielded around the turn of the century. This might seem a near-impossible task but Ward has tackled the job by extrapolating from existing design trends, taking into account the nature of future fighter missions, known Soviet production methods and areas of aerospace technology known to be under investigation in the Soviet Union.

He predicted the development of a twin-engined fighter in the 40,000lb (18,000kg) maximum take-off weight class and powered by two advanced turbofans developing around 18,000lb (8,100kg) of dry thrust and 27,000lb (12,250kg) thrust in afterburner. The aircraft would combine thrust vectoring with a canard delta configuration. Soviet literature has shown a high degree of interest in wing/canard layouts, says Ward. "When a canard is combined with vectorable nozzles, fly-by-wire and relaxed static stability, an interesting configuration results. Not only will the canard be an aerodynamic control device, but it can also be used to trim the vectored thrust during certain high angle-of-attack manoeuvres and STOL operations."

The traditional MiG formula of "speed and height" has resulted in a long series of impressive warplanes, albeit with some restrictions in performance and payload when compared to Western types. The Vietnam War showed how, under suitable tactical conditions, the lightweight, short-ranged and modestly armed MiG-21 could shoot down the heavier and more sophisticated F-4 Phantom. Ward argues that if high speed, good manoeuvrability and electronic countermeasures were to be combined with stealth technology at the conceptual design stage, the result could be a lighter lower-cost design. A drawing in his technical paper shows an aircraft whose wings and canards have EAP-style cranked leading edges and whose general lines show some degree of stealth faceting.

Very little is known about the MiG-33, although the MiG-35 is known to be a single-engined aircraft roughly in the size and performance class of the F-16. Both were probably started too soon to allow large-scale application of stealth technology. Like EFA and Rafale, they are more likely to feature reduced RCS than low

RCS. The first true stealth fighter from the Mikoyan bureau would thus be a follow-on MiG-37 design, a heavy fighter intended to match the USAF's Advanced Tactical Fighter in the late 1990s and beyond. Bearing in mind that the MiG-29 took about a decade from first flight to IOC, Ward's predicted in-service date of the year 2000 does not look unreasonable.

The "Mig-37" shown in our artwork is slightly heavier than Ward's "Mig-2000" but incorporates some of his conclusions, plus features

drawn from other artworks and models of US ATF-type fighters. Such a fighter would weigh around 50,000lb (22,700kg) and be powered by two thrust-vectored afterburning turbofan engines in the 30,000lb (13,600kg) thrust class.

Rounding rather than faceting is used for low-RCS but the degree to which this has been done is limited by the traditional Soviet preference for simple and easy-to-manufacture shapes. The wings and canards would be of all-composite construction, incorporating

RAM or even RAS in their leading and trailing edges. To simplify front-line maintenance, these surfaces are detachable, so can be repaired by replacement, with the damaged component being shipped back to a dépôt for repair. Extensive use would also be made of composites and RAM/RAS in the fuselage.

To minimise RCS, all missile armament is carried in an internal bay. By the late 1990s, even today's AA-8, AA-10 and AA-11 missiles would be somewhat dated. A more likely payload for a

future stealthy MiG would be four new "AA-12" fire-and-forget missiles with a range of about 50 miles (80km), plus a pair of short-range "AA-13" advanced dogfight weapons.

Given the pinpoint accuracy demonstrated by the cannon/laser ranger combination on the MiG-29, a similar fit can be anticipated on future fighters. In the interests of stealth, the optical head may even be made retractable, while today's 23mm calibre might give way to a new and larger, more lethal round of between 25 and 27mm calibre.

Above: This hypothetical "MiG-37" illustrates a possible Soviet approach to the problem of creating a stealthy tactical fighter. The canard-delta configuration has been much-studied in the

Soviet Union, and the rounded planform shown here would ensure that reflected energy was scattered over a range of directions. No one angle would offer an unduly high RCS. Rounding the

wing and fin tips reduces radar scattering by diffraction, while low-RCS slotted jetpipes allow a degree of thrust vectoring. Our artist has shown this example equipped with a fixed, protruding, EO sensor,

plus fin-mounted chaff/flare dispensers. Soviet designers have traditionally packed minor items of equipment into external fairings, and may find this hard to give up, despite its implications for RCS.

GENERAL DYNAMICS/McDONNELL DOUGLAS ADVANCED TACTICAL AIRCRAFT (ATA)

Least-known of the US stealth aircraft is the US Navy's A-12 Advanced Tactical Aircraft (ATA). As its designation suggests, the A-12 will be a strike aircraft. Intended to replace the veteran A-6 Intruder, it will have the performance needed to carry out long-range strikes against Soviet naval bases and surfaces ships and to cope with the air defences of Soviet client states such as Libya.

The A-12 remains highly-classified. In 1986 the Office of the Secretary of Defense ordered Navy Secretary John Lehman to provide data similar to that already circulating on the Air Force's ATF — basic details of cost, speed, and timescale. Despite this, very little information has entered the public domain. In late 1988, the programme was reported to be on schedule, as was the projected date for the first flight, but all details remained classified.

The aircraft will be a two-seater with a heavy payload and substantial range, a strike radius of about 1,000nm (1,850km) unrefuelled has been reported. The A-12 will be cheaper than many other future aircraft — a result of its subsonic performance. It will not be a STOL aircraft — the resulting performance and payload penalities were judged unacceptable — but will be able to fly at high subsonic speed at low level in all weathers.

Reported features include a wide fuselage with large internal weapons bay. Take-off weight could be about 55,000lb (25,000kg). Powerplant for the twin-engined aircraft will be a non-afterburning uprated derivative of the General Electric F404 turbofan.

According to USMC Deputy Chief of Staff for Aviation General Charles C. Pitman, the A-12 is "on the very edge of technology". The A-12 is expected to make greater use of stealth than the USAF's ATF and to incorporate more RAM in its construction. As a result, some EW experts are suggesting that the aircraft may not require active jammers.

The need for carrier compatibility probably ruled out some of the odder configurations thrown up by stealth technology. Northrop's unsuccessful ATA design, reported to have been a flying wing, was described by the magazine *Defense News* as being "essentially a scaled-down B-2".

Possible names for the new aicraft under consideration in 1988 included Avenger, Enforcer, Penetrator, Ghost, Shadow, Seabat and Stingray. By early 1989, "Avenger 2" was reported to be the front runner, leaving the Pentagon with the problem of deciding whether the rights to the name belonged to the DoD or to Grumman, manufacturer of the propeller-driven Avenger of early-1940s fame. Having lost the ATA competition, the Long Island company would hardly be pleased at seeing the name of one of its best-known designs of the past applied to a present-day product by its rivals.

Two names on the shortlist — Seabat and Stingray — probably give a clue to the aircraft's appearance, and are reflected in our artwork. Bill Sweetman had suggested that the A-12 might use faceting, but this seems unlikely, given the advances in stealth technology already demonstrated by the B-2.

The speculative configurations shown here in prototype markings has a dorsal intake incoporating long serpentine ducting to the engines. V-tails are rarely used at other than low/medium supersonic speed, but the use of artificial stability should allow their use in a high-subsonic mid-1990s design. The narrow light-coloured strips at the base of each tail surface are transparencies for lights used in an active-camouflage counter-illumination scheme.

The A-12 programme is reported to be running two years ahead of the ATF yet a prototype is not expected to fly until the mid-1990s. This later date seems surprising, even when allowing for the fact that the Navy has chosen not to have a time-consuming competitive fly-off of rival designs.

Talking to a meeting of USN pilots in the autumn of 1986, US Navy Secretary John Lehman described the aircraft's avionics and EW suites as "entirely new". In theory, the Navy is co-operating with the USAF to ensure a degree of commonality between the A-12 and the Air Force's ATF candidates. In practice, A-12

Above: The configuration of the US Navy's A-12 attack aircraft remains classified. This artist's impression of the aircraft in prototype markings shows possible stealth features. The use of underwing stores might seem surprising, but the external tanks would be dropped before coming into radar range of an enemy. The outboard stores are treated with radar-absorbent material, and are storage/launch tubes for Harpoon missiles.

avionics show little compatibility with the ATF designs.

The aircraft's multifunction radar is being developed by Westinghouse, and will almost certainly use advanced inverse synthetic array (ISAR) technology, a feature originally planned for the Norden Systems APQ-173 radar of the cancelled A-6F Intruder II. According to reports, the resolution

obtained will be good enough to allow the class of a ship target to be determined at a range of 90 miles (150km). The radar will have air-to-air modes, allowing the A-12 to carry AMRAAM. Although this may appear surprising in a strike aircraft, such a move had been planned for the A-6F Intruder II.

A navigation and targeting IR sensor is being developed by Westinghouse, the ESM

suite by Litton Amecon. Other reported contracts include the missile warning set (General Electric), VHSIC central mission computer (IBM), 8in (20cm) LCD colour tactical display (Allied-Signal Aerospace) integrated INS (Litton/Honeywell), air-data computer (Allied-Signal Aerospace), and a multifunction antenna (Harris). In March 1987 Congress was told by Assistant Secretary of Defense (C31) Donald C. Latham that the first 180 A-12 would not be fitted with INEWS or ICNIA. Some observers have even questioned whether any

newly-built A-12s will receive the INEWS system.

Target cost for the A-12 is $40 million a copy but a figure substantially above this is being predicted by some observers. All details of the A-12 budget are classified. During the production phase of the programme, it was expected that GD and McDonnell Douglas will compete for work but, in the spring of 1988, the DoD approved plans to assemble the aircraft at a McDonnell Douglas facility — Air Force Plant No. 3 at Tulsa airport, Oklahoma. The Government-owned site is conveniently located for both contractors and has 2.9 million square ft (270,000m²) of floor space.

Above: An A-12 in operational camouflage approaches the tanker. The refuelling probe rises from a cavity whose cover is designed to minimise radar

reflection when closed. Note the baffles in the dorsal air inlets. Any radar energy getting past these is faced with an S-shaped duct which conceals the engine.

The inlets would also incorporate Yehudi lights which could be activated to kill the dark shadows within their interior. The A-12 radar contract has been allocated to

Westinghouse after being reassigned from Texas Instruments and Norden by the US Navy. This system is expected to use inverse synthetic array technology.

YF-22A AND YF-23A ADVANCED TACTICAL FIGHTER (ATF)

Aircraft such as the F-15 were a natural evolution of earlier designs but, in the Advanced Tactical Fighter (ATF), the USAF hopes to make a revolutionary leap forward in aircraft capability, creating a fighter able to outfly all designs currently in production or even on the drawing board, while being able to operate easily in poor weather conditions.

Top speed will not greatly exceed that of current fighters, probably in the region of Mach 2.5, but ATF will be able to operate at such high speeds far more efficiently than current fighters, with less fuel consumption and greater endurance. Key requirements are the ability to cruise at between Mach 1.05 and 1.5, without the use of after-burning, and a combat manoeuvrability better than that of the F-16. The ability to manoeuvre and accelerate without using the after-burner will give the ATF a marked advantage over conventional types. Forced to use after-burning, it would have much less combat endurance. While the conventional fighter is forced to break off combat or risk running out of fuel, ATF will be able continued the fight.

Other performance-boosting features are expected to be the use of vectored thrust for STOL performance or even in-flight agility, a concept being tested on the canard-equipped experimental STOL F-15, plus variable-camber wing technology drawn from the AFTI/F-16 and F-111 MAW (mission adaptive wing) programmes. Avionics will include integrated fire/flight control systems with high-technology cockpit displays and large-scale use of built-in test equipment.

Lockheed has released several illustrations of ATFs. All show twin-engined canard delta aircraft with thrust-vectoring nozzles but even a superficial examination of these shows differences in configuration. Our Lockheed/ General Dynamics/Boeing YF-22A artwork combines features from several of these Lockheed drawings.

The configuration of the rival McDonnell Douglas/ Northrop YF-23A is thought to be more novel. In September 1988, the magazine *Defense News* quoted an unidentified source as saying that "Most of the so-called experts . . . are going to be embarrassed when actual definitive sketches are

Above: As the YF-22 climbs away, the glow of its two dimensional exhaust nozzles presents a minimal IR and radar target. Eyewitness accounts of F-117A flights have described seeing a yellow glow from that aircraft's exhausts. This seems surprising, given that it's twin turbofans are thought to be non-afterburning F404s.

released, because they (the experts) start with fairly standard concepts of what a fighter plane should look like. This is totally different."

Two opposing factors have influenced the ATF programme. The aircraft must have the performance needed to counter all current and projected Soviet threats, yet it must also be affordable in the number which the USAF requires. The need for performance tends to force up aircraft size and cost, while

affordability constraints demand that such parameters be limited.

ATF unit cost has been set at no more than $35 million, a figure which assumes a 750 unit buy at 72 per cent. Some USAF officials fear that the ATF specification will prove impossible to meet within the set price and are worried that a "design to cost" approach may see the requirement trimmed, eroding the new fighter's edge over future Soviet types.

Cost of an aircraft is proportional to weight and the gross weight of an ATF fully loaded for the air-superiority mission was set at 50,000lb (22,680kg), well below the 68,000lb (30,845kg) of the F-15C. To make this figure achievable, compromises have already been made.

Late in 1987 a USAF review of the programme concluded that it was on target to meet its weight projections but recommended that the

Stealth is an important quality of the ATF and one where compromise is undesirable. In May 1986, *International Defense Review* quoted the USAF Aeronautical Systems Division commander as saying that while "in the past we thought we could not get high maneuverability and stealth in the same aircraft", the ATF would be "one or two orders of magnitude" less detectable than the F-15.

About 45 per cent of the airframe of the production aircraft will be made from composites, probably bonded rather than mechanically fastened. The YF-22A makes large-scale use of reheatable thermoplastic composites, particularly for wing and fuselage skins, while the YF-23A team has used toughened versions of thermoset resins. Both aircraft could also make large-scale use of radar-absorbent structure (RAS). These materials, and the careful use of shaping, will be the ATF's main RCS-reduction measures. The need for stealth has apparently created difficult physical constraints for the avionics designer, presumably due to the dictates of shaping.

The first flight of a YF-23A prototype is expected to take place at Edwards AFB in the late summer of 1989. The YF-22A is due to fly by the summer of 1990. Each ATF contractor will deliver one prototype fitted with YF-119 engines, and a second powered by YF120s. Both engines are in the 32,000lb (14,500kg) thrust class. One airframe/engine combination will be selected for full-scale development, probably in 1991. First flight of a full-scale development aircraft is due in 1993, with delivery to start mid-1990s.

landing sink rate requirement be trimmed from 13ft/sec (4m/s) to 10ft/sec (3m/s) in order to reduce the structural demands on the landing gear components and structure. Even so, by early 1989 both teams were reported to be having trouble in meeting the 50,000lb (22,680kg) weight requirement.

Another important decision was to delete the engine thrust reversers. A standard NATO runway is 8,000ft (2,440m) long and 100 to 150ft (30 to 46m) wide. ATF was intended to be able to operate out of 2,000ft (610m) strips but this required the use of thrust reversers to reduce the landing run. Studies showed that reversers would have increased the aircraft's weight, cost and target signature, so runway requirements have had to be relaxed slightly.

Above: At the time these pages were cleared for press, no accurate drawing of the YF-22A or the YF-23A had been released. This artist's impression of the YF-22A is based on several Lockheed artworks. Like the "F-19" drawing on page 11, it assumes that RCS-reduction will be achieved by blending and rounding, plus large-scale use of RAM and/or RAS. Rounded wing and canard tips reduce RCS, as do the outward-canted tailfins. The pilot is seated under a radar-absorbent canopy. An LPI radar will be used to reduce detection by enemy ESM.

AIDS TO STEALTH

"Imagine a man with a powerful flashlight trying to find another man on a dark night", says Tom Amlie, former technical director of the China Lake Naval Weapons Center. "He might find him at 100-200 feet (30-60m). The other man can see the flashlight at a range of at least one-half mile (0.8km). To pursue the analogy a bit farther, if the second man has an automatic rifle and homicidal tendencies, the fellow with the flashlight could be in deep trouble."

It is a neat little story and one which formed part of Amlie's outspoken attack on the US over-dependence on radar, a central theme of a 1987 interview with *The Washington Post*. It is also a good analogy of the problem facing operators of stealth aircraft. The use of stealth technology to reduce the detectable signature of fighters and strike aircraft does much to reduce their vulnerability but, on its own, signature-reduction is not enough. The stealth aircraft's on-board systems must also be difficult to detect.

Ideally, a stealth fighter or bomber should emit no radar, radio, IR or EO energy which might betray its position. Many of the traditional avionics systems carried aboard military aircraft, such as high-powered radars, Doppler navaids, IFF transponders and conventional communications equipment, must be eliminated as far as possible and be replaced with stealthy equivalents. In practice, this will be hard to achieve. If passive replacements cannot be devised, the traditional equipment must be redesigned to keep the amplitude of its emissions as low as possible, preferably in areas of the spectrum less intensively monitored than the radio and radar bands.

RADARS

Most obvious candidate for redesign is the aircraft's radar. Conventional systems must give way to new Low Probability of Intercept (LPI) designs. Exact details of LPI

Above: **Warplanes such as the F-15 Eagle rely on their powerful radars for target detection, but such easily-detectable emissions would betray a stealth fighter.**

Below & Right: **A stealthy low probability of intercept (LPI) radar will use long pulses of low amplitude rather than the more detectable but traditional short high-** amplitude pulses. Its antenna will also be designed to have a narrower beam and smaller sidelobes, so will offer less stray radiation to hostile ESM receivers.

Radar Waveforms

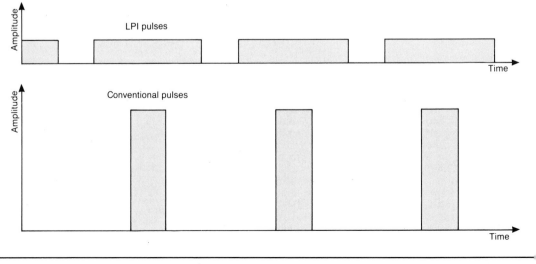

radar technology remain classified but many can be deduced.

For a start, the signal transmitted must be of a type which will be hard to detect by ESM. This involves using a wide-band waveform with a high duty cycle, ideally one which has noise-like characteristics. A conventional pulse radar has a low duty cycle and transmits powerful but narrow pulses of energy. A high duty cycle radar will transmit much longer pulses, but at a lower power level, and will spread this radiated energy over a

wide range of frequencies in the hope that it will become inconspicuous to an enemy ESM system effectively "buried" among the normal background of civil and military radar signals and communications links which clutter the microwave region.

The technique is not as simple as it sounds. One advantage of a low duty cycle is that the radar's receiver can listen for the returned echo at times when the transmitter is silent and can thus share the same antenna. The LPI radar will have to transmit and receive at the same time, so

must either use two antennas or rely on sophisticated signal processing.

To further reduce the chances of the signal being intercepted by an ESM system, it must be confined to the narrowest beam which will meet the tactical requirements for which the radar is designed. The use of a high frequency will give the narrowest possible beam from an antenna of fixed dimensions, while careful antenna design will minimise the size of the sidelobes (unwanted minor beams at different angles).

Above: **By means of the JTIDS data link, E-3 Sentry aircraft will be able to pass target information to NATO fighters, allowing the latter to avoid using radar.**

In the long run, it will be impossible to disguise a LPI radar's powerful (albeit much narrowed) main beam but denying the enemy any chance to exploit sidelobe radiation will be a major step forward. The chances of main-beam detection will be reduced largely by transmitting only in short occasional bursts, retaining the radar "snapshot" between transmissions, and updating target tracks by dead reckoning.

In an air battle involving stealth fighters, it is likely that at any one time only a few aircraft — AEW platforms and some long-range interceptors — would rely on active radar. Using LPI communications, these aircraft would pass target data to the others. It is possible to imagine tactics in which each stealth fighter in turn might use its own radar for a few seconds, then jink onto a new course while transmitting target information to the rest of the formation. Next generation radars such as those proposed for EFA and Rafale have a

Radar Beam Shapes

LPI narrow main lobe

Small side lobes

Conventional wide main lobe

Larger side lobes

large number of operating modes. Switching rapidly from one to another may help complicate the task faced by an enemy ESM system.

LASER RADAR

Many of the problems associated with microwave radar can be eliminated by using a laser radar. The very narrow beam would be difficult to detect and would have no sidelobes through which energy could leak. Performance would be dependent on weather and would be of short range. Air-to-ground seems a more likely rôle than air-to-air. By scanning the terrain ahead of the aircraft, the laser radar would be able to build up an image of FLIR-like quality, also obtaining range and velocity information which could be used for targeting and terrain following.

GEC Avionics has test-flown its LOCUS (Laser Optical Cable Unmasking System) on a US Navy A-6E. LOCUS is a small laser radar carried in a pod beneath the aircraft's starboard wing. The trials aircraft used in the "Real Night" programme has been fitted with a 1553B digital databus and a complete GEC-developed night-attack avionics suite. The standard of the avionics suite was built up gradually. Flight trials started in 1986 but the laser radar was not delivered until 1988.

LOCUS uses a carbon dioxide laser to scan a small 8 x 8 degree sector ahead of the aircraft. It was designed to detect a 0.4in (1cm) diameter cable at a range of 0.9 miles (1.5km), even in heavy rain, and to indicate the obstruction's position by overlaying suitable symbology on the FLIR imagery visible in the head-up display (HUD).

RECOGNITION

The high resolution offered by laser radars may also help in the critical and highly-classified field of passive target identification. Allied-Signal and Raytheon are already working on a new NATO Mk15 IFF (Identification Friend or Foe) system but active transponders of this type are hardly compatible with stealth operation. The interrogation pulse could easily be observed on an ESM system. If used in air combat, stealth aircraft would need a passive alternative.

Under the MSIP (Multi-Staged Improvement Program) upgrades applied to the F-14 Tomcat and F-15 Eagle, both aircraft are being given a degree of passive target identification. This area is highly-classified but is largely a matter of signal processing. There is a relationship between target shape and the characteristics of the reflected wave, so inverse scattering is one of the few clues which

Above left: **During this Dornier trial, an experimental laser radar produces recognisable images of a group of vehicles.**

Above: **The APS-137 radar in the nose of the US Navy S-3B Viking uses Inverse Synthetic Aperture Radar (ISAR) technology.**

Below: **The massive contra-rotating propellers on the Tupolev Bear create a distinctive and recognisable echo on western radars.**

Below right: **This Thomson-CSF photo is an example of the high-resolution imagery available from a radar which uses SAR techniques.**

will allow a radar to identify a beyond-visual-range target.

Aircraft approaching head-on may be identified by analysis of the radar returns from the engine inlets, since the signal will have been modulated by the spinning blades of the first-stage of the engine fan/compressor. Such modulation effects have been known for some time. The huge contra-rotating propellers on the Kuznetsov engines fitted to the Tu-95 and -142 Bear aircraft made them easily-recognisable radar targets on analogue radar displays, while early tests of the APG-63 radar used in the F-15 Eagle showed that the modulated radar return from the engine

compressors could be interpreted by the radar as a multiple target.

An obvious early goal of Western intelligence organisations whenever a new Soviet fighter enters service is to measure its head-on radar signature and the modulation created by its engines. Early in 1988. a time when the MiG-29 Fulcrum had rarely been seen by the West, I learned that its head-on signature had already been measured.

ISAR

The radar used on the A-12 strike aircraft will use Inverse Synthetic Aperture Radar (ISAR) technology. Described

earlier in the book as a research tool for the identification of "hot spots" on a stealth design, ISAR processes the Doppler shift resulting from target motion as a means of improving radar resolution. Its first military application was probably in intelligence gathering, with US ground-based space surveillance radars processing the Doppler shift from orbiting Soviet military satellites to build up a low-resolution image of the spacecraft.

The first USN aircraft to use the technique for tactical purposes was the Lockheed S-3B Viking anti-submarine aircraft. When first built and deployed as the S-3A, these

aircraft were fitted with a Texas Instruments APS-116 search radar. The new APS-137(V), introduced as part of the rebuild to S-3B standard, occupies the same physical space within the aircraft and adds less than 25lb (11kg) to the system's weight.

By carefully allowing for the much larger Doppler shifts created by the aircraft's own movement and the target ship's forward speed, the APS-137 is able to extract the Doppler effects due to pitch, yaw and roll of the different parts of the vessel, processing these to obtain a physical profile of the target vessel. Earlier ISAR work against satellite targets had been done by using computers to process recorded radar observations. The APS-137 does the same task in real time.

The same technique is now being applied to the radar of the A-12, presumably as a means of positively identifying surface ships at beyond visual range. In theory, it will also be possible to apply ISAR technology to an air-to-air radar, relying on the Doppler shift created by changes in target attitudes. Unlike the movements of a ship, these attitude changes will not be regular and rapidly repeating so the signal processing problems will be more difficult.

All nations working on passive target recognition keep their efforts highly classified. Nowhere was this

more apparent than in the 1987/88 competition between rival radar teams for the contract to supply a radar for the Eurofighter EFA. Although the USA was prepared to release much of the hardware and software technology from the Hornet's APG-68 radar to the Marconi/AEG team which was offering a developed version of the set, it was made clear that this would not include target-recognition algorithms. Even within the four-nation consortium, national secrecy still prevails. Each nation will develop its own target-recognition software.

In air-to-air combat, passive target recognition would be a valuable aid to a stealthy fighter such as the ATF. Low RCS would deny a similar capability to its opponent. By reducing the amount of back-scattered radar energy to a minimum, stealth measures would rob the opponent's radar of the information which its target-recognition algorithms would need.

INFRA-RED

Radar is not the only technology being studied for beyond-visual-range target identification. In 1987, the USAF's Rome Air Development Center requested proposals from industry for innovative approaches to the problems of real-time identification of air and ground targets at ranges of 170 miles (270km) or more. The resulting study contracts were expected to cover the extraction of target signature data from the information obtained via radar, laser, IR and ultraviolet, optical and even acoustic sensors.

Given good weather conditions, infra-red or other types of electro-optical sensor may be used for target recognition and fire-control purposes. In the late 1950s and early 1960s, Hughes Infra-Red Search and Track Systems (IRSTSs) were fitted to the F-101 Voodoo, F-102 Delta Dagger and F-106 Delta Dart. The sensor covered a sector of up to 50 degrees on either side of the aircraft centreline and could be cued towards targets by data from GCI radar sites transmitted automatically to the interceptor by datalink.

Targets could normally be detected at a range of a few miles (up to 5km). In theory, the equipment could only indicate bearing, but crews found that range could be estimated by observing the strength of the IR signal and the look-down angle of the sensor. Target speed and heading could be deduced by observing that rate of change of the target's azimuth position. By slaving the radar to the IR sensor, the interceptor was less likely to be fooled by ECM or chaff.

Units assigned to the air-defence rôle may have found the IR data useful but such systems never proved popular with tactical fighter squadrons. Although the US Navy fitted the AAA-4 IR sensor to its early-model Phantoms, the equipment's distinctive chin fairing was also present on the USAF's F-4C model, the sensor was never installed on the latter aircraft. The F-4D started life without the fairing but it was later retrofitted to house the aircraft's radar homing and warning system. In 1985 Hughes retrofitted an IRST into an F-4D of the North

Dakota ANG and flight tests were successful enough to make the idea of a retrofit scheme seem attractive.

IR SENSORS

On the F-4E, the chin location formerly occupied by the IR sensor was used to house a 20mm M61 cannon, giving the Phantom built-in cannon armament for the first time. Some USAF F-4Es carried the Northrop ASX-1 TISEO (Target Identification System Electro-Optical) in the

Above left: **Hughes APG-65 radar for the F-18 uses target-recognition software whose algorithms are kept secret by the US Government.**

Above: **Electro-optics in action — this F-4 Phantom is fitted with a wing-mounted TISEO TV sensor, and carries a GBU-15 "smart" bomb.**

Right: **More than 300 USN F-14A Tomcats are fitted with a Northrop Television Camera Set (TCS) target identification system.**

wing leading edge. This was a small stabilised TV camera offering two levels of magnification and able to present imagery on the normal cockpit CRT displays. Tests showed that in good conditions the system could detect a Tu-95/142 Bear at a range of more than 40nm (74km) or a MiG-23 Flogger at more than 10nm (18km). Although carried by some F-4s in the final stages of the Vietnam War, it never saw combat use there but is reported to have seen action with the Israeli Air Force.

In a similar move, the US Navy fitted its F-14A Tomcats with a Northrop AXX-1 Television Camera Set (TCS) for long-range target detection and identification. When the F-14D was developed in the mid-1980s, General Electric was selected to develop an IRSTS (Infra-Red Search and Track System) with Martin Marietta acting as a second source. This was originally developed by the USAF, with USN participation, but shortage of money caused the USAF to drop out in 1986. The USN, which opted to press ahead with the programme, has encouraged the development of improvements to the signal processing intended to increase the detection range of the system. The Navy sees

the combination of IR and TV as an essential sensor for the automatic passive detection and tracking of targets at long range, so the F-14D has a twin pod able to house both the TCS and IRSTS units.

ELECTRO-OPTICS

From 1992 onwards GE and Martin Marietta will compete with each other for US Navy IRSTS orders but on the USAF's Advanced Tactical Figher they are working as collaborators rather than rivals. On the Lockheed/Boeing/General Dynamics YF-22A, the lead company on that aircraft's IRSTS is GE, while Martin Marietta leads the effort to create the EO Sensor System (EOSS) planned for the Northrop/McDonnell Douglas YF-23A.

Early study of the first heavily-retouched photo of the Lockheed F-117A showed the presence of an unusual feature on the nose, directly under the windshield. Widely interpreted as a "refuelling receptacle", it is probably an electro-optical target-acquisition and tracking sensor.

Little work is being done in Western Europe on similar long-range EO sensors, although Ferranti has carried out tests against aircraft

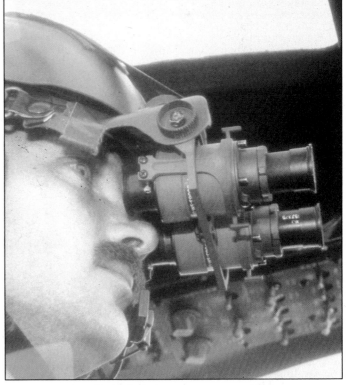

Left: **On these early-model F-4Bs, the chin fairing carried an AAA-4 IR sensor. Results proved poor, so it was dropped from later F-4s.**

Above: **Originally used by helicopter aircrew, night vision goggles (NVG) are a stealthy alternative to terrain-warning radar.**

targets as part of its work in support of the British Aerospace/Ferranti/GEC Avionics TIALD (Thermal Imaging Airborne Laser Designator) targeting pod being retrofitted to some RAF Tornado GR1 strike aircraft. When the Eurofighter EFA enters service in the mid-1990s, it is expected to carry a FLIR able to help with long-range identification of day and night targets.

SOVIET SENSORS

The Soviet Union has equipped its latest generation of fighters with EO sensors. On the MiG-29 Fulcrum, a hemispherical transparency, positioned just ahead of the windshield and slightly offset to the starboard side, houses stabilised optics for an infra-red sensor and a laser rangefinder. These units can be coupled to the radar and the pilot's helmet sight.

The pilot can thus direct the radar or the EO system to any target which he can see. If the helmet sight does not already incorporate cueing marks which can direct the pilot's gaze to targets detected by the radar or EO sensor, such a development can only be a matter of time. In combat, the two long-range sensors complement each other. A target lost by one can still be tracked by the other. Given GCI data via a secure datalink, the Fulcrum pilot will probably be able to carry out a high-altitude attack (or a low-altitude attack in clear weather) using only IR and laser rangefinder data. If the target had no laser-energy warning receiver, it would receive no warning that it was being intercepted.

When the West obtained its first close look at a Su-27 Flanker in 1987, when a minor collision took place between one of these Sukhoi interceptors and a Royal Norwegian Air Force P-3B Orion operating over the Barents Sea, close-up photographs taken by the Norwegian crew showed that this aircraft also carried an EO sensor, probably the same unit fitted to Fulcrum, which was fitted in the same location, slightly offset to starboard. Also visible on the photographs was the presence of a second sensor mounted within the cockpit and slightly offset to port. This looks rather like a large version of the sort of telescopic sight used by snipers. It is probably a telescope incorporating stabilised optics, an airborne

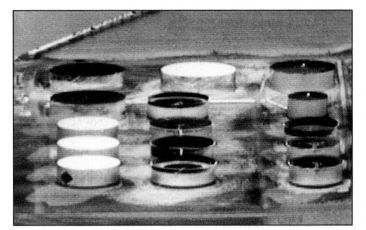

Above: **This infra-red air-to-ground image of oil tanks shows the level of liquid in each. Such information can be useful during an attack.**

Below: **The spherical housing ahead of the windshield of the MiG-29 houses stabilised optics shared by an IR sensor and laser rangefinder.**

equivalent to the British Aerospace Steadyscope. This could act as a back-up to the EO sensor and may offer more powerful magnification to aid target recognition.

DIGITAL MAPS

Radar is also widely used as a navaid and as a method of steering the aircraft in terrain following flight. FLIR systems are one passive alternative to radar but the pilot tasked with manually flying a long mission at very low level using only the small field of view presented by FLIR-derived HUD imagery has an unenviable task. The development of powerful airborne computers has made possible a stealthy replacement for the conventional terrain-following radar. Known as terrain-reference navigation (TRN), this relies on careful measurement of the profile of the terrain passing beneath the aircraft and its comparison with digitally-stored geographic data.

Measurement of the terrain is done using a radar altimeter. At first sight this might seem a weak point of the system, particularly if fitted to a stealth aircraft. In practice, radar altimeters have a narrow beam-width and low power output, directing their energy downwards rather than forwards, so are thus a poor target for enemy ESM systems.

The UK was the first Western nation to specify a requirement for a terrain-referenced navigation (TRN) system suitable for use in a manned aircraft. Three UK companies, British Aerospace,

Right & Below: **A terrain-referenced navigation (TRN) system compares radar altimeter readings with pre-stored geographic data, so can pinpoint its location. An aircraft relying on terrain following radar will tend to gain height by "ballooning" over obstacles (top right), but the TRN-equipped aircraft (bottom right) can predict the terrain ahead, so can fly closer to the ground.**

TRN Grid

TRN compares ground with stored database

Right: It's not necessary to own a spy satellite to create digital maps like these. TRN systems will work with Landsat or Spot data.

Ferranti and GEC Avionics, have offered systems to the UK MoD to meet a requirement for upgrading the Royal Air Force's Tornado GR1 strike aircraft.

The UK does not have the monopoly on TRN navigation. In the USA, Harris is working on its Digital Terrain Management Display (DTMD) system and is competing against Hughes to develop a Integrated Terrain Access and Retrieval System (ITARS) for the USAF. In France, *SAGEM* has been testing INS systems modified to incorporate TRN algorithms since 1981, while *Thomson-CSF* has developed the *Dracar* digital map generator.

PENETRATE

All of these systems offer the same basic facilities but use slightly different technology. The system on which most information has been released is probably the Ferranti Penetrate (Passive Enhanced Navigation with Terrain Referenced Avionics). At the 1988 Farnborough Air Show, the company displayed imagery obtained during early flight tests of its Penetrate systems which had been flown earlier that year in pod-mounted form on a Royal Aerospace Establishment two-seat Hawker Hunter fighter.

The database used in the Penetrate system contains elevation data which defines the terrain shape, cultural

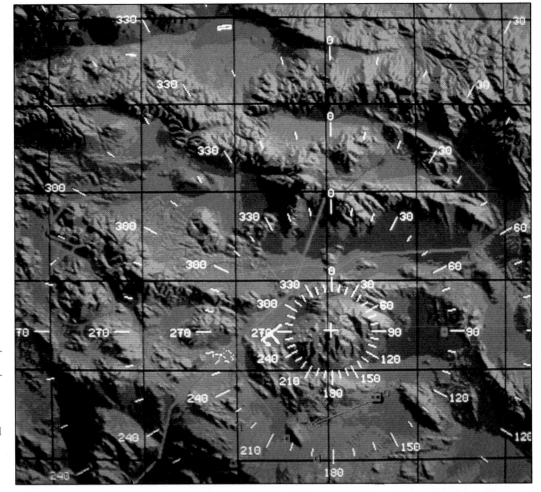

Right: It's not necessary to own a spy satellite to create digital maps like these. TRN systems will work with Landsat or Spot data.

data such as details of buildings and other man-made features, information on pylons and other potential obstructions. It also contains intelligence data and information on the mission to be flown.

Intelligence data comes in two categories. Details of the threat radii and lethality of enemy anti-aircraft systems are relatively constant. They

only need to be updated if a new system is fielded, if modifications improve the performance of existing systems or if new information shows that earlier estimates were inaccurate. Much faster-changing are the details of enemy deployment — the current location and number of threat systems.

When the aircraft is in low-level flight, Penetrate

continuously computes the height above ground level (the g level) needed to fly over the terrain ahead of the aircraft. The pilot is presented with data in two forms — head-down map and image displays and as enhancements overlaid on the normal view as seen through the HUD.

TRN systems work best when coupled to INS. They could be teamed with a compass/Doppler navaid and the resulting degradation of accuracy would probably be acceptable by many operators. The processor power required is proportional to the square of the desired accuracy — doubling the accuracy requires four times the processor power.

DATABASES

A conventional terrain-following radar (TFR) can only "see" the terrain ahead of the aircraft and within radar range. It has no information on terrain concealed by ridge lines. This is not shown until the aircraft has reached a position where the radar beam can illuminate the concealed terrain. Thanks to its database, a TRN system "knows" the terrain over which it is flying and can predict the profile of the

Terrain Following System

Terrain Reference System

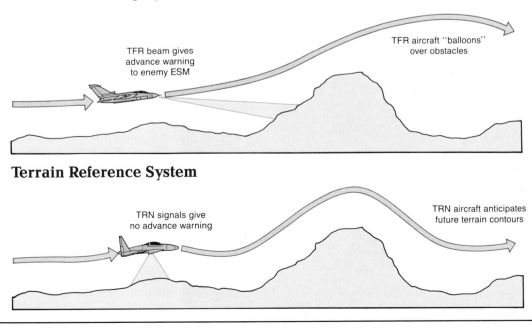

TFR beam gives advance warning to enemy ESM

TFR aircraft "balloons" over obstacles

TRN signals give no advance warning

TRN aircraft anticipates future terrain contours

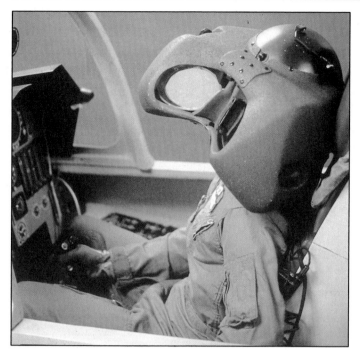

this becomes available, the risk will be no greater than that of flying in "total clag" (widespread low cloud, mist and/or rain) with a TFR.

For routine navigation of long-range stealth aircraft, such as the B-2, other passive navaids are required. Over a long mission, an inertial navigation system slowly drifts, building up an ever-increasing error. This can only be rectified by obtaining an accurate positional fix. One possibility for long-range stealth operations might be celestial navigation by means of an automatic star tracker. Northrop systems of this type were used on the short-lived Snark intercontinental cruise missile, of the late 1950s, and on the SR-71 Blackbird. A good star tracker can locate and track stars even in hazy daylight but is limited under poorer weather conditions

unless the aircraft is operating at very high altitude.

Several companies have created accurate navaids by integrating an INS system with a terminal for the US GPS (global positioning system) navigation satellite network. For example, Litton Italia has combined a LISA-4000 strap-down inertial reference unit with a five-channel P-code GPS receiver to create its private-venture LISA-6000. A GPS terminal is normally a bulky item of hardware but Northrop has been able to put most of the circuitry needed to create a GPS receiver on three specially designed integrated circuits. Having shrunk the size of a GPS receiver, the company can now offer a combined INS/GPS system mounted within a casing similar in size to that of a normal INS. One of the first applications for a combined INS/GPS is likely to be the Eurofighter EFA.

ground well ahead of the aircraft's current position, even if this region is concealed by a ridge or peak. By using this information, the TRN system can initiate pull-up and descent manoeuvres at the optimum time, minimising sudden unwanted gains in height (or "ballooning") of the aircraft flight path.

TRN obviously requires terrain irregularities in order to "fingerprint" and identify its current location. Deprived of these irregularities when flying over water or flat ground, the system must rely on INS data. The use of Kalman filtering (powerful software for combining multiple inputs) allows gyro drift to be estimated, says Ferranti, maintaining system accuracy until TRN-suitable ground is once more overflown. The accuracy of a good TRN system is a few tens of metres in the horizontal plane and about 10 to 20ft (3 to 6m) vertically.

Burn-Through Range

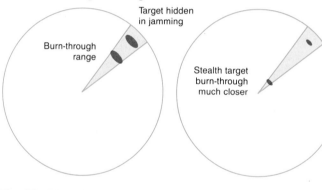

Top: **The Visually Coupled Airborne System Simulator programme could provide technology for the cockpit of the YF-22/23 ATF.**

Below: **Every four-vehicle battery of these SA-6 SAMs relies on a single Straight Flush radar, so is vulnerable to stealth.**

Above: **Even when hidden by a jamming strobe, a target will eventually become visible once its echo is strong enough to burn through the jamming (left). Reduce target RCS and you reduce the echo strength. The target must come much closer (right) before the new burnthrough range is reached.**

DEFENCES

According to US sources, the air defences of the Warsaw Pact include about 10,000 radars, 4,000 interceptors, 12,000 radar-directed anti-aircraft guns and 13,000 SAM systems. To further complicate the problems faced by Western stealth aircraft, the Soviet Union is also deploying new and more capable IR-guided missiles, while millimetre-wave and laser-directed weapons are taking their place alongside those operating at more traditional frequencies.

Large-scale exports of Soviet military hardware to North Africa, the Middle East, Southern and South-east Asia, sub-Saharan Africa, Latin America and South America effectively guarantee that if Western stealth aircraft are committed to action in any conflict, they are likely to face Soviet-designed air defences.

Dealing with Soviet-style air-defence systems is not easy. Most serious studies of the problem have concluded that the only solution is a "mix" of soft- and hard-kill technologies — systems able to confuse enemy anti-aircraft systems and weapons able to destroy them or at least force a temporary shut-down.

Reducing aircraft RCS provides advantages when designing self-protection jammers. Since most EW techniques rely on swamping the echo from the target with noise, or seducing the hostile

NAVAIDS

The obvious question must be — would pilots be prepared to fly at night and in bad weather using only a Penetrate-type navaid and perspective display? At present, the answer is probably no — at least for peacetime flying. The limited height accuracy makes banking sharply rather hazardous. In combat, however, the risk may be acceptable. Ferranti already offers the possibility of using a forward-scanning laser (effectively a laser radar) to provide what it calls "additional integrity". When

Above: This *Luftwaffe* Tornado has a BOZ chaff pod and Cerberus jammer. Stealth aircraft will also require EW systems.

Below: On the B-52, highlevels of jamming power were required to swamp the bomber's huge radar echo. Less power is needed to mask

the B-1Bs reflection, so the designers of this EW suite were able to allocate more weight to sophisticated signal processing.

B-1B Defensive Avionics

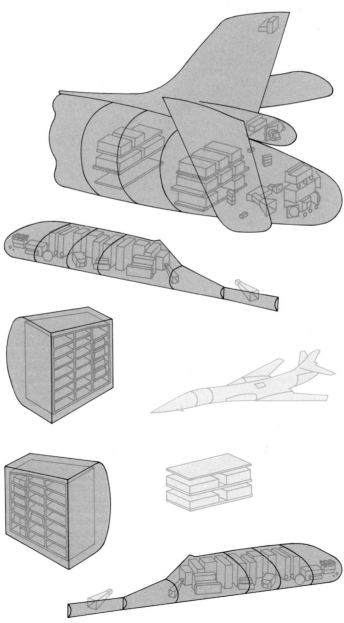

radar away from the true target by providing it with an acceptable but false substitute, any reduction in the size of the genuine echo must be of benefit.

EW engineers use the term "J/S ratio" to describe the ratio between the strength of the normal radar return from an aircraft and the signal which the hostile radar receives from the jammer. As the distance between the radar and the target is reduced, this ratio degrades, with the true echo becoming stronger and stronger until it is detectable through the jamming.

JAMMING

The term "burn-through range" is used by engineers to describe this vital distance at which the EW system gives no further protection. Its value depends on the power of the radar transmitter, the sensitivity of the receiver, the power of the jammer and the RCS of the target. The need to keep burn-through range as large as possible led Soviet designers to install a massive 600kW transmitter in the Fox Fire radar carried by the MiG-25 Foxbat.

If the RCS of an aircraft is reduced, the amount of jamming power needed to achieve the same burn-through range falls by the same amount. Since high levels of jamming power involve large, bulky and power-hungry transmitters, stealth is obviously good news for the designer of EW systems. If the aircraft plans to rely on the use of chaff rather than jamming, the

reductions in the amount of chaff needed are similar to those for jamming power.

Over the life of the B-52, some $2,600 million has been spent on EW upgrades. The current system weighs about 5,500lb (2,500kg) and consists of 238 LRUs (line-replaceable units). Given that the B-1B has a radar echo only 1 per cent of that of the older bomber, it would at first sight seem reasonable to assume that the lower levels of jamming power needed would result in a lighter EW suite. In practice, the Rockwell aircraft carries about 5,000lb (2,250kg) of EW equipment, virtually no weight saving.

The likely reasons are not hard to guess. If RCS is reduced by a factor of four while keeping the amount of jamming power constant, the burn-through range will be halved. Reduce it by a factor of ten and the burn-through range will fall to less than a third; while an RCS of one hundredth of the original value will reduce burn-through range to a tenth of its original value.

Rather than accept all of the potential weight saving which a lower level of transmitter power would allow, the USAF will have opted to have extra power in hand in order to increase burn-through range well beyond that available to the B-52. The ALQ-161 system on the B-1B is also likely to devote more of its weight to signal-processing circuitry, allowing the use of the most advanced deception jamming techniques.

EW SYSTEMS

EW systems must be updated to adapt to the latest threat technologies. Even today no single EW technique can cope with all types of radar-guided weapon. Next-generation ECM suites will have to incorporate the normal radar bands, plus millimetre waves and IR wavelengths. They will also be tightly co-ordinated both with the aircraft's ESM and missile-warning system and with the systems which release towed or expendable decoys.

Some indication of future trends in EW was provided in the spring of 1988 when French electronics giant *Thomson-CSF* revealed the direction which its own electronic-warfare efforts were taking. Stealth technology and low-level operations may reduce the vulnerability of future combat aircraft, explained *Thomson-CSF* Technical Director Pierre

SA-3 and SA-6 missiles in the conflicts of the 1960s and 1970s. A recent US Department of Defense study of combat losses in the decade from 1975 to 1985 revealed that 90 per cent of the tactical aircraft downed fell to IR-guided air-to-air missiles or IR-guided SAMs.

CHAFF AND FLARES

In the past, such IR threats were detected visually and countered by manoeuvring and/or the release of flares. This worked well against threats such as the AA-2 Atoll or SA-7 Grail. These older missiles were essentially "tail-chase" threats but the latest models of missile have better seekers, offering all-aspect attack capability and good resistance to countermeasures.

Flares will have some effect against such weapons, particularly the newer types being developed in the late 1980s. Current dispensers are used to release chaff, IR cartridges or expendable active decoys. Future trends are likely to be the use of "smart" dispensers, able to release decoy payloads only

Left: **Even zero RCS would do nothing to protect an aircraft from this Stinger SAM. IR signature must also be kept to a minimum.**

Above: **Matra's Sycomor chaff-dispensing pod is used on the Mirage F1, and could see service during the 1990s on the semi-stealthy Rafale.**

Baratault, but the importance of electronic countermeasures is undiminished.

Low-peak radars, such as pulse Doppler radars and missiles fitted with solid-state active seekers, force an increase in EW receiver sensitivity, while new jamming techniques designed to counter techniques such as monopulse radars demand higher levels of transmitter power. "Detailed analysis of potential threats indicates that all of the most significant technical characteristics (of EW systems) will have to be increased by one or two orders of magnitude." To complicate the problem, these future high-power transmitters and sensitive receivers will be required to operate simultaneously. Radar, IR and laser warning systems, jammers and decoys must be integrated into a coherent defensive system, which in turn must be fully integrated into the aircraft which carries it.

TOWED DECOYS

One relatively new type of EW system is the towed decoy. Widely used by warships since the early 1940s as a method of countering acoustic homing torpedoes, towed decoys were not

seriously promoted for aircraft use until the late 1980s. These devices would take the form of a small radar jammer towed behind the aircraft it is protecting. Being vulnerable to destruction or accidental loss, this must be kept as simple as possible, with most of the signal processing being carried out by avionics mounted within the aircraft and linked to the decoy by electrical conductors within the towing cable.

Eurofighter's EFA will carry an internationally-developed DASS (defensive aids support system) decoy system, while Raytheon and Hughes started full-scale development of an Advanced Airborne Expendable Decoy in 1988. Flight tests of this USN-funded system using A-6 and F-111 trials aircraft have gone well and production is expected to begin in 1993 or thereabouts. Other US efforts are studying possible towed IR or multi-spectral decoys able to deal with the most advanced threats.

For a long time the primary threat to aircraft was seen as being radar-guided weapons, so the bulk of Western EW funding was applied to the creation of RWRs and radar jammers. This was the result of the large-scale use of SA-2,

in the direction of the threat, and also by the development of multi-spectral expendable cartridges.

IR JAMMERS

Countering the more sophisticated IR threats will require the use of IR jammers but to date such systems have only been installed aboard helicopters and transports. The technology needed to create IR jammers for fighter use was not available; the existing models of IR jammers were large, power-hungry and unable to mimic the high nozzle and efflux temperatures of after-burning engines. In the case of a stealth aircraft, the low IR signature would in theory make current IRCM technology usable but, in practice, new types of IR jammer will probably be created for deployment on stealthy and non-stealthy fighters alike.

The earliest IR jammers used electrically-powered or

Below: **Flares remain an effective counter to IR-guided missiles, and are cheaper to develop and deploy than IR jammers.**

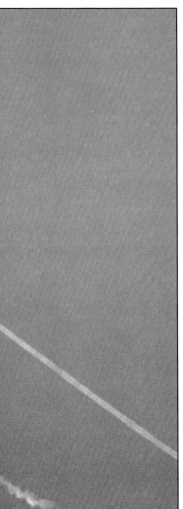

Above: **ALQ-159 IR jammer on the tail of a Chinook. Many current units of this type were developed for helicopter applications.**

fuel-heated hot elements as their source of IR energy but later, by the early 1980s, IR tubes were being used. For a fighter-based IR jammer, a more likely power source would be an IR laser. In 1988 Loral was given a contract under the USAF's "Have Glance" programme to develop a laser-based IRCM system. The system uses a gimbal-mounted low-powered laser to detect and jam incoming IR missiles. It will begin flight testing in 1991 in a pod-mounted F-111 installation. Initially intended for strategic aircraft, it will later be miniaturised for use on tactical fighters.

EO JAMMING

As stealth technology makes radar a less useful targeting aid, passive electro-optical tracking devices will pose a growing threat. In response, the US is developing new types of electro-optical countermeasure (EOCM). One current programme is "Coronet Price", a large pod-mounted system developed by Westinghouse and due to begin flight trials in 1989. Full-scale development could begin in 1991. Very little information on this sytem has been released. It is thought to use a low-powered laser to

Below: **Most RWR systems incorporate a small CRT screen which shows the bearing and nature of detected threats.**

Below: **Five antennas, two electronics units, a control unit and a display are all that is needed to locate radar threats to a helicopter.**

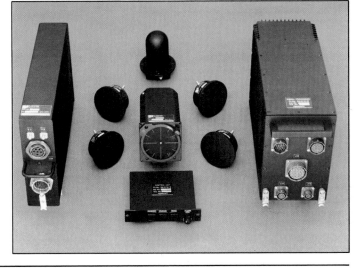

detect and jam passive systems such as TV/FLIR automatic trackers, or even long-range TV tracking aids. A similar system intended for helicopter use is being developed by the USMC under its "Cameo Bluejay" programme. EO threats such as laser rangefinders are addressed by another USAF programme which was started in 1985.

Since the ATF and A-12 will operate passively for much of the time, these stealthy aircraft will make extensive use of a sophisticated ESM system. This will allow them to make minimal use of active radar, while still giving their crew adequate information of nearby threats.

ESM SYSTEMS

A next-generation ESM system must be able to cope with radar, millimetre-wave, IR and laser threats. It must be able to determine the location and nature of all threat systems, warning aircrew when they are being tracked, have been targeted or are being engaged. It should be possible for stealth aircraft to detect enemy fighters by ESM, then launch fire-and-forget missiles. Not until the missiles' active seekers were energised would the enemy realise that he was under attack.

ESM needs to be backed up by a reliable missile-warning system able to detect passively-guided rounds, or those whose radar parameters are unknown. First attempts to develop a system of this type involved specialised radar-warning receivers designed to detect changes in radar threat signals which intelligence-gathering had identified as being indicative of SAM missile launch. Equipments of this type were designed to be effective against only one or

two types of SAM. Creation of a more general-purpose missile warner initially relied on detecting the IR energy for the missile's rocket motor. Early equipments of this type were not very successful and had a high false-alarm rate.

An obvious alternative was to use a low-powered aft-facing radar. One successful example is the Sanders ALQ-156, a tiny pulse-Doppler radar which provides 360 degree coverage for US Army CH-47 Chinook helicopters. In 1988 the company was given a US Navy contract to develop a version suitable for use on tactical fighters. In the UK, Plessey has developed the Missile Approach Warner (MAW) for use on the RAF's Harrier GR5s (AV-8Bs) and is now adapting the system for use on the Tornado. MAW is a low-powered pulse-Doppler radar which has been designed to trigger the release of flares or other decoys at the optimum moment.

Active warners have two great operational advantages. They can detect unpowered projectiles, such as anti-aircraft artillery rounds, and can measure range. Their *Achilles heel* is that they emit radar energy which might be detected by enemy ESM systems. Designers of radar warners try to keep the level of power emitted to an absolute minimum but cannot eliminate this tell-tale energy.

Data from both the ESM and missile-warner need to be integrated into a single display able to inform aircrew when they have been detected, tracked or engaged. Given a degree of artificial intelligence, such equipment might also be able to suggest

the best countermeasure or mix of countermeasures.

To meet the EW demands of the mid to late 1990s, the United States has embarked on what has been described as ''the most ambitious and expensive program in electronic warfare history''. Phase one demonstration and validation contracts for the Integrated Electronic Warfare System (INEWS) have been awarded to two teams — Sanders Associates, teamed with General Electric, and TRW, teamed with Westinghouse.

INEWS will bring a major improvement in the USAF's ability to locate and identify hostile emitters. Working in conjunction with the radars

carried by the ATF and A-12, it will cue the aircraft's EO system. It is also due to be fitted to the LHX helicopter. Under the ''Seek Spartan'' programme, technology from INEWS will also be applied to other USAF aircraft.

COMMUNICATIONS

Just as the location of German Navy U-boats was often betrayed by their use of HF radio during the Second World War, a stealth aircraft could be detected by its radio communications. Much of the technology needed for covert communications has already been pioneered by today's frequency-hopping and spread-spectrum radio

Above left: The USAF's Advanced Tactical Fighter (ATF) will introduce new developments in man/machine-interfacing.

Above: **AGM-88 HARM, seen here on a German Tornado, is the most effective anti-radiation missile. The EW pod is Germany's Cerberus.**

Below: **The EF-111 Raven which currently protects US strike formations will play the same rôle in helping the stealth aircraft of tomorrow.**

Right: **AGM-88 HARM anti-radiation missiles, (wings and fins not yet installed), are wheeled toward a FLIR-equipped A-7 Corsair.**

systems. For the ATF, the USA is developing the Integrated Communication Navigation Identification Avionics (ICNIA) system.

Based on common digital and RF processing modules built up from advanced VLSI (very-large-scale integration) circuits, ICNIA will combine the functions of current communications equipment, such as HF SSB, VHF, SINCGARS, UHF, Have Quick, EJS and JTIDS, navaids, such as VOR/ILS, MLS, Tacan and GPS, plus transponder and interrogator facilities compatible with the Mk XII and Mk XV IFF systems. Despite this multifunction complexity, the system will be about half the size of all the conventional hardware it will replace. Like the INEWS EW suite, ICNIA will probably have to be retrofitted into early-model A-12 attack aircraft but should be ready in time for use in the ATF.

Just like today's fighters and bombers, stealth aircraft will need the support of self-contained EW systems. At present, US strike aircraft require large-scale support from jamming aircraft, chaff bombers and "Wild Weasel" SEAD (Suppression of Enemy Air Defence) aircraft. In the short term, the use of stealth aircraft will enable much of this militarily unproductive "tail" to be eliminated. As counters to the new technology start to emerge, making defences more effective, it is virtually certain that support aircraft such as stand-off jamming platforms and Wild Weasels will once more have a rôle to play in helping their stealthy colleagues.

SUPPORT AIRCRAFT

Stand-off jammers mounted in aircraft such as the EA-6B and EF-111 are best used against early warning and GCI radars, where their high power can prevent the enemy predicting the direction from which strike aircraft or fighters may be coming. Deprived of this tactical information, target acquisition and tracking radars must carry out their own search for the incoming formations.

There is a limit to what even the best EW techniques can do. Defence suppression is also needed to ensure that an aircraft will survive in hostile airspace. This is largely a job for anti-radiation missiles (ARMs). Weapons of this type first saw service during the Vietnam War on dedicated anti-radar aircraft known as "Wild Weasels". A more general term would be SEAD aircraft.

SUPPRESSION

Few nations can afford the high cost associated with dedicated anti-radar aircraft. Outside of the USA, West Germany is the only NATO ally to have ordered SEAD aircraft — the Tornado ECR. Based on the standard Tornado IDS, the ECR carries two AGM-88A HARM missiles, two AIM-9L Sidewinders for self-defence, a jamming pod, a chaff/flare dispenser pod, plus two external fuel tanks. It lacks the twin 27mm Mauser cannons of the strike version. These were deleted to make room for the internally-mounted EW avionics.

The first prototype (a rebuild of IDS development aircraft P.16) flew for the first time in the autumn of 1988. Firing trials of HARM from Tornado were successfully completed at Manching by July 1987 and production deliveries to the West German Air Force started in November of that year.

Deliveries of 35 production ECR aircraft should begin in the second half of 1990. These will serve with *JBG38* at Jever and *JBG32* at

Lechfeld. All should be in service by the end of 1991. Italy is considering rebuilding some of its IDS fleet to the ECR standard. The only alternative would be to purchase new ECRs from its Panavia partners — the Italian assembly line closed in 1986.

The sole anti-radar aircraft in Warsaw Pact service is the Foxbat F version of the MiG-25 interceptor. This is similar in appearance to the Foxbat D ELINT aircraft and has a dielectric panel on the fuselage side just aft of the radome. It is armed with AS-11 anti-radiation missiles.

WILD WEASELS

A developing trend is the installation of ARMs on many types of strike aircraft as well as on dedicated SEAD types. The HARM may be carried on any aircraft which has digital avionics and sufficient computer capacity. The US Navy was ahead of the USAF in this respect, since its main HARM carriers are standard F/A-18 Hornets and A-7 Corsair IIs, the types which gave the weapon its combat début during operations against Libya in April 1986.

In August 1986 the US Navy began to fit HARM to its EA-6B Prowler EW aircraft. The EA-6B has proved an effective HARM carrier. The effectiveness of any add-on ARM installation can be enhanced by linking the missile seeker to the aircraft's ESM system, so that high-priority threats which it detects may be automatically assigned to the ARMs. Prowler's on-board ESM system is well-suited to this task. The unique mixture of hard- and soft-kill capability offered by the aircraft was summed up by one pilot following the April 1986 US attack on targets in Libya. "As soon as they come on, you squirt 'em, with electrons or with missiles", he told a US reporter. The USN also plans to fit HARM to the A-6E. Wind tunnel testing required to clear HARM for use on the F-14 Tomcat was completed in the summer of 1988.

When first deployed in Europe with the 52nd TFW, the F-4G Wild Weasel served with dedicated anti-radar squadrons. However, a 1981 reorganisation saw the force restructured into mixed "hunter/killer" formations in which the APR-38 equipped F-4Gs, intended to locate enemy radars, would rely on the accompanying F-4E fighter-bombers to help with the task of destroying them.

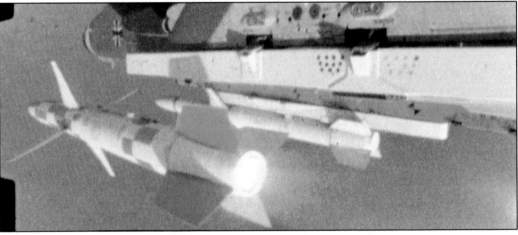

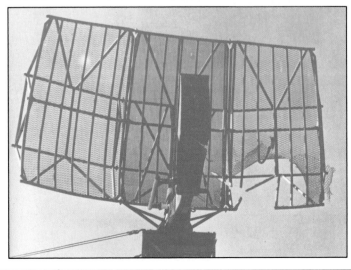

Top: F-16s now fly alongside Wild Weasel F-4Gs during USAF anti-radar operations, flying as "hunter-killer" teams. The GD fighter will soon be able to carry and fire HARM as well as Shrike.

Above: HARM ignites its rocket motor after a trials release from a West German Tornado. Further export orders for this defence suppression missile are anticipated.

Left: During a 1980 flight test at China Lake in the USA, an unarmed HARM round gouged this hole through the target antenna.

that the weapon will in some tactical circumstances have to get from the launch aircraft to a ground based SAM-guidance radar faster than a SAM can complete its trip from the launch rail to the aircraft.

In the late 1980s, the company was known to be working on a light ARM known as STAR (Supersonic Tactical Anti-Radar) missile, Weighing less than 550lb (250kg) and powered by a *Matra/Onera Rustique* ramjet, it would have cruised at Mach 2 +. This project has now given way to a lightweight air-breathing weapon which the company simply describes as an advanced anti-radiation missile.

Despite years of stop-go development work, progress with anti-radiation and decoy RPVs has been slow. Israel is the only nation with decoy RPVs in service, having used them to good effect during its battles against Syrian-manned air defences in the Beka'a valley during the 1982 invasion of Lebanon. No anti-radiation RPV is yet in service but progress with recent designs such as "Tacit Rainbow" is described later in one of this books colour artworks.

In 1987 the USAF's 52nd TFW began to replace these F-4Es with the new Block 30 version of the F-16. These new-build aircraft incorporated what the USAF described as "improved electronic guidance and weapons delivery systems". They arrived in Europe equipped to carry the AGM-45 Shrike ARM but General Dynamics hinted at a possible later installation of the AGM-88 HARM.

OTHER SYSTEMS

Under the USAF's "Seek Eagle" programme intended to gather data on the compatibility of various inventory weapons with current aircraft, the F-16 flew with HARMs in the autumn of 1988. Some F-16Cs are now fitted with facilities for HARM, including a data link which will allow them to accept threat data from F-4G Wild Weasels during "hunter/killer" operations.

Other nations are expected to order HARM. Australia is expected to place an initial

Right: **Decked out in a high-visibility paint scheme, Northrop's Tacit Rainbow anti-radar drone flies over a US test range.**

order for between 80 and 90 missiles, having completed carriage and separation trials on the F-111C in January 1988. Spain will install HARM on its F-18s.

Lightweight self-protection ARMs are another relatively new development. Weapons of this type would be carried in addition to a strike aircraft's normal armament. First to be announced was the British Aerospace ALARM, a weapon whose parachute-borne target search and near-vertical attack profiles remain unique. Problems with the original design of the rocket motor

delayed flight trials until the end of 1986. A new powerplant has now been developed, by the West German company Bayern Chemie, but the missile is unlikely to enter service before 1990. It will arm the Eurofighter EFA when this aircraft enters RAF service in the mid-1990s.

Rafale will probably be equipped with a new self-protection ARM currently in the early stages of development at MATRA. The company sees high speed as an essential quality in a weapon of this type, arguing

SRAM

In a nuclear conflict, the task of suppressing enemy air defences can be assigned to a dedicated nuclear missile. The Boeing AGM-69A SRAM was developed to meet the needs laid down in USAF requirement SOR 212 in 1964. This called for a nuclear-armed missile able to suppress all known or projected SAM defences. Some 1,500 rounds were delivered between 1972 and 1975, at a unit cost of $300,000, and deployed at 16 SAC bases.

SRAM was a great success. Flying at speeds of up to

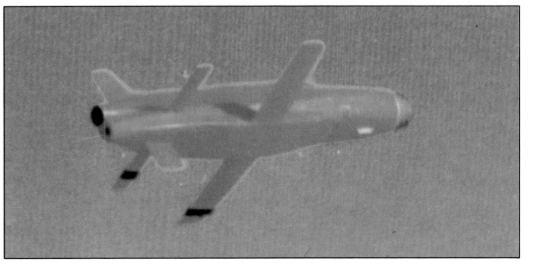

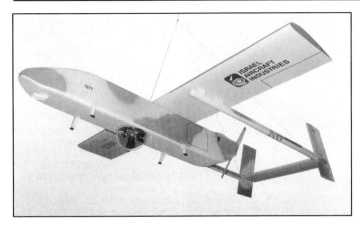

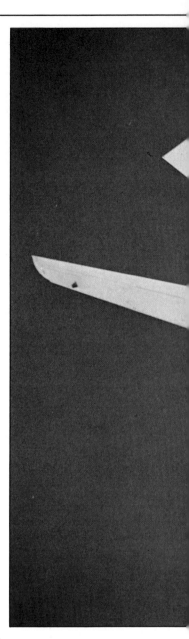

Mach 2.5, it had a maximum range of 34 miles (55km) if released at low level and programmed to follow a flightpath. Released on a ballistic flight at high altitude, it could reach up to 100 miles (160km) from the launch aircraft. By early 1977 more than 70 had been fired, with only two failures (both during launches from B-52s).

SRAM UPGRADES

One valuable feature was a high degree of in-flight agility, allowing the weapon to engage targets on either side of the flight path, or even to the rear of the launch aircraft. Testifying before the Senate Armed Services Committee in March 1977, General Alton D. Slay, USAF Deputy Chief of Staff showed a film of such an attack, describing how "you cross directly over the target and fire the SRAM at the target behind you. It is really moving out there as you can see. The SRAM made a 180 degree turn and it is attacking the target . . . We've found that particular feature to be very, very handy in our bomber force, the ability to fire to the side and rear."

According to Slay, its ability to penetrate defences was "because it is so fast. It is a supersonic missile and has extremely low radar cross-section about (deleted) square

metres, and ALCM is (deleted) times that radar cross-section." RCS of ALCM is known to be less than a tenth of a square metre, so the figure for SRAM is probably around 0.02m².

"There is nothing we know that can shoot it down", he told the committee. "I don't know how to attack SRAM, and I am very familiar with everything we have got, and everything we have got on the drawing board. I can't attack SRAM today . . . if someone gave me free rein on the purse strings and said 'develop a defense against a SRAM', I could probably do it, but I don't know how today."

For the Rockwell bomber, SAC proposed a new variant known as AGM-69B. This was basically the same missile with a new W-80 nuclear warhead plus a new motor with a ten-year shelf life. A buy of 2,014 had been planned, at a unit cost $670,000, but like the B-1A, the project was abandoned.

In the decade which followed, the basic AGM-69A continued to serve with SAC. Despite a motor upgrade programme in the late 1970s which introduced a longer-life motor, the USAF realised that the weapon's rocket motor and electronics were deteriorating in storage, while the now-elderly W-69 nuclear warhead did not meet the latest safety standards. With

the new B-1B entering service and the stealthy B-2 taking shape at Northrop, the USAF decided in 1983 to develop a replacement missile.

System definition studies of what was to become SRAM II began in 1985 and, in December 1985, the USAF ordered Boeing to begin the development task. SRAM II will be about two-thirds the size of the AGM-69A and the B-1B will be able to carry 20 rounds in an internal launcher. A new high-performance Hercules rocket motor and extensive use of composite materials gives the new missile a longer range. Litton is developing the ring-laser gyro inertial guidance system which will give greater accuracy than the AGM-69A guidance package, while the flight-control computer forming part of the guidance system will use very-high-speed integrated circuit (VHSIC) technology.

ACTIVE SKINS

As stealth technology becomes more widespread, Western aircraft will find themselves faced by Soviet stealth fighters and SAM batteries equipped with LPI radars and stealthy missiles. When that time comes, Western stealth designers will be able to look to the avionics industry for new aids to stealth.

In its futuristic forward-looking study "Forecast 2", the USAF predicted that one of the key technologies for tomorrow's aircraft and avionics would be the use of "outer skins containing embedded phased arrays to permit aircraft to sense and communicate in optical and other frequency bands, and in any direction from any

Below: **Like a hungry mosquito in a darkened bedroom, an anti-radar drone can loiter waiting for an opportunity to attack. If no emitters are present, or if the intended victim shuts down, the drone climbs back to cruise height to await a fresh signal on which it may home. An endurance measured in hours keeps radars silent.**

Anti-Radar Drone

Transit to loiter area

Loiters over enemy territory

Target identified

Terminal dive

Launch vehicle

aircraft attitude". The concept was rapidly dubbed "smart skin". These phased arrays would consist of arrays of microscopically tiny active transmitting elements buried within the aircraft skin. Given suitable signal processing, these would work together like the active elements of a phased array antenna.

The most obvious first use of smart skins will be for communications. Radar applications would be expected to follow, but these require increasing levels of power. Addressing an Air Force Association symposium in June 1986, Brigadier General Eric B. Nelson, AFSC Deputy Chief of Staff for Plans and Programs, revealed another potential application of smart skins. Future US warplanes might try to match their apparent radar signature with that of ground clutter. An antenna array on the underside of a low-flying aircraft could be used to sample the ground clutter from the terrain being overflown. "If you can make the topside of the aircraft look like the clutter in a frequency and power sense, then you have done something nearly ideal — you have made an (electronic) chameleon out of your airplane."

It may read like science fiction but science fiction has a habit of becoming science fact. The conformal array radar which Raytheon was contracted to build in the autumn of 1988 is a first step towards developing the technology needed for smart skins, bringing forward the day when these will help to make tomorrow's stealth aircraft vanish amidst the ground clutter.

Above: **The weapons bay of an FB-111 bomber opens to reveal the ultimate defence-suppression weapon — the nuclear-tipped SRAM.**

Below: **Long obsolete, the tiny Quail decoy equipped SAC's B-52 fleet in the 1960s and 1970s. Able to fly as fast as a bomber, this jet-powered** drone carried equipment which boosted its RCS to B-52 proportions, allowing it to mimic the bomber which had released it.

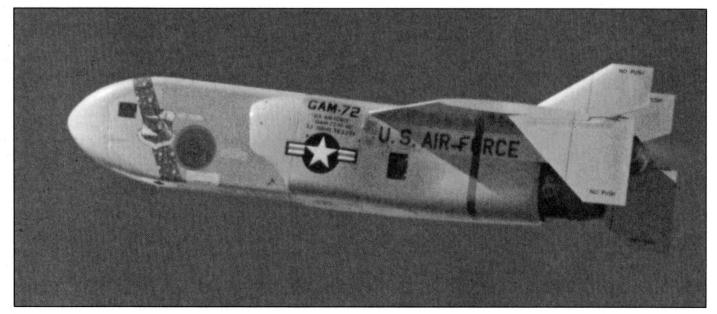

McDONNELL DOUGLAS F-4G PHANTOM

Rôle: ''Wild Weasel'' fighter
Length: 63ft 0in (19.2m)
Height: 16ft 6in (5.03m)
Wingspan: 38ft 5in (11.71m)
Max. take-off weight:
61,795lb (28,030kg)
Max. speed: Mach 2.2
Ceiling: 56,120ft (17,100m)
Max. range: c.2,000nm
(3,700km)
Armament: 16,000lb
(7,250kg) of ordnance
Powerplant: two General
Electric J79-GE-17 turbojets,
each with 11,870lb (5,384kg)
dry thrust, 17,900lb (8,119kg)
with after-burning

For the definitive F-4G, currently the USAF's front-line ''Weasel'', a batch of 116 selected F-4E fighters with long fatigue lives were rebuilt from 1977 onwards at the USAF's Air Logistic Centre at Ogden AFB, Utah. Each aircraft required about 14,000 man-hours of work which lasted for almost four months. Stripped of their 20mm cannon and ammunition drum, these aircraft were fitted with new mission avionics including an advanced radar homing and warning (RHAW) system, plus self-defence systems such as the ALQ-119 or -131 jamming pods and ALE-40 chaff dispenser.

The earlier F-4C Wild Weasel used the ALR-46 to detect and home on to hostile radar but this was replaced in the F-4G by the APR-38, a system based on an IBM superheterodyne receiver. Antennas for this equipment are located in a new glass-fibre chin fairing, which replaced the original fairing used by the M61 cannon, and on the tip of the vertical fin. Incoming signals are detected, analysed and compared with the extensive on-board library of threat signatures contained in the aircraft's Texas Instruments signal processor. The resulting data is presented on a Loral control indicator suite (CIS) whose displays are located in the front and rear cockpits.

Deliveries began in April 1978 with the arrival of the first production F-4G at George AFB, California, and all 116 aircraft had been delivered by the end of 1980.

Conversion cost was around $2.8 million per aircraft. To keep the fleet up to strength, a second batch of 18 low-hour F-4Es was reworked to the F-4G standard, the first being delivered in June 1987.

Like all other US EW aircraft, the F-4G is being upgraded to keep abreast of new threats. By the early 1980s, the USAF had issued contracts for an ambitious Performance Update Program

Left: **Elderly airframes and cancellation of the planned new RHAW receiving system threaten the long-term viability of the F-4G force.**

Below: Despite its age, the F-4G remains the standard equipment of the USAF's Wild Weasel squadrons. Creation of an anti-radar Phantom proved a difficult and demanding task. Engineers tasked with adding the new avionics needed to create this aircraft and the earlier F-4C Wild Weasel discovered that space was at a premium within the Phantom's tightly-packaged fuselage. This artwork shows an F-4G in the current blue/grey camouflage scheme, and equipped with AGM-88 Harm anti-radiation missiles, an ALQ-131 jamming pod and a single IIR-guided AGM-65D Maverick.

(PUP). This was to be carried out in two phases which would run near-concurrently.

Phase I involved upgrading the signal processor from 64K to 256K capacity. This digital computer is a central component of the APR-38 system. It processes the incoming data, interfaces with the guidance systems of the aircraft's anti-radiation missiles (ARMs) and, to a greater or lesser degree (depending on the operational mode being used), controls the other elements of the system.

The new computer is known as the Sperry CP-1674 Weasel Attack Signal Processor (WASP) and has eight times the memory and seven times the speed of the unit it replaces. It can perform more than a million instructions per second.

In its initial form, the APR-38 was somewhat limited in flexibility, with major updates requiring a change of hardware. Software control now makes it completely flexible. More complex tactical situations can now be handled and the time needed to process signals has been reduced, minimising the time for which the F-4G must be exposed to a hostile emitter in order to identify and locate it. Anti-radar ordnance can also be delivered on target more quickly. As new threats continue to emerge, the system software grows in size but the new expanded computer will be able to cope with continued growth.

Work on the WASP started in October 1982 and trials began in 1984. Deliveries of new processors started in the autumn of 1988, with hardware being delivered to the 37th TFW at George AFB, California.

Phase II started in March 1983, when E-Systems was awarded a $31 million contract by McDonnell Douglas for the development of a new Direction Receiver Group of increased frequency range. The award was made following a year's competitive work by E-Systems, Litton Amecom and Bunker-Ramo and was expected to result in eventual production contracts worth more than $200 million.

As work on the latter system progressed, E-Systems found itself faced with demanding environmental and packaging restrictions. The company delivered a prototype receiver in March 1987 but this seemed likely to need a major redesign which would have stretched the programme by two more years. On 23 March 1988, TAC cancelled the contract. The F-4G fleet would continue, fitted with the Sperry WASP processor, but long-term plans would be focussed on a new SEAD aircraft.

Rival airframes competing for the Follow-On Wild Weasel (FOWW) contract are the F-15, F-16, Tornado, the ATF, the A-12 or even a reworked F-4G. Selection of the winning candidate is expected in the autumn of 1989. The new aircraft's EW systems will be the subject of a separate development programme.

GRUMMAN EA-6B PROWLER

Rôle: Electronic warfare platform
Length: 59ft 10in (18.24m)
Wingspan: 53ft (16.15m)
Height: 16ft 3in (4.95m)
Max. take-off weight: 65,000lb (29,484kg)
Max. speed: 533kts (987km/h)
Service ceiling: 41,000ft (12,500m)
Armament: None
Powerplant: (EA-6A) two 8,500lb (3,855kg) Pratt & Whitney J52-P-6A turbojets; (EA-6B) two 11,200lb (5,080kg) Pratt & Whitney J52-P-408 turbojets.

Production deliveries of the EA-6B Prowler started in 1971 and more than 100 have now been delivered, with production continuing at about six per annum. By stretching the basic A-6 Intruder airframe by 54in (137cm), Grumman was able to accommodate an extra two seats, for specialist EW operators, and to pack within the fuselage and on underwing pylons the complex avionic units of the ALQ-99 jamming suite.

Designed for stand-off or escort jamming missions, this complex installation was created by an industrial team headed by AIL and including AEL and IBM. The ALQ-99 is packaged in five external pods each containing two transmitters, a receiver and the associated antennas for them. Other equipment is located in the fuselage and in a fin-top fairing.

The system can operate in automatic mode, with the operators acting as monitors, or in manual model. Its high-powered jammers are designed to counter the threat posed by Soviet-bloc early-warning, GCI and SAM-guidance radars. Each

of 25 aircraft was delivered, built to the EXpanded CAPability (EXCAP) standard, and able to handle six threat bands. Even this modification was to prove short-lived. By July 1975 production had standardised on the Improved CAPability (ICAP) model. This covered two additional bands, allowing the system to "take out" threats in bands ranging from C to J. This version also offered better response time and introduced a new multi-format display.

ICAP remained the definitive build standard for a decade before being replaced by the ADVanced CAPability (ADVCAP) version. This introduced a new advanced receiver processor group which required a new antenna array to be fitted beneath the fuselage and an enlarged fin-top fairing. Jamming capability was improved, as were navaids, displays and the self-protection chaff/flare dispensing system. Other changes included an additional stores station under the outer wing.

Unlike the A-6 Intruder on which it is based, Prowler spends most of its time at high altitude. Despite the use of

Above: **The triple-triangle radiation warning logo on the nose of the Prowler is a stark reminder of the high power levels which the aircraft's jamming transmitters can emit.**

Right: **Operating from carrier decks, Prowler has been in action against Libya. It has also flown sorties over the Gulf, using its EW systems to locate Iranian Silkworm batteries.**

transmitter has an output of about 2kW and can generate spot, dual-spot, swept-over or noise jamming signals.

Given the rapidly-evolving nature of the EW threat, equipment must be regularly upgraded in order to maintain its effectiveness. Few programmes illustrate the "cat and mouse" game of EW so vividly as Prowler. In its basic form, the ALQ-99 system was designed to cope with three threat bands but only the first 23 production aircraft were equipped to this standard. In 1973 the first of a new series

Above: The US Navy's costly fleet of EA-6B Prowler EW aircraft will not become obsolete when the stealthy A-12 Advanced Tactical Aircraft enters service.

Designed to screen today's Intruders and Hornets from enemy radar, Prowler will be even more effective at concealing stealthy attack aircraft. Since less

power will be needed to guard a low-RCS target, the aircraft will be able to simultaneously spread its jamming power over a much greater number of threat emitters.

uprated engines in the Prowler, the drag created by its underwing pods and fin-top fairing create some performance penalties. Maximum level speed falls to 533kts (987km/h), while 6,300ft (1,900m) is carved off the service ceiling. More disturbing for the aircrew who fly the type is the increased stalling speed. Typical EA-6B operating weight is between 10,000 and 15,000lb (4,500 and 6,800kg) greater than that of the A-6E, eroding its stall manoeuvring margins. Since first entering service in 1971, the EA-6 has had a higher accident rate than the basic A-6 Intruder.

Under the Vehicle Improvement Program (VIP), the US Navy, Grumman and NASA have investigated several modifications which might improve Prowler's aerodynamic performance. Some effort was put into wind tunnel testing a scheme which would have allowed partial extension of the wing-edge slats during manoeuvres but this was soon rejected. It would have involved expensive reworking of the wing and slat tracks; even then slat deployment would have been limited to speeds of less than 250kts (460km/h).

Engineers have now devised an alternative scheme in which the leading edges of the outer and inner wing are given a slight droop and the mid-span leading-edge slat and full-span trailing edge flaps are recontoured. These changes increased lift by between 25 and 30 per cent in cruising flight but affected directional stability. The latter problem was remedied by fitting an 18in (46cm) extension to the vertical fin above the fin-top fairing and adding small strakes ahead of the leading edge of the wing roots.

Another modification programme will give the aircraft more thrust. In 1987 Pratt & Whitney was given a contract to develop the PW1212 engine, a 12,000lb (5,440kg) thrust derivative of the J52. The revised engine will have the US military designation J52-P-409 and will be created by modifying the existing powerplants, adding new components where necessary, such as an improved LP turbine, a HP turbine based on that of the commercial JT8D-219 and a redesigned 12th stage for the compressor. Performance goals for the uprated engine include the extra 800lb (360kg) of thrust and a 20 per cent improvement in engine acceleration. The latter feature will improve single-engine rate of climb and be useful when flying late "wave-offs" (overshoots ordered by deck-landing control officer) or "bolters" (aircraft which fail to engage arrester gear and overshoot) on aircraft carriers. First flight of an EA-6B fitted with the uprated engine and aerodynamic modifications is due to take place in late 1989.

CRUISE AND ATTACK RPVs

Low radar cross-section was always seen as an important quality in US cruise missiles. The Boeing ALCM and General Dynamics Tomahawk were designed to have an RCS of around 0.05m², about one hundredth of that of a jet fighter, and less than a thousandth of that of a B-52 bomber. The need to reduce RCS yet further was always appreciated. The AGM-68B ALCM-B which currently arms the B-52 and B-1B force was given a reprofiled nose, intended to minimise RCS, and a more streamlined tail section which would reduce the radar and IR signature.

Boeing studied other methods of reducing the RCS, such as using more carbon fibre and other composite materials in the airframe. The longer-ranged ALCM-C planned in the early 1980s could well have incorporated a further degree of RCS-reduction but it was cancelled in favour of the all-new and stealthy General Dynamics AGM-129 Advanced Cruise Missile (ACM).

Like other US stealth programmes, the ACM is highly classified; no photos or drawings of hardware were released until the spring of 1989. ACM differs from ALCM in one important respect. The current Boeing missile has a fuselage of triangular cross-section, and has pop-out wings, features intended to allow it to be carried on a rotary launcher within the parent aircraft's weapons bay. Designing for stealth imposes its own constraints on airframe shape, so engineers were not so free to design for minimum stowed bulk. Early reports even suggested that ACM's wings might be fixed, rather than folding.

In practice ACM does have folding aerodynamic surfaces, but despite this it cannot be carried on the existing rotary launcher, so a new pattern of external carriage has been developed for the weapon. Although ACM is scheduled to enter service on the B-52, in the longer term it will be the main cruise missile armament of the Rockwell B-1. Wind tunnel testing of the new external carriages has shown that drag is well above the predicted value. Much design work remains to be done on these units but, by early 1989, the US General Accounting Office was warning that the extra drag could cut up to 640 nm (1,185km) from the Rockwell bomber's planned 4,684nm

(8,675km) mission range specified for the ACM-carrier rôle.

Some current models of RPVs show evidence of stealth technology; one of these — Teledyne's Model 324 — has been used as the basis for the stealth cruise missile artwork at the centre of this page. Developed for Egypt and flight tested in 1987, the Model 324 inherited many characteristics of the earlier AQM-91A Compass Arrow reconnaissance drone, such as a flat underside, dorsal engine installation and composite construction. Our hypothetical cruise missile uses the same basic configuration but adds cropped wings and inward-canted tailfins. The air-launched Teledyne Model 350 uses a similar airframe to that of the 324 but uses lateral intakes. It was developed as a possible solution to the US Joint-Service Common Airframe Multipurpose System (JSCAMPS) requirement for a stealth stand-off weapon.

Two models of advanced cruise missile are being planned for Air Force and Navy use starting in the late 1990s or early 2000s. The USAF weapon is the Long-Range Conventional Cruise Missile (LRCCM), while the USN missile is designated Advanced Sea-Launched Cruise Missile (ASLCM). Both would carry conventional warheads and be used against land targets. Congress has suggested that the two efforts be pooled.

Both services are emphasising long range and high accuracy, requirements which could lead to the use of advanced turbofan or propfan engines, plus laser radar and/or imaging infra-red guidance. The USAF has specified a miss distance of only 3ft (0.9m). Stealth is also an Air Force goal and is probably a Navy one also.

Left: Northrop's AGM-136A Tacit Rainbow (seen here in high-visibility trials markings) was one of the first US "black" programmes to be unveiled. After release from aircraft such as the B-52, this jet-powered anti-radar drone will fly for over 80 minutes. The airframe is largely plastic.

Above: This curious Lockheed concept dates from the mid-1980s, and shows a low-RCS cruise missile. Armed with sideways-firing sub-munition dispensers, it could be used to attack high-value area targets such as airfields or armoured formations.

An unexplained feature of the design is the presence of wing-mounted Sidewinder missiles. A possible air-combat role must have been envisaged.

Above: Creating a long-range ballistic missile is a formidable challenge to any aerospace industry, so a stealthy cruise missile might be an easier basis for future Third-World nuclear forces. This hypothetical design uses several design concepts drawn from Teledyne's Model 324 RPV, a reconnaissance system developed for Egypt. Declassification of the USAF's AGM-129 Advanced Cruise Missile (ACM) came too late for this General Dynamics weapon to feature in our artwork, but a photo on page 78 illustrates its general configuration.

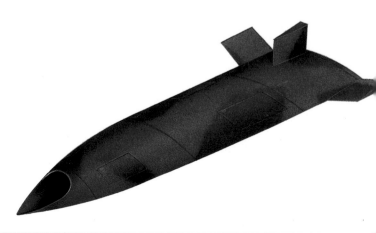

Eight US companies have carried out preliminary studies for the USN and at least four are expected to be given two-year research contracts in 1989.

One method of reducing the RCS of future cruise missiles may be to move to higher speeds which would allow the missile to be made as a wingless lifting body. At the 1987 Paris Air Show, the French government pavilion displayed a model of a *Configuration Avancée pour Missile à Stratoréacteur*. Intended for flight at hypersonic speeds, this had a shallow elliptical cross-section and inlets tucked well in below the body. If built and flown, it would probably be a difficult radar target and could form the basis for a future stealthy cruise missile. In the early 1980s Northrop used a similar configuration (but with a single nose inlet) for its proposed ND-10 stealthy sub-munition carrier. Carried inverted as a conformal store beneath the fuselage of its parent aircraft, this would have rolled through 180 degrees after release, before starting its jet engine and heading for the target area.

Ground attack using sub-munitions was also the goal of a stealthy canard cruise missile proposed by Lockheed in the mid-1980s. Looking rather like a cross between the Boeing ALCM and the Saab-Scania JAS-39 Gripen aircraft, this probably relied on small size and composite construction to minimise its radar signature.

Reduced RCS will be a feature of many future tactical air-to-surface missiles. At the 1988 Farnborough Air Show, Matra announced that its Apache stand-off missile had entered full-scale development and incorporated some "improvements in stealthiness", while RCS-reduction is also a feature of the planned NATO collaborative MSOW (Medium-range Stand-Off Weapon) being studied in the late 1980s by two international industrial teams.

Above: Like the surface/ship launched General Dynamics Tomahawk, Boeing's AGM-86 Air Launched Cruise Missile (ALCM) was designed with low RCS in mind, and even the original ALCM-A test model proved a difficult air target. The sculpted nose profile seen on this ALCM-B production round was a late modification made during development testing. It was done to reduce ALCM-B's radar signature, a move intended to counter improvements to the Soviet air defence system. Production was cut back in favour of the stealthier AGM-129 ACM.

Below: Attempts by Boeing to develop this piston-engined anti-radar RPV have suffered from "stop/go" orders by the US Congress. The weapon was flight-tested in 1984, then abandoned. In 1987 Congress ordered that the project be revived as the YGM-121B Seek Spinner, but work was suspended in 1988. Now known as Brave 200, it is seen as a ground-launched Tacit Rainbow equivalent.

Left: In the early 1980s, this little-known Northrop proposal for the ND-10 air-launched stealthy submunition carrier gave the world an unclassified glimpse of US stealth technology. Although an artwork showing the weapon and its post-release rollover manoeuvre was featured on the cover of a US aerospace magazine, it attracted surprisingly little attention from aviation journalists attempting to learn more about "black" programs.

Right: When France displayed this model of a "Configuration Avancee pour Missile a Stratoreacteur" at the 1987 Paris Air Show, it was trying to illustrate the technology needed for hypersonic flight. The chosen configuration — a wingless lifting body with inlets similar to those first proposed for the Rafale fighter — also promises a low RCS. Could this be a possible shape for the successor to today's ASMP supersonic cruise missile?

GENERAL DYNAMICS/GRUMMAN EF-111A RAVEN

Rôle: electronic warfare aircraft
Length: 76ft 0in (23.16m)
Height: 20ft 0in (6.10m)
Wingspan: 31ft 11in (9.73m) swept, 63ft 0in (19.2m) unswept
Max. take-off weight: 88,948lb (40,347kg)
Max. speed: 1,227kts (2,272km/h)
Ceiling: 45,000ft (13,700m)
Tactical radius: 807nm (1,495km) in the escort rôle
Armament: none
Powerplant: two Pratt & Whitney TF30-P-3 turbofans, each of 18,500lb (8,390kg) with after-burning

When the USAF decided in the late 1960s to develop a new dedicated electronic-warfare aircraft to replace the obsolescent Douglas EB-66, the simplest solution would have been to swallow its pride and purchase the US Navy's EA-6B Prowler. For two years, such a scheme was considered but studies concluded that the Grumman aircraft lacked the performance and endurance needed for stand-off and escort jamming operations on the NATO central front.

Although the air vehicle was found wanting, there was nothing wrong with Prowler's sophisticated and complex ALQ-99 EW system. The obvious high-performance platform for EW duties in the 1980s was the F-111A strike aircraft but the problem of squeezing the ALQ-99 into the General Dynamics aircraft was to pose problems. A 1974 study contract was assigned not to GD but to Grumman. The Long Island company not only had first-hand knowledge of the ALQ-99 but was already familiar with the F-111 as a result of the abortive US Navy F-111B programme.

In its basic form, the ALQ-99 needed three operators, a situation which had forced Grumman to stretch the Intruder fuselage to make room for two more crew members. In theory, a larger four-man cockpit could be squeezed into the F-111A but only by redesigning the entire forward fuselage or by reducing internal fuel capacity. Luckily for the USAF, experience with the ALQ-99 ICAP (Interim Capability) model showed that it would be feasible to devise a version of the system which was automated to a degree which would allow it to be controlled by one man.

In January 1975 Grumman was awarded a contract to convert two F-111As as prototypes for the EF-111A Tactical Jamming System (TJS) configuration. The first flew on 10 March 1977. Operational testing identified a number of problems with the modified EW system (designated ALQ-99E) but these were corrected in time to allow a programme involving the rework of 42 aircraft to be agreed in November 1979.

Between 1980 and 1985, the ex-USAF aircraft were stripped down and then rebuilt with the addition of some new components to a build standard with a fatigue life of about 8,000 hours. They retain the existing engines and their troublesome inlet system.

The aircraft retains its nose-mounted APQ-110 terrain following radar and APQ-160 navigation radar but the cockpit is reworked for the new rôle. The pilot's station on the port side has only minor alterations, posing no problems to an experienced F-111A "driver", but the right-hand station for the EW operator takes the cockpit a decade ahead in avionics technology and into the world of digital displays.

A rebuild of the lower fuselage and weapons bay created a new avionics bay and a large ventral "canoe" fairing, while the fin top acquired a Prowler-style fairing. These changes provided the space needed for the ALQ-99 EW system, an ALQ-137 CW deception jammer, for self-protection, and two environmental-control systems able to deal with the heat produced by the EW equipment.

The system is thought to cover frequencies from VHF to J-band. These are divided into eight bands designated 1, 2, 4, 5, 6, 7, 8 and 9. Output power is sufficient to be effective at ranges of up to 124nm (230km). According to Grumman, five EF-111As can

Right: In the late 1970s and early 1980s, Grumman rebuilt a batch of obsolescent F-111A strike aircraft as EF-111A Raven electronic-warfare platforms. Deployed with the USAF, the aircraft carries an eight-band ALQ-99E jamming suite, a highly-automated derivative of the system fitted to the US Navy's Grumman EA-6B Prowler aircraft.

Above: **Technologies old and new share the EF-111A cockpit. The pilot's displays (nearest the camera) are largely 1960s-vintage** **analogue systems inherited from the F-111, but the EW operator is equipped with the latest in digital technology and CRT displays.**

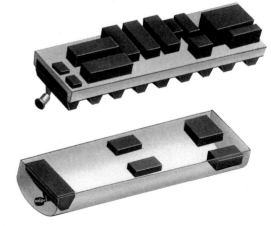

Above: The rebuild to EF-111A standard added a long ventral "canoe" fairing under the centre fuselage. Mounted above this in what had been the weapons bay is a 4,300lb (1,940kg) electronics pallet which houses the exciters, transmitters, computer, and other main units of the ALQ-99E system. The sides of the "canoe" form a large radome, through which the antennas can direct their energy.

Above: The Canadair-built fintop fairing weighs around 950lb (430kg) and is largely devoted to ALQ-99E antennas. Those in the front radome cover the forward sector. Aft of these is a row of vertically-mounted receivers, then side-facing antennas which provide port and starboard coverage. Other antennas face aft.

maintain stand-off jamming coverage of a strip of terrain running across central Europe from the Baltic right down to the Adriatic.

Approval of full-scale production was given in 1979. The first aircraft (a rebuilt prototype) was delivered to the USAF in 1981 and aircraft were deployed to Western Europe in 1984. The final example was delivered in December 1985.

RFPs (requests for procurement) for the upgrading of the EF-111A were issued in January 1984, their purpose being to cope with "fast-moving technology and the rapid upgrading of many foreign air defences". It was planned that the aircraft's internally-mounted ALQ-99E

would be improved, particularly in hardware areas such as the encoder, processor and exciter. At first it was hoped that modification kits could be devised so that the aircraft could be modified by USAF Logistics Command personnel during routine dépôt maintenance but this seems to have been shelved in favour of factory-assembled improved jammers.

On 3 October 1984, Eaton AIL and General Dynamics were given a $961 million contract to develop the improved jamming equipment and to deliver the first three production units of the upgraded ALQ-99. The first should have been delivered to GD in September 1987 for installation in an EF-111A but

the target date came and went. Cost overruns and schedule slippages escalated and by the early summer of 1988 USAF Systems Command realised that the programme would swallow a further $970 million if continued to completion and that some two and half more years of work would be needed. The USAF issued a stop-work order on 20 May 1988 and cancelled the contract on 3 June.

Given that the aircraft still needed upgrading, the USAF began a study of alternative schemes. Grumman is now working on a scheme known as the EF-111A Avionics Modernization Program (AMP). One possibility being investigated involves fitting

the new receiver/processor developed for the US Navy's EA-6B into the USAF aircraft, a move which would provide the threat-identification facilities needed by the Air Force in the mid 1990s.

Several potential modifications have been reported. The deployment of AGM-88 HARM missiles on the US Navy's EA-6B Prowlers in August 1986 raised speculation that the USAF might fit the weapon to the EF-111A, while other sources have suggested that the aircraft will probably be retrofitted with a low-band radar and communications jammer during the early 1990s. The aircraft could remain in front-line service until the year 2010.

STEALTH IN ACTION

The West has traditionally faced the problem of trying to match Warsaw Pact quantity with NATO quality, relying on Western technology to reduce the gap between the size of its forces with that of the Soviet war machine. During the late 1970s and early 1980s, improvements in Soviet technology eroded this differential, causing President Reagan to launch a new doctrine called "competitive strategies" in the mid-1980s. A key feature of this will be stealth technology.

At first sight, the effects of reducing RCS do not seem particularly valuable. By inserting diminishing values of RCS into the radar range equation — a mathematical formula which defines the basic relationship between the various parameters of a radar and its range performance — it becomes obvious that a halving of RCS does not result in a halving of target detection range. Range varies with the fourth root of RCS, so halving the RCS reduces range by only 16 per cent to 0.84.

It has been reported that the Folland Gnat lightweight fighter of the late 1950s could only be detected by radar when closer than the larger Hawker Hunter, but the difference is unlikely to have been significant. The smooth lines of the Avro (later Hawker Siddeley) Vulcan bomber are also said to have made this aircraft a difficult radar target although it probably did not translate into any great military advantage.

A key factor in determining the degradation in range is the figure obtained by dividing the reduced RCS by the original figure. To determine the reduction in radar range, the result must be raised to the power of 0.25:

reduced radar range =

$$\left(\frac{\text{reduced RCS}}{\text{original RCS}}\right)^{0.25}$$

Assume that an aircraft has a RCS of 100m² — a value probably typical for a head-on B-52. Reducing RCS by 50 per

Physical Size Compared to RCS

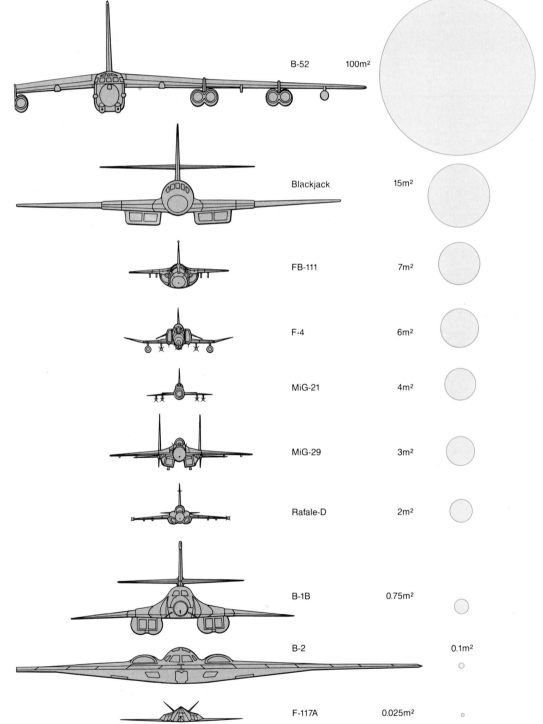

B-52	100m²
Blackjack	15m²
FB-111	7m²
F-4	6m²
MiG-21	4m²
MiG-29	3m²
Rafale-D	2m²
B-1B	0.75m²
B-2	0.1m²
F-117A	0.025m²

Above: Thanks to stealth technology, the RCS of an aircraft is no longer proportional to aircraft size. In this diagram, the aircraft are drawn to a constant scale, but RCS steadily reduces from that of the B-52 and Blackjack to that of the B-2 and F-117A stealth aircraft.

Right: A stealth aircraft may not be detected until it comes within the relatively long minimum range of this Soviet SA-5 Gammon SAM.

cent reduces radar range to:

$$\left(\frac{\text{reduced RCS}}{\text{original RCS}}\right)^{0.25} = 0.5^{0.25} = 0.84$$

The B-1A is known to have an RCS one-tenth of that of the B-52, so the range resulting from this improvement is reduced to:
$$(1/10)^{0.25} = 0.56$$
A radar tracking a B-1A instead of a B-52 would thus have its range reduced by 44 per cent. If it could just detect a B-52 at a range of 100 miles (kilometres), it could only track a B-1A at 56 miles (km). Substitute a B-1B (which has a RCS a tenth of that of the B-1A and one hundredth of that of the B-52), and the range is reduced to:
$$(1/100)^{0.25} = 0.32$$
Radar range is thus reduced to 32 per cent. Reduce RCS by a further factor of ten by substituting an Advanced Tactical Fighter, and the range is reduced to 18 per cent. Reducing even this small RCS by a further factor of 10 will give a value close to that of the F-117A stealth fighter, reducing radar range to around 10 per cent of the original value.

Figures similar to the above have been widely published as being typical of the effects of reducing RCS. Reducing radar range by 45 or even 70 per cent by a ten or one hundredfold reduction in RCS gives a valuable bonus to the attacker, forcing the defender to double or even triple the number of surveillance radars needed to guard a long border, but hardly constitutes "radar-invisibility".

In his 1985 book *Radar Cross Section Lectures*, Professor Allen B. Fuhs pointed out that the degradation in real-life military situations may be

Above: **Production B-2 bombers will look just like this prototype — the rules of stealth leave little freedom for modifications.**

Below: **Reductions in target RCS have a marked effect on radar range, particularly when against radars using area and volume search modes.**

Radar Range and Reduced RCS

RCS	Reduced radar range		
	Tracking	Area search	Volume search
0.1	0.56	0.32	0.18
0.01	0.32	0.1	0.03
0.001	0.18	0.03	0.006
0.0001	0.1	0.01	0.001

much greater. For a tracking radar, the figures given above do apply, but in order for a target to be tracked it must first be acquired.

SEARCH RADAR

A ground-based or naval search radar tasked with locating an incoming target uses a moving radar beam to search a selected area in a time defined by the antenna scanning rate. According to Fuhs, the degradation in range resulting from reduced RCS is more secure than for a tracking radar and is given by:

$$\text{reduced range} = \left(\frac{\text{reduced RCS}}{\text{original RCS}}\right)^{0.5}$$

A reduction of RCS by a factor of 10 will cut detection range to 0.32, whereas reduction by factors of 100 and 1000 will give detection ranges of a mere 0.10 and 0.03 of the original range respectively.

A radar mounted on an aircraft has an even more difficult task, being required to search a volume of airspace in a given time. The formula for degradation now becomes:

$$\text{reduced range} = \left(\frac{\text{reduced RCS}}{\text{original RCS}}\right)^{0.75}$$

Reducing the RCS is now even more effective. Reduction factors of 10, 100 and 1000 now give range reductions to 0.18, 0.03 and 0.006 respectively.

MISSILE RADAR

Reduced RCS also makes the problem of detecting a low-flying target more difficult, since the latter is more readily hidden in ground clutter. In October 1977 Dr William J. Perry, then US Under Secretary of Defense for Research and Engineering described the improvements which Soviet radar engineers would have to make in order to intercept US cruise missiles. He told reporters that during a recent successful Soviet live-warhead look-down/shoot-down trial using the radar and missiles being developed for the MiG-31 Foxhound, the supposedly cruise missile target drone used "was about the size of the US T-33 training aircraft".

RCS reduction will also blunt the effectiveness of SAM systems. Look up the performance of any anti-aircraft missile in a reference

book, or even the manufacturer's brochure, and a maximum range figure will inevitably be quoted. Much more difficult to find is the missile's minimum range. Immediately after leaving the launch rail, a round is not fully under the control of its guidance system but must be brought on to the desired trajectory. This is particularly true in the case of SAMs, where the round will take an appreciable time to reach full flying speed. On some boost-slide weapons, the control fins are locked until the rocket motor has burned out, only then does the weapon begin to guide.

For the sake of argument, let us invent a hypothetical "Missile X", a medium-range SAM with a maximum range of 25 miles (40km) and a minimum range of around 5 per cent of maximum — 1.25 miles (2km). In designing the range of the acquisition radar used to locate a target, the designer will have to allow some performance in hand, so as to ensure that by the time the target is within range, it shall have been designated for attack and the missile launcher will have slewed on to the correct bearing and be prepared for firing. The longer the range of the surveillance radar, the larger, heavier and costlier it will be, so the designer is not free to set any maximum range specification he likes. Let us assume that the radar is designed to detect a typical target at three times the maximum range of the missile — 75 miles (120km).

JAMMING

If the enemy introduces stealth technology and reduces the RCS of a target by a factor of 100 (the sort of improvement which the B-1B shows over the B-52), then the maximum range of the acquisition radar falls — according to the equations given by Fuhs — to only a tenth of its design value. Instead of detecting the target at 75 miles (120km) range, the radar associated with "Missile X" will not achieve detection until 7.5 miles (12km).

By the time that the target is first detected, it will be well within the missile's lethal envelope. Most of the weapon's 25 mile (40km) range will have been wasted and the newly-detected target will be already less than six miles (9km) from the system's minimum range.

Like ground clutter, the radar noise created by chaff

Typical Missile Ranges

Missile	Max range (km)	Min range (km)	Min as % of Max (%)
Crotale	8.5	·0.5	5.9
Roland	6.3	0.5	7.9
Rapier	7	0.5	7.1
Sea Sparrow	18	1	5.6
SA-6 Gainful	35	4	11.4
SA-5 Gammon	250	80	32
R-550 Magic	10+	0.3	2
AIM-7F Sparrow	50-100	0.6	0.6-1.2

Below: **Designers of air defence systems aim to create a network of overlapping radar fields of coverage, ensuring that all enemy aircraft will be illuminated and detected, eventually coming within the lethal radius of SAM systems or other weapons.**

Above: **SAMs and air-to-air missiles have maximum and minimum ranges. Targets must be between these limits.**

Right: **Most current interceptors, such as the MiG-31 Foxhound, are totally dependent on powerful radar for target detection.**

Defences against Non-Stealthy Aircraft

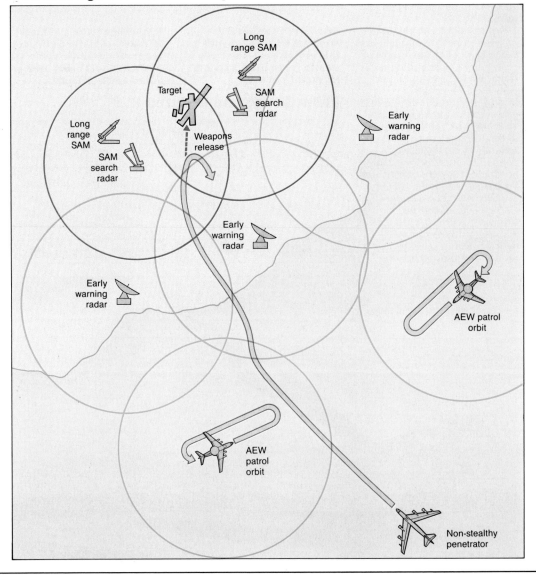

or radar jamming will also help to mask the low-RCS target. Reducing the aircraft's RCS also helps in the EW battle. It can reduce the amount of jamming power needed, allowing designers of jamming equipment to either reduce volume, weight and power consumption of their systems or even to use new jamming techniques made practicable by the stealth aircraft's relative radar invisibility.

The small radar "size" of a stealth aircraft also makes it easier to shelter behind the protection of a stand-off jamming aircraft. The powerful signal from an aircraft such as the EF-111A

Below: **Reducing radar detection range by a factor of around two-thirds makes the hypothetical defences shown on the opposite page near-useless. The attacker can pick his way between the radars, releasing weapons outside of the defensive SAM's reduced lethal radius.**

was designed to mask a conventional fighter. It will be even more effective when screening the tiny radar target presented by a typical stealth aircraft.

Such then, is the theory of how stealth will affect the air defences pitted against it. In practice, these theoretical performance gains must be translated into the operating tactics for future air combat, they will also make possible new operational rôles and force the development of new hardware able to allow stealth aircraft to operate to the limits of their potential.

F-117 IN ACTION

The first stealth aircraft to enter US service was the Lockheed F-117A. Although widely referred to as "the stealth fighter", it could more accurately be described as a stealth fighter-bomber. Its primary missions are reconnaissance and ground attack operations.

Over Warsaw Pact territory, the F-117A would probably fly at relatively low altitude, probably around 5,000ft (1,500m). Unlike conventional strike aircraft, which must make use of the concealment offered by ground clutter and terrain masking for survival, the F-117A will be able to rely on its low RCS for protection. It will thus be able to cruise at the heights best suited to both the location of tactical targets and the delivery of ordnance.

In areas of high threat, the F-117A will probably descend to lower altitude in order to take advantage of ground clutter and to reduce its exposure to anti-aircraft systems. What it is unlikely to be able to do is to fly a terrain-following attack. It has no terrain-following radar (TFR). Indeed, the tell-tale radar signals from such a system would deprive the aircraft of its radar invisibility. Using a ground-based ESM system to observe an approaching TFR-equipped strike aircraft has been described as like watching the sun rise!

The main hostile systems attempting to locate the aircraft would be microwave radars, equipments operating at the very frequencies which stealth technology is intended to counter. Radar and missile sites would have greatly-reduced coverage, as would the Ilyushin Mainstay and Antonov Madcap early-warning aircraft.

Extensive flight testing in Nevada has pitted the F-117A against US radars, missile

Defences against Stealth Aircraft

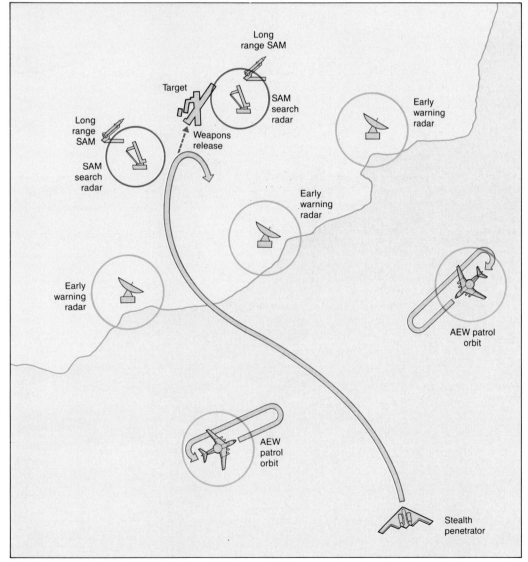

systems and fighters, also against captured or otherwise "acquired" Soviet systems and US simulations of latest-generation Soviet equipment. Reports of deployments to the UK and other locations outside the USA are at least in part the result of reported test flights which have taken the aircraft close to the Soviet frontier to assess its capability against the real thing. According to a November 1988 report in the magazine *US News & World Report,* such tests have been conducted from "at least one isolated air base near the Soviet Union".

Enemy installations singled out for F-117A attack would probably include tactical nuclear missiles, runways and hardened shelters used by nuclear-capable strike aircraft, major command posts, communications centres, bunkers used to store nuclear or chemical weapons, essential logistical targets such as repair and maintenance facilities and large or otherwise troublesome SAM sites.

In many ways, the F-117A will be an ideal SAM hunter.

Above: Electro-optically guided weapons such as this SLAM air-to-ground version of the Harpoon anti-ship missile emit no signal which might betray their approach.

Right: The successful US air strikes against Libya in 1986 required a large force of A-6E Intruders and USAF F-111s. Supporters of stealth claim that a smaller number of F-117A fighters could have done the job equally well. Early studies of the mission did consider using the Lockheed aircraft.

Stealth on the Battlefield

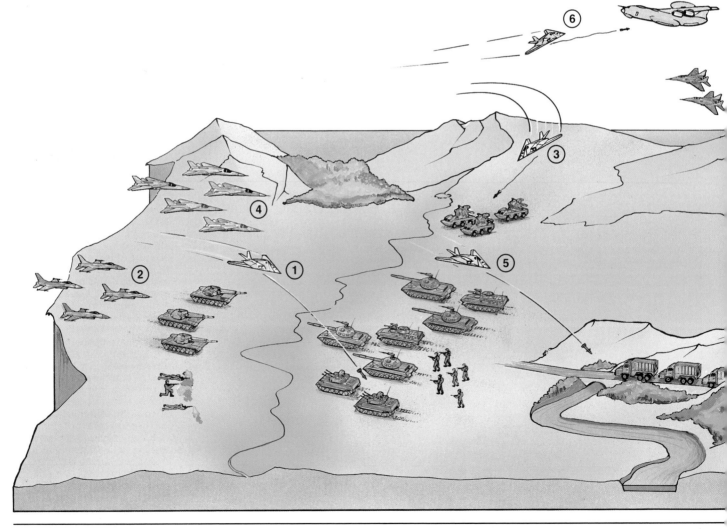

Since all it needs to do to detect a SAM site is to listen on its ESM equipment for the powerful signals from the SAM site's radar, it can thereby detect such emissions long before being detected itself. Thanks to its low RCS, it will be able to fly well within the lethal radius of a SAM system before being detected. Allowing a few seconds for reaction time at the SAM site, it may in some cases be getting close to its minimum range by the time that the site is ready to fire. There is little

that can be done to restore the effectiveness of the radars attempting to locate such a stealthy hunter. A stealth aircraft's low RCS prevents the radar from switching to less ESM-interceptable tracking modes, while the use of a higher-powered radar will simply make the site more detectable.

Remove the chemical and nuclear components of the target list mentioned earlier and it starts to read a little like the list of objectives attacked during the 1986 US

air strikes on Libya. The operation, conducted as it was under cover of darkness would have been a near-ideal operational début for the F-117A, a fact which apparently did not escape the attention of those who planned the raid. The desire to maintain high security on what was still a ''black'' programme probably resulted in the Lockheed fighter being rejected for the mission.

B-2 IN ACTION

Like the F-117A, Northrop's B-2 bomber is essentially a medium/high altitude aircraft. If ever launched in anger from its bases in the continental USA, the new bomber would operate much like today's B-52 and B-1B force, refuelling in flight from KC-135 and KC-10 tankers.

First warning that the B-2 force was on its way would come from Soviet high-frequency over-the-horizon radars. These would detect the tankers and any other SAC bombers such as the less stealthy B-1B and the utterly non-stealthy B-52.

Performance against the B-2 would be somewhat lower but, nevertheless, sufficient to warn that the Northrop bombers were on their way. As the SAC formations moved to within the minimum range of the OTH radars, they would slip out of radar coverage.

While still hundreds of miles from the Soviet border, the B-2s would probably be detected by Soviet VHF surveillance radars, sets such as the P-14 Tall King. These would give some idea of the aircraft's location but the resulting data would be much less accurate than would be the case with conventional targets. At shorter ranges, even these radars would lose sight of the big flying wings.

Detecting the intrusion of the B-2 force into Soviet airspace would be difficult. The Soviet strategic air defences were originally designed to cope with the B-52, an aircraft probably detectable by ground-based radar at ranges of up to 300nm (550km). Deployment of the B-1B in the late 1980s has in theory cut the detection range to less than

Left: **Stealth aircraft will be useful not only in their own right, but also as force multipliers able to boost the effectiveness of conventional non-stealthy aircraft. This diagram shows possible tactical and strategic rôles for stealth aircraft.**

At the far left, an F-117A stealth fighter attacks the self-propelled AA guns defending a Warsaw Pact armoured formation (1), clearing the way for a formation of incoming A-16 (F-16 derivative) strike aircraft (2). Another launches anti-radiation missiles at an SA-8 unit (3), knocking out a threat which might counter a wave of F-111 interdictors (4). Other possible tasks for the Lockheed aircraft include destroying vital choke points which would hamper the arrival of second-echelon formations and resupply convoys (5). Another hampers the effectiveness of enemy fighters by downing a Soviet Mainstay AEW aircraft (6) (a tactic predicted by author Tom Clancy in his best-selling novel *Red Storm Rising*).

Strategic rôles for the B-2 include attacking long-range SAM systems (7), mobile ICBMs (8), and fixed high-value targets such as airfields (9) and command facilities (10). Many of these missions will also be carried out by the next generation of stealth aircraft.

100nm (185km). Assuming that the B-2 has a RCS at least as low as a tenth of that of the B-1B, the detection range against this aircraft drops to less than 50nm (90km).

Any system deployed as a replacement for Tall King will have been designed in the late 1970s with the B-1A as a potential target. The B-2 will reduce its range to a third or less of that expected against the B-1A. Even had its designers anticipated targets with a RCS of a lower order of magnitude (i.e. the B-1B) and obtained a full 300nm (550km) detection range against them, the deployment of the B-2 will have negated up to half of such a radar's range performance.

DEFENCES

Given the high cost of long range radars and the sheer size of the Soviet periphery, the Soviets face a massive bill in attempting to deploy a radar network able to detect the B-2. Any new set designed for use against even B-1 targets will be much more expensive than the older and simpler Tall King generation of equipment and many more will be needed to provide full radar coverage.

Much the same logic applies to the fleet of Ilyushin Mainstay AEW aircraft now entering service. Assuming that its designers worked with the B-1B in mind, radar range against a B-2 will be reduced by up to half. Maintaining an

Above: **Wartime targets for the B-2 might include mobile defence systems such as the Soviet Union's advanced SA-12 Gladiator SAM.**

Below: **France's ASMP supersonic cruise missile (seen here on a Mirage 2000N) trades stealth for high penetration speed.**

adequate defence would thus involve a greater number of AEW aircraft flying tighter racetrack patterns.

Even when inside Warsaw Pact airspace, the B-2 is likely to remain at altitudes of 30,000ft (9,000m) or more in order to minimise fuel burn. Cruise heights of this order will also reduce structural loads on the aircraft's composite airframe, prolonging the new bomber's service life.

By the time that radars had found the attackers, it would be too late to scramble interceptors. If the latter were able to detect the stealth aircraft on their near-ineffective radars, this would probably occur only after the US aircraft had already struck their targets.

Targeting information for the B-2 would be obtained by US reconnaissance satellites such as the camera-equipped KH-12 and the Lacrosse imaging-radar spacecraft. For as long as these valuable assets remained operational, they would pass information back to SAC on the latest movements of Soviet mobile ICBMs and the positions of Soviet mobile air-defence missiles such as the SA-10 Growler and SA-12 Gladiator. After analysis, these data would then be relayed to the B-2 fleet via the nuclear-hardened Milstar communications satellite network.

Stealth aircraft will probably operate individually,

Left: **The radar-equipped Mainstay derivative of the Ilyushin Il 76 Candid is the first really effective Soviet AEW aircraft.**

Below: **The first of two AIM-120A AMRAAM rounds lights up during an F-15 "one-versus-two" attack against two target drones.**

Above: **Although costly, the Hughes AIM-120A AMRAAM (seen here on an F-14) will give the USAF and USN a major boost in firepower.**

or at most in small groups. It has even been suggested that B-2 bombers searching for and attempting to destroy mobile ICBMs would have to work singly to avoid the risk of fratricide caused by exploding nuclear weapons.

Once close to their targets, the B-2s are likely to descend to heights of between 10,000 and 15,000ft (3,000 and 4,500m) to give their own infra-red and electro-optical sensors and low-probability of intercept (LPI) radars a better chance of locating and identifying their quarry.

The most heavily defended targets would be attacked using Boeing SRAM 2 missiles. Free-falling bombs would probably be reserved for second strikes, less well-

defended targets and hardened targets such as deep bunkers, the destruction of which would require the more powerful nuclear explosions available from gravity bombs.

AIR-TO-AIR

With the arrival in service in the mid-1990s of the USAF's stealth F-22 or F-23 Advanced Tactical Fighter, the art of air combat will be markedly changed. During the studies which led to today's Western fighter programmes, future air combat conditions were extensively modelled by computer. These studies have shown the effect which developments such as stealth fighters and long-range "fire-

and-forget" missiles will have on the air battles of tomorrow. Under most tactical conditions, the aircraft which first detects the other will win the resulting engagement.

In fighter-versus-fighter combat, stealth can give the side which has it a massive combat advantage. Faced with a non-stealthy opponent, the pilot of a stealth fighter will not be interested in dogfighting. His goal will be to get to within missile firing range, fire his missiles, then turn and escape — while not being detected himself.

Take the case of two fighters approaching one another head-on, both being equipped with radars having a maximum detection range of 50nm (90km). In the best

tradition of war gaming, let us call them Blue and Red. If Blue can detect Red at full radar range, while using stealth technology to deny Red warning that an attack is imminent, then Blue enjoys a time slot during which he can fire his long-range air-to-air missile at an unsuspecting target aircraft.

LONG RANGES

Once the closing distance has come within weapon range, Blue can launch fire-and-forget missiles, such as the Hughes AIM-120A AMRAAM (Advanced Medium Range Air-to-Air Missile) or the Matra MICA (*Missile d'Interception et de Combat Aérien*), and then turn away to avoid being engaged. Missiles of this type fly much of the way to the target under autopilot control with no discernible radar emissions. Approaching head-on, they will give their quarry little or no warning that he has come under attack. By the time that Red had detected either the missiles or the other fighter, a counter-attack would result in Red missiles attempting a tail-chase engagement of the retreating Blue fighter, a tactical situation unlikely to result in a kill.

In practice, it is not quite as simple as that, of course. Red may not be able to detect Blue by using his own radar but his radar-warning receiver would have no trouble in detecting the signals from Blue's radar, which would betray the aircraft's approach.

To be combat effective, a stealth fighter needs stealth sensors such as the low probability of intercept (LPI) radar or passive sensors described in an earlier chapter 'Aids to Stealth', supplemented perhaps by threat data passed by secure datalink from an AEW aircraft or ground-based radar network. Given an opponent armed with AMRAAM/MICA type missiles, even a traditional non-stealthy fighter will use active radar with caution.

HELMET SIGHTS

In today's fighters, the radar is often used to cue the missile seeker heads, directing them to the target prior to launch. This is a proven technique but, if used at long range or by a stealth fighter, it will warn an ESM-equipped enemy that an attack is under way. For stealth aircraft, a better solution using no active radiation is required.

At short ranges, there are several passive methods of cueing a missile. Many types of short-range IR-guided missile have a seeker head able to operate as a target detector, carrying out an autonomous pre-launch search for its victim. A more recent trend involves the use of a helmet sight which can be used to direct the missile seeker in the direction of the pilot's gaze.

Below: **Honeywell's Integrated Night Vision System (INVIS) projects an infra-red image into the eye of each crewman, allowing night combat operations.**

NATO has been woefully slow in teaming air-to-air missiles with helmet sights. At the 1984 Defendory military exhibition in Greece, I was assured by one company that the possibility of linking the European ASRAAM (Advanced Short Range Air-to-Air Missile) to a helmet sight was being considered. My suggestion that the company might find a visit to the nearby Armscor stand to be of interest came as a surprise. While Western Europe was content to study helmet sight-aimed dogfight missiles, the South African company had used the show to unveil its V3/Kukri IR-guided dogfight missile and its associated helmet sight.

I later learned that although the South African missile was operational in 1984, the helmet sight was not. Even so,

the incident left me with a distinct impression that NATO was dragging its heels in this field. South Africa was probably the first Western nation to deploy such a system and its lead has been followed by the Soviet Union, which has fielded a helmet sight on the MiG-29 Fulcrum, and also on the Sukhoi Su-27 Flanker.

ELECTRO-OPTICS

At longer ranges, a more sophisticated solution is needed. One possible solution was first proposed in the 1970s by Dornier. In studies of its proposed Tirailleur missile, the West German company proposed that the launch aircraft be fitted with a pod-mounted passive sensor suite, with a single gimballed optical system being shared between

Above: **An onboard inertial unit within the AIM-132 ASRAAM should bring the missile within range of stealthy targets.**

Below: **With the smaller MiG-29 Fulcrum, the Su-27 Flanker is fitted with an electro-optical seeker and helmet-mounted sight.**

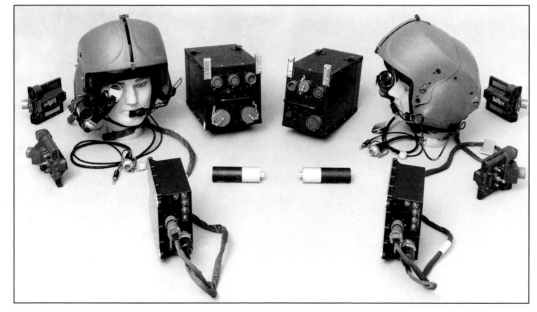

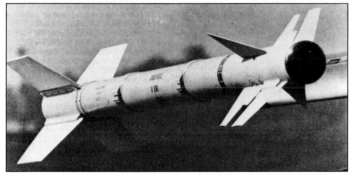

Top: **Unlike the Honeywell system shown on the opposite page, this Hughes helmet-mounted display projects imagery into both eyes.**

Above: **First Western air-to-air weapon system to rely on a helmet sight was the Armscor Kukri, a South African heat-seeking missile.**

a TV sensor and a laser rangefinder. The TV system would be used for target acquisition, with the target image being relayed to the pilot via a cathode-ray tube (CRT) display in the cockpit. Elevation and azimuth data would be obtainable from the optical system. Range would be obtained either from the laser or by a brief radar transmission. In order to cope with the effects of weather — always a problem in Western and Central Europe — the EO system would have been linked to the aircraft's radar, INS and fire control system.

Targets at beyond visual range (BVR) can in theory only be engaged by using active radar. On a stealth fighter, this would use low probability of intercept (LPI) techniques and transmission time would be kept to a minimum — just long enough to take a radar "snapshot" of the combat area and to obtain the target co-ordinates needed by an AMRAAM-type missile.

Passive seekers are once more beginning to look attractive, particularly when launched from "stealth" fighters the elusive nature of which would give the victim no clue that he was under attack. If the enemy fighters

are using their radars, an air-to-air anti-radiation missile (ARM) could prove an effective long-range weapon. AMRAAM and ARM rounds launched in salvo could present the enemy with an awkward tactical problem. While both rounds were flying towards the target under autopilot control, the victim might not realise he was under attack.

Once the AMRAAM seeker became active, the target aircraft would receive an immediate ESM warning, but the act of turning on a radar to look for the attacker, or activating a jammer to counter the AMRAAM would provide an attractive target for the ARM.

ALTITUDES

One effect which the prospect of full-capability look-down/shoot-down radars is having on US fighter tactics is to force a re-evaluation of operating altitudes. Warsaw Pact air defences are largely configured for the task of engaging low-altitude intruders, targets which were difficult for earlier systems designed to deal with high-altitude threats. Once the ATF is in service, USAF strike

aircraft may abandon current 100 - 200ft (30-60m) operating heights in favour of medium altitudes of around 15,000ft (4,600m), relying on stealth aircraft such as the F-117A and ATF to suppress the enemy defences.

Stealth technology can also boost the performance of other weapon systems. When the Advanced Cruise Missile (ACM) programme was launched in the early 1980s, it was hoped that some of the resulting technology might spin off into other programmes, such as stealthy RVs for ballistic missiles and new types of decoys and penetration aids. These would take advantage of the latest developments in RAM and would probably be shaped in a manner intended to reduce RCS. Warheads of this type could negate an ABM or SDI-type system. A scientific adviser to the US Navy Chief of Operations has been quoted as saying that stealthy RVs would create a "major problem for guaranteeing strategic early warning".

Dr Donald Hicks, Under Secretary of Defense for Research and Engineering told the magazine *Armed Forces Journal International* in 1986 that "Our forces will never have total immunity from the enemy's defense ... stealthy platforms must be equipped with stand-off weapons — weapons which themselves should also be stealthy."

SHIPS AND MISSILES

In June 1983, the Japan Self-Defence Agency's Technical Research and Development Institute placed an order with Mitsubishi Heavy Industries for a modification programme to the company's ASM-1 anti-ship missile. This called for the standard pattern of light alloy wings on the missile to be replaced by plastic wings reinforced with radar-

absorbing ferrite. Revealing the scheme late that year, the Japanese newspaper *Asahi Shimbun* quoted Defence Institute officials as saying that the new wings would delay the detection of incoming ASM-1s by enemy vessels, making it difficult for the ships to either confuse the missile seeker or attempt to shoot down the round with gun or missile fire. Institute officials also said that the same stealth technology could be applied to the follow-on shore-launched SSM-1. Given the fact that metal surfaces angled at right angles to one another act as prominent radar reflectors, it is hardly surprising that ships are large and conspicuous

radar targets. Many ship features seem to have been designed with a straight edge and set square. Deck and superstructure meet at right angles, as do the vessel's hull and the sea surface, while most above-deck features abound in large flat plates and right angles.

As a result, RCS of a ship can be as high as 10,000 square metres. In his book *Introduction to Radar Systems*, Merrill Skolnik suggests that as a first-order approximation, the RCS of a ship in square metres is numerically equal to its displacement in tons.

When Britain's Royal Navy sent a force of minesweepers to the Gulf in the summer of 1986, these vessels faced the

Above: **General Dynamics and Westinghouse have teamed to offer this rocket-powered Advanced Air-to-air Missile (AAAM) to the US Navy as an eventual replacement for the long-range AIM-54 Phoenix.**

Right: **Despite its massive size, this Soviet Kirov class battlecruiser has an RCS close to that of a Western frigate. Clean lines and sloped superstructure minimise the radar echo.**

Below: **A rival AAAM design exists in the form of this air-breathing Hughes/Raytheon design. The integral rocket/ramjet powerplant promises long range and high speed.**

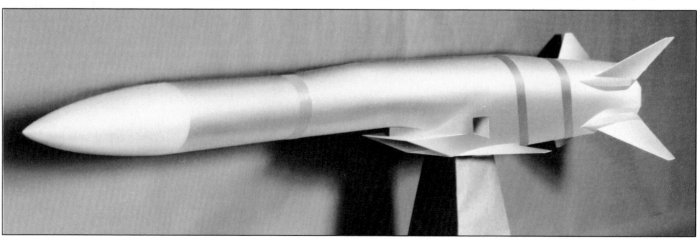

threat posed by radar-guided anti-ship missiles such as Iraq's Exocets and Iran's Silkworms. To provide protection against these weapons, the superstructures of the tiny vessels were swathed in hastily-applied blankets of RAM.

WIDESPREAD STEALTH

By the mid-1980s, designers were proposing features such as inward-sloping superstructure, rounded hulls and deck edges and the rapid dispersion and cooling of funnel gases. In the summer of 1988, it was revealed that the Japan Maritime Self-Defence Force would employ a novel low-RCS hull form on four new 1,900 ton destroyers. Hull panels in the mid and aft sections of these vessels would be sloped inwards at an angle of about seven degrees to minimise the energy returned towards the radars of low-flying strike aircraft and anti-ship missiles. Similar sloped panels would also be incorporated on the service's planned Aegis destroyers, along with other more advanced stealth features and countermeasures.

Tanks and other AFVs could also benefit from RCS reduction. The US and British Armies have already tested radar-absorbent camouflage netting and are unlikely to be the only ground forces to have done so. Treating artillery shells or mortar bombs with RAM to reduce their RCS will hamper the effectiveness of battlefield radars currently used to locate artillery units. This would allow artillery units to spend more time firing against known targets and less unproductive time travelling in "shoot and scoot" manoeuvres.

The last word concerning the combat effectiveness of stealth technology can be left to Professor Fuhs. In his book *Radar Cross Section Lectures*,

Above: **Japan's SX-3 (FS-X) may look like a standard F-16, but the use of Japanese-developed radar-absorbent material should greatly reduce its RCS.**

he makes the observation that "The advantage of a certain ECM technique can be nullified in a week or two. The advantage of a built-in low RCS requires a decade for an opponent to nullify." That is bad news for America's enemies in the 1990s but in the long run it is also a warning for the NATO Alliance. When Soviet stealth fighters and bombers enter service, probably in the mid to late 1990s, the West will face the problem of creating weapon systems able to deal with them.

COUNTERS TO STEALTH

This book has already described the stealth technology used to make aircraft and missiles "grow and become small" or to "vanish and come unknown". This chapter will look at the technologies needed "to begin our strife to destroy him". Such techniques will already be under investigation in the Soviet Union and it will be only a matter of time before the deployment of Soviet stealth aircraft to force the West to deploy suitable defences.

Writing in the magazine *Air Force* in 1986, senior editor Edgar Ulsamer has suggested the creation in the US defence community of a watchdog organisation tasked with maintaining the security and secrecy around low observable technology, also the setting up of a "Red Team" to predict the methods of countering US stealth aircraft which the Soviet Union may attempt to devise.

Measurement of the radar signature of stealth warplanes will obviously be a high priority for any nation faced with such threats. It seems safe to guess that when the

B-2 made its maiden flight from Palmdale, non-US clandestine radars both friendly and unfriendly would have attempted to illuminate the big bomber. Any spy learning of the operating routes of the F-117A might attempt to measure its RCS by indirect passive means, relying on US air-traffic control radars to provide the illuminating energy.

Given knowledge of the threat, the problem breaks down into two main areas. Sensors able to detect low-RCS targets must be developed, along with weapons able to attack these elusive opponents.

The obvious short-term move is to develop better radars. Work in this direction has been spurred by the threat posed by small cruise

Right: A variant of Marconi's Martello radar was a candidate in the mid-1980s competition to select a radar for a joint military/civil US radar network.

Below: The MiG-25 Foxbat was designed to intercept high-flying bombers, but by 1977 missile firing trials against simulated cruise missiles had begun.

Right: The E-3A was designed before the era of stealthy targets but a planned upgrade programme will improve its effectiveness.

Below: With the collapse of the UK's Nimrod AEW.3 programme, Boeing's E-3 Sentry has become NATO's only effective AEW aircraft.

missiles such as the US ALCM and Tomahawk and the Soviet AS-15. In October 1977 came news that the Soviet Union had successfully intercepted a target simulating a cruise missile. This initially drew denials from the Pentagon but in late December Dr William J. Perry, then US Under Secretary of Defense for Research and Engineering, admitted that a successful Soviet live-warhead trial had taken place. The target drone used ''was about the size of the US T-33 training aircraft'', he told reporters, and had taken place ''at an airfield where MiG-25 Foxbat aircraft are stationed''.

FUTURE RADARS

Stealth technology will reduce the RCS of manned aircraft to values comparable with, or even lower than, those associated with ALCM and Tomahawk, thus increasing the problems which designers will face when trying to extract every last drop of performance from conventional radars.

Obvious measures which may partly offset the effects of stealth technology involve increasing a radar's power or improving its ability to combine several faint echoes into one strong one. A stealth aircraft may seem bird-sized in terms of echoing area but moving-target indicator (MTI) techniques will allow the tiny echo to be picked out from among slower-moving natural targets such as birds or even insect swarms.

Some indication of the ability of conventional radars to detect low-RCS targets can be gleaned from the new joint civil/military radar surveillance network due to enter service in the mid-1990s. When drawing up its specifications for a suitable surveillance radar, the US authorities specified that the equipment should be able to detect targets as small as 0.1 square metre at a range of 100 miles (160km).

To meet this specification, three teams offered radars, two of which were based on existing sets. General Electric proposed a version of its FPS-117 radar, the equipment used in the US/Canadian North Warning Network, while Raytheon teamed with Marconi Radar Systems to offer a version of the UK company's Martello 737 radar used in the NATO air defence radar modernisation plan. Westinghouse proposed a new set based on a novel type of antenna. The other teams used conventional ''billboard'' phased array antennas but the Westinghouse design used small phased array which acted as a feed for a larger conventional reflector.

In the summer of 1988, Westinghouse won the competition to supply the new radars. At the 1988

Farnborough Air Show, I asked Westinghouse if the 0.1 square metre figure represented the likely RCS of a future Soviet threat. It did not, they claimed, but was simply a measure of radar performance taken from an earlier specification. It seems unlikely however that the US DoD would have allowed a radar to be procured for the joint US Federal Aviation Administration/USAF Joint Surveillance System if it was not confident that the equipment could deal with the potential air threats of the late 1990s.

RADAR FREQUENCIES

A potential problem for Western stealth aircraft is that a significant number of Soviet air-defence search radars operate not at microwave frequencies (1 – 20GHz) but in the UHF band (300MHz – 1GHz) or in the even lower-frequency VHF band (100 – 300MHz). In the past, these equipments have often been dismissed as examples of Soviet technological backwardness. VHF and UHF radars are relatively easy to design and manufacture, the reason why all the early Second World War radars were of this type.

The need for smaller size, better low-altitude coverage and improved target discrimination soon led to most radars being built to operate at microwave frequencies but, even today, UHF and VHF frequencies still have some military advantages. For one thing, their antennas tend to be bulky. This is a problem for the user but it does give virtual immunity from attack by anti-radar missiles – it is just not possible to cram a VHF homing antenna into a missile seeker. They also offer good long-range performance. To see the reason for this requires a detour into basic radio theory.

High frequency microwave radio signals require a direct line of sight between the transmitter and receiver. Thus transmitted signals can be obscured by terrain features and maximum range is constrained by the curvature of the Earth. Operating at such frequencies makes long range communications difficult, and the first radio stations used the much lower LF or MF bands. At these frequencies the "surface wave" effect becomes apparent. The signal emanating from the antenna tends to hug the Earth's

surface, travelling well beyond the horizon.

Significantly longer ranges can be obtained by operating in the higher frequencies of the HF band, where the "sky wave" phenomenon is important. Part of the signal rises into the sky and reaches the highly charged ionosphere layer between 50 and 250 miles (80 and 400 km) above the Earth's surface. The ionosphere refracts the signal, curving its path back to the ground, where it reaches distances of over 500 miles (800km) away. This sky wave forms the basis of most long-range radio communications and the effect is exploited in the new generation of over-the-horizon radars described later.

Above: **The envelope of a non-rigid airship makes a near-perfect radome for a surveillance radar, and the helium atmosphere will not effect performance.**

Below: **This model shows the gondola of one proposed USN solution to the problem of detecting low-RCS targets — the Airship Industries/ Westinghouse YEZ-2A.**

Top right: **The envelope of the YEZ-2A AEW airship is intended to carry a massive radar antenna, but budget cuts threaten the future of this promising AEW concept.**

Right: **The massive antennas of the Cape Dyer station of the DEW line look impressive, but this network of North-facing radar stations is obsolescent.**

ability to detect and track stealth aircraft.

Luckily for the operators of stealth aircraft, UHF and VHF radars are no panacea, so they still make up a small portion of the total number of threats. Long wavelengths create their own tactical and engineering problems.

For instance, such radars tend to be physically big, since large antennas are needed in order to obtain adaquately-narrow beam-widths and high antenna gains. A side effect of the relatively wide beam created by even a large VHF antenna is that the radar's resolution in azimuth is poor.

When the designer sets out to combine VHF operating frequencies with mobile operation, the resulting systems are often reminiscent of the Second World War German Freya and are cumbersome to deploy.

OTH RADARS

One of the most promising methods of detecting a stealth aircraft is by means of over-the-horizon (OTH) radars. In the United States, research on equipment of this type has been under way for about 25 years, with the aim of developing better defences against conventional bomber threats. The aim was to create long-range radars able to track aircraft which are masked from the view of conventional ground-based radars by the curvature of the earth's surface.

Radars of this type direct a powerful sky wave towards the earth's ionosphere. This is refracted and returned towards the earth's surface, illuminating a distant patch of terrain or sea. Any targets present in this area create radar echoes which follow the reverse route back up to the ionosphere and thus back to the receiver of the OTH radar.

One problem in such dependence on sky waves is that the signal is redirected not by reflection but by refraction, so propagation conditions cannot be calculated by simple geometry. The amount of refraction experienced depends on the frequency of the signal and the density of the ionosphere. The latter varies with time, as does the height of the ionosphere. Variations occur on both daily and annual cycles and cannot be predicted accurately. As the amount of refraction being experienced alters, so also does the distance between the transmitter and

At the still higher VHF and UHF bands, the skywave is not refracted back to the ground and is lost. There is still a useful degree of ground-hugging surface wave, however, which allows radio reception some way over the horizon. The previously mentioned "obsolete" UHF and VHF radars also make use of this effect, giving much longer ranges than direct line-of-sight microwave systems.

VHF PROBLEMS

In designing a stealth aircraft, RCS engineers work to defeat the 1 – 20GHz microwave frequencies used by most radars. Equipments operating at lower frequencies will be less affected by RAM and other RCS-reduction measures, giving them some

OTH Radar System

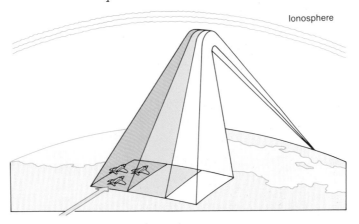

Ionosphere

Above: **General Electric's FPS-118 over-the-horizon radar bounces HF signals off the ionosphere in order to track aircraft flying far out over the Atlantic. The beam can be electronically steered in azimuth, while range is adjusted by varying the frequency (and ionospheric bounce behaviour) of the transmitted signal.**

the location where the sky wave returns to the earth's surface a distance known to radio operators as the "skip distance".

Studies of a possible US OTH system began in the early 1970s and system definition work was completed by November 1973. The contract to develop a prototype of what was then called the over-the-horizon backscatter (OTH-B) radar was awarded in March 1975 but the programme soon ran into difficulties with both cost and timescale. A restructuring began in December 1976 which put the effort on a more realistic basic, allowing technical feasibility tests four years later.

The initial goal of the programme was to develop and test a limited coverage prototype radar. Based in Maine, this was used to assess the level of technical performance required by an operational system. At the same time, further work was carried out on basic OTH radar technology in order to increase the effectiveness of the final system. Areas explored by this research effort included ionospheric modelling and prediction, adaptive beam-forming, low-sidelobe antennas and computer algorithms for signal processing and radar control.

The prototype system was handed over to the USAF in

***Above:* The Pave Paws phased-array radar on the US East and West coasts are anti-SLBM systems, intended to detect sneak attacks by missile firing submarines.**

***Below:* Based at Shemya in the Aleutian Islands, the Cobra Dane radar covers the Eastern tip of the USSR, including the strategic Kamchatka Peninsula.**

May 1980, allowing the start of nine months of system performance tests. These gave the confidence needed to make the decision in October 1981 to proceed with the development and deployment of an operational system, a contract for which was awarded to General Electric in June 1982. This called for the upgrading of the experimental system in Maine

to a fully operational 60 degree azimuth coverage Initial Operating Sector (IOS) of the East Coast Radar System.

US COVERAGE

Official designation of the system is AN/FPS-118. Four sites are planned. Coverage of the east coast is handled by the upgraded Maine installation where the transmitter antenna is at Moscow/Caratunk, while the receiver antenna is more than 100 miles (160km) away at Columbia Falls. These sites cover three 60 degree sectors. From north to south, these are numbered one, two and three. Between them they cover an arc extending from southern Greenland to the Caribbean.

Each sector has its own transmit and receive antenna. These are large — 3,630ft (1,106m) long and between 35 and 135ft (10.7 and 41m) high. Feeding these arrays is the task of twelve 100kW transmitters serving six frequency bands covering the entire HF spectrum from 5 to 28MHz. Each sector transmitter site swallows more than four megawatts of electrical power and pumps out a total of 1.2MW of RF power.

The receiver site is built on an equally gargantuan scale. Once again there are separate antennas for each sector. Each is 4,980ft (1,518m) long and teamed with a 65ft (19.8m) high backscreen. Signals received are processed on-site, then analysed at the operations centre, a 32,500 square foot (3,020m²) building equipped with 28 VAX computers and 30 display consoles for detection and tracking, target correlation and identification and for control, monitoring and maintenance. The centre uses 2MW of electrical power and 180 tons of air conditioning equipment is needed to keep the electronics cool.

Early trials showed that Sector 1 of the Maine radar could track USAF F-15s and F-16s flying from the USA to Reykjavik in Iceland. In October 1986 the US Air Force announced that the radar had tracked President Reagan's aircraft "Air Force One" all the way to Iceland as he flew out for his summit meeting with the Soviet leader. The East Coast System passed its initial tests in December 1986 and became operational in 1987. On 20 October of that year it detected its first Soviet targets, two Tu-142F maritime patrol aircraft. These were detected at a range of 1,050nm (1,945km). Maximum range of the FPS-118 was originally to have been 1,800nm (3,330km)

US Defensive Radar Coverage

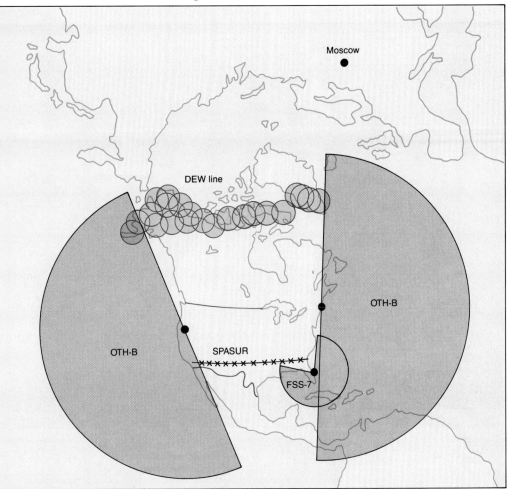

Below: If the US is to be able to detect future stealthy Soviet stealth bombers and cruise missiles, much of the current radar network must be updated.

Above: By the 1970s, the US radar early-warning network had shrunk to this emasculated form. Congress was unwilling to make the major investment needed for

modernisation. Development by the Soviet Union of the Backfire bomber and AS-15 cruise missile finally provided the impetus for the deployment of new radars.

but this was later extended to 2,000nm (3,700km).

By 1990 the West Coast System should be in place at locations in Oregon (transmitter), Northern California (receiver) and Idaho (operations centre). This system will cover three 60 degree sectors numbered four, five and six. Built to an improved standard which includes a larger 8,000ft (2,438m) receiver antenna, the West Coast System is expected to have a better performance against small and stealthy targets. Changes and modifications introduced there will later be retrofitted to upgrade the original East Coast System.

Sectors 9 and 10 will be southwest and northwest facing, from sites in Alaska, and will cover the Aleutian islands. The operations centre will be at Elmendorf AFB, the transmitter and receiver at Gulkana and Tok respectively. Tok will be the first receiver site to use a new pattern of antenna which does not require a backscreen. A final site is planned for the central USA. This will have its operations centre at Grand Forks AFB, North Dakota, and will cover four 60 degree

sectors — numbers 8 (southeast), 9 (southwest), 11 (east) and 12 (west). There will be no north-facing sectors; OTH radars cannot cover the polar region. This is due to the interaction between the ionosphere and the earth's radiation belts, a phenomenon which results in the *aurora borealis* and which makes HF propagation unpredictable. The entire OTH-B system is due for completion in the late 1990s at a cost of $2.5 billion.

RELOCATABLE OTH

A second pattern of OTH radar is under development in the USA. Under a US Navy contract, Raytheon is designing a tactical OTH radar with a range of up to 1,800 miles (2,900km). As its designation suggests, the AN/TPS-71 Relocatable OTH Radar (ROTHR) is much smaller than the FPS-118 and is designed to allow rapid deployment to prepared sites. It consists of two parts — a transmitter and a combined operation centre/receiver — spaced at sites up to 110 miles (180km) apart.

Being redeployable, the ROTHR can be located within a matter of weeks in geographic locations which will allow the US to establish emergency long-range coverage of areas not normally within the OTH

radar "umbrella". Typical applications may be the monitoring of routes likely to be used by Soviet bombers flying towards USN task forces or the tracking of Soviet naval task forces.

The possibility that OTH radars could be used to track stealth aircraft emerged in the summer of 1986 when Dr. D. H. Sinnott, a senior principal research scientist of the Australian Department of Defence's Research Centre at Salisbury, stated during a defence conference in Canberra that the entire airframe of a stealth aircraft would reflect energy at HF frequencies.

An OTH radar system has a severe limitation in terms of minimum range. Since the radar signal must reach the ionosphere, reflect and then return to the earth's surface, an OTH radar cannot detect targets operating within a radius of about 500nm (900km). Aware of this fact, the crew of a stealth aircraft would be able to initiate a change in course or other evasive tactics once they were confident that their aircraft was no longer visible to the OTH radar.

The enemy would be aware that the aircraft was on its way but this is seen as no problem by the USAF, given that any US strike mission against Soviet territory would

be in response to a Soviet attack on the United States. "What stealth is intended to do is to fix it so that an aircraft can deliver its ordnance to a target within the enemy territory. Now, it's not designed to keep the other guy from knowing that the war has started. What you want to do is counter the things that are going to shoot at you and kill you", a senior US defence official explained during an Associated Press interview in late 1986.

According to Western defence analysts, the Soviet Union now has two operational OTH radars (some sources say three). These are

aimed towards the continental USA and apparently serve as a warning device to monitor the USAF's ICBM fields. In theory, they could also be used to watch for US bombers but at present large gaps exist in their coverage, gaps which would limit their usefulness in such a rôle.

OTH PROBLEMS

Other nations are likely to deploy their own OTH systems. Radars of this type are effective only when searching the airspace over water. Radar clutter from land masses make interpretation of the returned signals

Left: Both of these USAF operators are seated at modern digital displays incorporating synthetic symbology, but the display at top right shows raw analogue radar imagery.

impossible, at least with 1980s processing technology. OTH radars are thus attractive only to nations which have a significant ocean-surveillance task to fulfil.

On the other side of the globe, Australia has the need for an OTH system and vast tracts of desert in which to locate antennas. Under the Jindalee programme, a single test site has been built at Alice Springs in the centre of the country. This will later form part of a three-site operation system due to enter service in the mid-1990s. The other sites will be in the north-east and the south-west.

It remains to be seen just how effectively OTH and VHF radars could "hand over" stealthy targets to microwave band radars. Much of the secret test flying of the F-117A and earlier XST stealth fighters in Nevada against threat systems will have been intended to investigate this problem. The results obtained must surely have been a major target for Soviet-bloc espionage. Construction of an XST-style stealth testbed must be a high priority task for the Mikoyan, Sukhoi and Yakovlev design bureaux. Until such an aircraft is available, Soviet radar engineers will have to rely on RPVs as semi-stealthy test targets.

Another possible technique for detecting stealth aircraft

Below: The DEW line station at Fylingdales in the UK was intended to detect ballistic missile attacks. Upgrading will come just in time to cope with stealthy warheads.

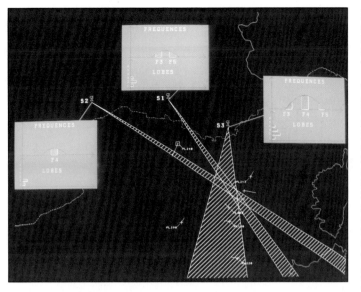

Above: Triangulation locates the position of a hostile emitter. Stealth aircraft must remain radar- and radio-silent while in range of enemy ESM stations.

Below: When teamed with an improved missile now being studied by the US and Germany, this Patriot radar should be able to engage low-RCS air targets.

involves inter-netting a series of fixed-site and mobile radars, using them intermittently as active search systems and for the rest of the time as passive direction-finders. This was first done as a way of avoiding ARM attacks. The enemy is faced with a series of blinking emitters which ESMs and ARMs "see" as only intermittent signals whose

location and characteristics change rapidly. Even if one or more sites can be attacked and knocked out, the network will continue to function.

Detection of stealth targets would involve the use of a group of netted radars able to transmit on a wide range of frequencies. As a result of the inevitable compromises in the design process, stealth measures cannot be equally effective at all angles and frequencies. The greater the number of frequencies and directions of the signals arriving at a stealth aircraft, the greater the chances that one or more might create a usable echo.

NEW TECHNOLOGIES

In the longer term, new technology will have to be applied to the problem of locating and tracking stealthy opponents. Defence of the continental USA against air-breathing threats of the late 1990s and beyond (including cruise missiles and stealth bombers) is the goal of the Air Defense Initiative (ADI) programme, a lesser-known effort running in parallel with

Above: SAM systems which don't use radar will pose a threat to stealth aircraft. Shorts' Javelin is command guided and has an IR surveillance system.

the highly-publicised Space Defense Initiative (SDI). ADI is running seveal years behind SDI. Full-scale development is unlikely to be ordered until the mid-1990s.

In the meantime, studies are underway of possible ADI system architectures. The battle-management problems associated with ADI and SDI are very different but, even so, alternative architectures being studied by companies such as General Dynamics, Hughes and Raytheon will probably be tried out on the SDI's National Test Bed.

It is unlikely that any one single technology will dramatically decrease the vulnerability of stealth aircraft. By pooling the information from several sensors, not one of which is itself giving reliable data, the "signal-to-noise" ratio may be improved to the point were stealthy targets can be distinguished.

BI-STATIC RADARS

One important sensor will always be microwave radar, future versions of which will be designed with the stealth threat in mind. Despite plans to update the E-3 fleet, a new type of airborne radar will be needed in the future. The most likely end result would

be a new airborne early-warning aircraft based on the Boeing 747 airframe and fitted with a large "smart" radar operating in the UHF band (0.3 – 1GHz) or in D band (1 – 2 GHz). These relatively long wavelengths would be less affected by stealth technology than those currently used and be good for the task of picking out small radar targets from background clutter.

In 1987, Grumman, Hughes and Westinghouse were all given contracts to study airborne radars working at these frequencies. This was expected to lead to one or two companies being given contracts to develop flight test hardware by the mid-1990s.

One promising countermeasure to stealth is bi-static radar. In a normal (mono-static) radar, the transmitter and receiver are at the same location and often

share a common antenna. In a bi-static radar, they are located some distance apart and several receivers may share a single transmitter. An aircraft which relies on shaping or faceting to reduce its RCS is designed to ensure that an incoming radar signal is not reflected directly back to the radar. This works well against a conventional mono-static radar but could result in the incoming radar energy being "dumped" in the direction of a listening receiver forming part of a bi-static system.

Being passive, receiver sites are immune to the attentions of threats such as directional jammers, anti-radiation missiles and "Wild Weasel" aircraft. In a bi-static radar, there are several potential ways of protecting the transmitter. The concept known as "sanctuary radar" involves installing the

transmitter in a safe location from which it may serve a number of front-line receiving sites. Suitable locations for the transmitter could be far back from the battle area, either at a ground location heavily protected by air defences or in a high-flying aircraft. Another possibility would involve mounting the transmitter unit in a geo-stationary satellite.

Below: One possible stealth detector is bi-static radar, a system whose transmitter and receiver are in different locations. The "sanctuary" concept shown here is probably the ultimate bi-static system. Ground-based receiving sites operate in conjunction with a transmitter in a high-flying aircraft (whose position is measured using ground-based DME stations), or even in a satellite.

Bi-Static "Sanctuary" Concept

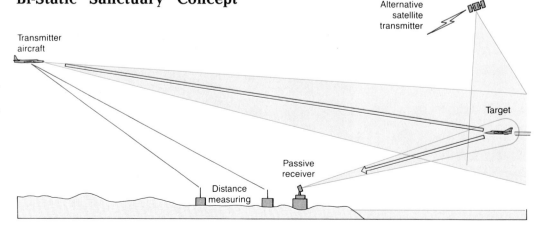

Transmitter aircraft

Alternative satellite transmitter

Target

Passive receiver

Distance measuring

Above: **The Soviet SA-8 Gecko uses radar guidance, but has a back-up optical tracking mode which would be effective against stealthy targets such as the F-117A.**

Below: **Advanced IR-guided weapons such as the Stinger SAM (seen here in vehicle-mounted form) might be able to home in on the jetpipes of stealth fighters.**

US stealth designers take the bi-static threat seriously. Early in the B-2 programme it was feared that the RAM material due to be used in production would not be effective against bi-static radars. Tests carried out using B-2 components in the early 1980s soon showed that this was not the case. In wartime, any assumption by the defender that attacking

stealth aircraft had not been designed to cope with bi-static radar might prove to be, in the words of Bill Sweetman, "terminally erroneous".

ADVANCED RADARS

Perhaps the best prospect for an anti-stealth radar is a technique only just emerging from the laboratory. This is known as a "carrierless radar". Tiny low-powered radars of this type are already used for some commercial applications such as creating images of the interior of concrete structures. However, larger and vastly more powerful systems could be developed for air surveillance and target tracking.

At first sight, the concept of a carrierless radar seems like a contradiction in terms. Engineers use the word "carrier" to describe the basic radio-frequency signal to which modulation is applied. Such modulation can be speech or data (in the case of a communications link), pulses (in the case of pulsed radar) or variations in frequency (in the case of a continuous-wave radar). Remove the carrier and it might seem that nothing is left to carry the modulation.

All the radar engineer needs is a pulse (probably of rectangular shape) with which to illuminate his target. Using a mathematical technique known as Fourier Expansion,

any waveform can be broken down into a series of sinusoidal components — a main component, known as the fundamental, and multiples of this fundamental, known as harmonics. Vary the shape and frequency of the waveform being analysed and the resulting "mix" of fundamental and harmonics will also change. For every shape of waveform, a "cocktail" of these components can be obtained.

The exact operating principles of carrierless radar are classified but the broad idea seems to be to reverse the process. Instead of transmitting the desired waveform, transmit the correct mix of frequencies which will recreate it. These could mostly be of low power and could stretch across most or even all of the frequency bands used for radar. The resulting synthesised pulse would not be affected by radar-absorbent materials.

OPTICAL SYSTEMS

Stealth technology may also be partially nullified by the use of sensors operating at frequencies far above those of traditional microwave radars. Millimetre-wave radar is one possibility; another is laser radar. In the spring of 1988, the US Navy started flight tests intended to evaluate the use of high-power lasers. During these tests, a ground-based MIRACL (Mid Infra-Red Advanced Chemical Laser) at the White Sands missile range illuminated Teledyne BQM-34S Firebee drones equipped with a 53in (135cm) diameter sensor/reflector mounted under the port wing. The circular unit was steerable and was matched, for aerodynamic reasons, by a second dummy unit under the opposite wing. These tests were part of research into laser weapons; previous tests using standard drones had resulted in two Firebees being destroyed by the laser energy. Some of the technology, and some of the test results, may be applicable to future laser radars.

During the Vietnam War, the Soviet Union modified SAM systems such as SA-2 and SA-3 to reduce the vulnerability to growing US EW expertise. One technique involved the provision of back-up electro-optical guidance modes. Being passive, these were not vulnerable to radar jamming, although their communications links still offered a warning that aircraft

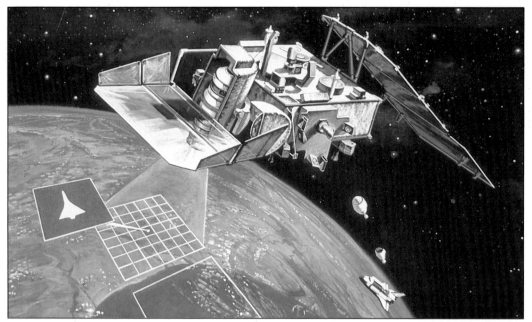

dimensional mosaic array IR sensor would attempt to pick out the IR signature from trials aircraft against the IR radiation from the terrain background. The orbital angle was specially chosen so that the spacecraft would be able to observe the northern coastlines of Alaska and Canada, areas which would present what scientists expected would be the most difficult terrain background for an IR detector system — rocky tundra and broken ice.

The grounding of the US Space Shuttle fleet in 1986 following the loss of the "Challenger" was a major setback. Instead of being used for orbital trials, the USAF's classified AFP 888 spacecraft and its onboard Teal Ruby infra-red surveillance sensor were placed in storage at

were coming under attack. During the decades which followed, US spending on EW systems has run into billions (US) of dollars per year, while the Soviet Union has pressed ahead with its use of back-up EO modes.

Infra-red (IR) and ultra-violet (UV) sensors are also being investigated, particularly for use on space-based platforms. Such systems are seen in the USA as a possible long-term alternative to OTH radars. Much effort was initially placed into the study of space-based tracking radars. One possible space-based sensor might have been a large constellation of satellites each carrying a phased array radar. Networked together, they would have a similar performance to that of a single large space-based radar but would be much less vulnerable to attack by anti-satellite weapons.

The more likely method of tracking an aircraft from space is by looking for its IR signature. To test the feasibility of this idea, the USAF ordered the development of a sensor codenamed "Teal Ruby". This was fitted to a classified AFP 888 spacecraft and scheduled to be orbited in March 1986 at an inclination of 72 degrees by the US Space Shuttle.

SPACE SYSTEMS

Once in orbit the 4,800lb (2,177kg) spacecraft would direct its 11ft (3.4m) sensor assembly — effectively a large telescope mounted on a yoke and spindle — towards pre-selected test sites on the earth's surface. A cryogenically-cooled two-

Above left: **The Teal Ruby infra-red sensor was devised as a research tool into the problems of detecting air targets by observing their IR signature from orbit.**

Left: **The SA-10B Grumble was designed with low-RCS targets in mind, while its mobility will help it avoid attack by B-2 bombers tasked with destroying SAM sites.**

Below: **The likely operating altitude and location of aircraft such as the TR-1, EF-111 and E-3A could bring them within the firepower of long-range Soviet SAMs sited at forward operating locations. Once the SA-10 and -12 are available in large quantity (probably in the late 1990s), the survivability of such high-flying platforms will become questionable. Less vulnerable stealthy replacements will eventually be required.**

Ranges of Soviet SAM Systems

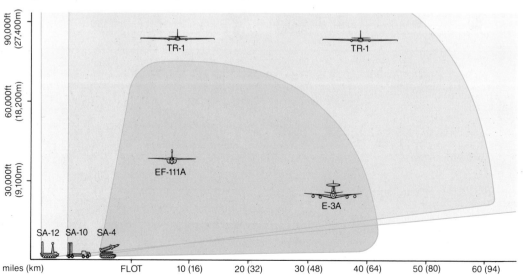

Rockwell International, while studies began into ways of getting it into orbit aboard an expendable launch vehicle.

Reconfiguring the satellite for a new launch vehicle would take a long time. By the time the redesign task was completed, the Shuttle was expected to be operational once more. The decision was further complicated by the DoD decision to "mothball" the as yet uncommissioned Shuttle launch pad at Vandenberg AFB, California.

Every possible signature of a stealth target is being considered as a possible tracking aid. Sophisticated ESM systems might be able to intercept even the most covert transmissions such as those from low probability of intercept (LPI) radars or laser rangers, while at short ranges the sound or even the atmospheric turbulence created by the aircraft's passage through the air might be utilised as a trackable "signature".

SOVIET MISSILES

As was the case with sensors, the fielding of weapons able to engage and destroy a stealth aircraft will probably occur in several stages. Improved versions of current missiles will later give way to new weapons custom-designed with low-RCS targets in mind.

Since the USA has been openly developing small cruise missiles since the mid-1970s, it is only to be expected that the latest generation of Soviet SAMs has been designed to deal with such low-RCS targets. One of the first was the SA-10 Grumble, a weapon whose development may have been protracted by the need to cope with cruise missiles.

Deployment of the original SA-10A version began in 1980. By 1985 more than 60 sites were operating. The total by the late 1980s was probably close to 100. All early deployments of this vertical-launch missile were near high value targets such as key command and control, military and industrial locations — more than half were near Moscow. The latest version is the mobile SA-10B which uses eight-wheeled vehicles to carry the missile launchers and the radar. Each transporter/erector vehicle carries a cluster of four launcher/containers, while the radar vehicle is fitted with a planar-array radar.

According to the US Department of Defense, at

Above: **The massive SA-12A Gladiator may have been developed to protect mobile ICBMs. If so, it will pose a threat to B-2s attacking SS-24 and SS-25 units.**

Below: **The Improved Hawk is NATO's most common medium range SAM. Further upgrades are needed to counter future Soviet stealth aircraft developments.**

least 500 SA-10 sites would be needed in order to create an effective defence against cruise missiles. A system of this size would have at least some capability against stealth aircraft. The SA-10 systems are inter-netted (a technique described earlier when describing anti-stealth radar operations) and in 1987 the US DoD confirmed that the weapons have "a capability against low-altitude targets with small radar cross-sections such as cruise missiles".

The SA-12A Gladiator will be a much more significant threat, particularly to B-2 operations. Like SA-10B this is a mobile system, in this case on tracked rather than wheeled vehicles, and was first fielded in the mid-1980s. Two vehicles in each battery

carry a single large phased array antenna. One has an antenna about 15ft (4.5m) square, which may be for target acquisition, while the other has a slightly smaller unit which could be for fire-control. The other vehicles carry four ready-to-fire vertically launched missiles. Each round is 24.6ft (7.5m) long and 20in (50cm) in diameter. Guidance is thought to be by semi-active radar.

NATO MISSILES

NATO's main tactical SAM is still the Raytheon Improved Hawk. Given the high cost of the follow-on Patriot system, the older weapon will still be in widespread service when Soviet stealth aircraft enter service. Latest in a long series of I-Hawk upgrades is Phase III, which modifies the continuous wave (CW)

illumination radar, to provide single-scan target detection, and adds a fan beam to the high-power illumination radar, to make possible the new Low-Altitude Simultaneous Hawk Engagement (LASHE) operating mode a method of running multiple engagements against saturation raids.

Phase III also updates the platoon command post, to incorporate Patriot-type displays and symbology, and allows I-Hawk units to accept tactical information from nearby Patriot systems. Raytheon hopes that I-Hawk can be kept effective into the early years of the next century. Among the modifications being planned is a new Agile Continuous Wave Acquisiton Radar (ACWAR) intended to replace the current high-altitude Pulsed Acquisition Radar and low-altitude CW Acquisition Radar.

The US Navy is also upgrading its SAMs. In August 1987 Raytheon was given a $231 million contract to develop the new vertically-launched Block 4 version of the Standard missile. This will incorporate a short tandem booster and digital technology from the Patriot and

Above: **Jamming strobes designed to mask large targets will be even more effective when used to protect stealth aircraft.**

Left: **The Standard missile can now be vertically launched, and the USN is developing a further-improved Block 4 version.**

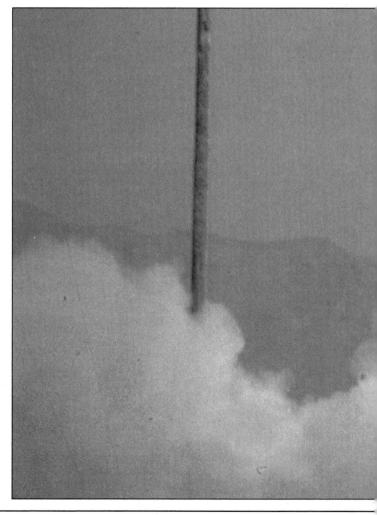

AMRAAM missiles. It will be deployed aboard all but the older CG-47 cruisers and on the new Burke-class (DDG-51) destroyers.

Several new patterns of SAM are under study in the West. Early in 1987 the Governments of Belgium, France, Italy, the Netherlands, Norway, Spain and the UK ratified a European Staff Target for a new medium SAM, a tactical air-defence missile able to replace the Improved Hawk. In April 1988, France, Italy, Spain and the UK agreed to collaborate on studies of the proposed Medium Surface-to-Air Missile (MSAM). A similar agreement signed in the early summer of 1988 committed the same partners to 18-month feasibility studies of a Family of naval Anti-air Missile Systems (FAMS). These would include systems for point, area and medium-range defence. The short-range system could be amalgamated with the NATO Anti-Air Warfare System (NAAWS), a weapon already under study by France, Italy, the Netherlands, Spain, the UK and the USA.

West Germany's TLVS (*Taktisches Luftverteidigungssystem*) is due to enter *Luftwaffe* service in the year 2005. MBB, AEG and Siemens are all collaborating on the new missile which is seen as a mobile system able to provide all-sector defence against all air threats, including tactical ballistic missiles and "low-flying objects with small radar cross sections". A battery will consist of a multi-function radar, an engagement control station and several fire units. All will be mounted on wheeled vehicles and be linked by a jam-resistant communications network and a back-up system based on fibre-optic cables.

NEW SYSTEMS

In France, Thomson-CSF and Aérospatiale are working on another medium SAM. The *SAMP (Système sol-Air Moyenne Portée)* will be a land-based weapon, while the *SAAM (Système de défense surface-air anti-missile)* is for naval use. Both systems will use Aérospatiale vertically-launched missiles, a Thomson-CSF Arabel I/J band multi-function phased-array radar, plus common computers and displays. The radar is expected to be able to handle approximately 50 tracks and

Above: **The display of a Patriot fire-control system shows several air targets. How well will the system cope with stealth aircraft?**

Below: **The current version of Patriot (seen here on flight test) will eventually be replaced by the Advanced Tactical Patriot.**

to engage up to 10 targets at the same time, with rounds being fired at rates of up to one per second.

The USA has no all-new long-range SAM on the drawing board but has plans to greatly improve the current Patriot system. The USA and West Germany are collaborating on the Advanced Tactical Patriot. Intended to offer better capability against ballistic missiles, stealth aircraft and stand-off jammers, this will have a better radar, larger rocket motor, giving greater range, a new 35GHz (K-band) seeker with three operating modes (including fully-active) and an improved warhead and fuze. Flight tests could begin in 1989.

DUAL SENSORS

Almost nothing is known about future Soviet SAM systems. The only weapon of which details are available is the SA-X-15. A derivative of the naval SA-9, it will be fielded as a replacement for the SA-8 Gecko. Since the naval version would have been designed to defend warships against attack by Harpoon and Tomahawk missiles, a good performance against low-RCS targets can be anticipated.

Stealth threats also demand the introduction of improved or even all-new air-to-air missiles. Given the specific advantages and weaknesses of semi-active radar (SAR) and IR guidance, many air arms equip their fighters with a "mix" of both types. This is often done by combining lightweight IR short-range

different types of guidance. The pioneering Second World War Hs 298 and X-4 had tried radio-command and wire guidance. Wire was never seriously considered for post-war air-to-air missiles but several designs tried radio command, radar beam-riding and even active-radar homing, finally settling for the IR and SAR systems widely used by most air forces today.

Active radar was in theory a promising alternative to SAR, freeing the launch aircraft from the tactical limitation of having to keep its radar antenna pointed at the target throughout the time of missile flight in order to illuminate the target. An active radar seeker would carry its own transmitter, greatly increasing its weight and complexity, but leaving the fighter free to turn away either to avoid short-range combat or to attack another victim.

At a time when all electronics were based on

Above: **In air combat, warhead size can compensate for guidance inaccuracy. This 1950s-vintage Genie missile carried a nuclear warhead.**

weapons with longer-ranged SAR missiles but the Soviet Air Force prefers to deploy many of its light and medium-weight missiles in both IR and SAR forms.

One possible short-term improvement to existing missiles is to fit both types of seeker into the same missile. By switching from one to another as necessary, the weapon could use whatever method is giving the best results. The US Navy is known to have studied the feasibility of fitting a combined SAR and IR seeker within the nose radome of the AIM-7 Sparrow.

AIR-TO-AIR MISSILES

By the mid to late 1990s, fire-and-forget dual mode guidance will be an essential feature in the air intercept missiles (AIMs) of all nations facing a stealth-equipped opponent. Like the SAMs described earlier, such missiles will have to rely on mid-course updating and inertial guidance to bring them close enough to a stealthy target for seeker activation and final homing.

A key component of such missiles will be miniature active-radar seekers. When developing the first post-war air-to-air and surface-to-air guided missiles in the late 1940s, designers were prepared to try many

Above: The radar-guided AIM-120A AMRAAM missile (seen here below the wing of an F-16) will boost the firepower of the GD warplane.

Left: **Phoenix was the first air-to-air missile with mid-course guidance, a feature essential to most future anti-stealth missiles.**

bulky, fragile and power-hungry thermionic valves (tubes), the few active seekers to be built and tested proved both heavy and unreliable, as were the few experimental weapons to which they were fitted. Missiles built to carry them were massive. The UK's Vickers Type 888 (Red Dean & Red Hebe) which started trials in the mid-1950s weighed about 1,300lb (600kg). Like the US Navy's 1960-vintage Bendix AAM-N-10 Eagle, this was soon cancelled. The only anti-aircraft missile to enter service with an active-radar seeker was the seven-ton Boeing Bomarc SAM.

AMRAAM

Active-radar seekers remained impractical until the mid-1960s when the US Navy began flight testing the AIM-54 Phoenix. Despite its massive 990lb (450kg) weight, even this missile used its active mode only in the final stages of flight, flying longer-range interceptions under SAR or pre-programmed operating modes for much of the way to the target. Only at short ranges could the missile be launched in active mode.

By the mid to late 1990s, the ability to fly close to a target before engaging a terminal guidance mode will be an essential feature in the AIMs of all nations facing the threat of stealth aircraft or missiles. It will be available to the USAF and other NATO air arms with the long-delayed fielding of the Hughes AIM-120 AMRAAM, a missile which combines an active radar seeker with updatable inertial mid-course guidance. Developed to replace the AIM-7 Sparrow, AMRAAM is smaller and lighter, yet has a range of between 30 and 40nm (55 and 75km).

Despite delays and problems, the USAF has never faltered in its commitment to AMRAAM. According to General Lawrence A. Skantze, commander of Air Force Systems Command, "The capabilities of the numerically-superior Soviet fighter force are improving to the point where the initial engagement will likely result in unacceptable losses to our aircraft and pilots . . . With its active radar, longer range and greater speed (AMRAAM) will allow us to launch and leave before entering the enemy's lethal zone. Despite the Soviets' improved capability and greater numbers, AMRAAM will enhance our survivability and maintain our essential air superiority."

The FY 1989 budget contained $20 million for work on an improved version of AMRAAM. Worried by apparent duplication of effort, Congress ordered that only

half of this money could be spent until the DoD had established a joint programme office to oversee the development of next-generation air-to-air missiles.

ADVANCED MISSILES

Development of the US Navy's new Advanced Air-to-Air Missile (AAAM) started in 1988 with the awarding of contracts to two industrial teams, Hughes, working with Raytheon, and General Dynamics with Westinghouse. AAAM will be lighter than Phoenix but will have a longer range. An F-14 Tomcat will be able to land back on a carrier while carrying eight rounds, rather than four Phoenix as at present.

The two teams have taken different technical approaches. GD and Westinghouse have opted to use a dual-band semi-active radar/EO guidance and rocket propulsion. Their design is based on the Advanced Missile System (AMS), a proposed weapon which GD studied for a decade.

The Hughes/Raytheon design is based on a dual-mode active-radar/IR guidance system and an integral rocket/ramjet powerplant. This will provide a slower acceleration than the rival team's rocket — the benefit will come at ranges beyond two-thirds of maximum when the ramjet-powered missile will be faster.

Congress wants to see this USN programme become a

Left: The Rafale A prototype demonstrates an air-to-air armament of four Matra MICA "fire-and-forget" missiles and two wingtip-mounted Magic heat-seekers.

Below: Early test firings of MICA were from ground launchers. According to Matra the weapon is in the same performance class as the US AMRAAM.

USAF/USN operation. The official Air Force position is that the service has no requirement for an extended-range missile, so it is confining its rôle to that of monitoring the USN programme. If a requirement were to emerge, the AAAM would be purchased and could arm the F-15C/D Eagle and the F-22 or F-23 Advanced Tactical Fighter. The AAAM is seen as having a much better capability against stealth targets than AMRAAM and this factor may be enough to guarantee an eventual USAF order.

Several AMRAAM-type missiles are under development in Western Europe. Matra claims that its *MICA (Missile d'Interception et de Combat Aérien)* will match the performance of the US missile. Two alternative models of seeker are planned — a passive IR unit for air-combat mission and an active-radar seeker for interception sorties.

Selenia's *Idra*, based on the earlier *Aspide* Sparrow-derivative, uses tail-control and fixed wings rather than Sparrow-style moveable wings. Guidance is based on a strap-down inertial system, a spread-spectrum fast-hopping data link for mid-flight updating and a J-band monopulse pulse-doppler active seeker incorporating a planar array antenna and digital signal processing. The rocket motor would be a dual boost unit which could either carry out both burns one after the other, to obtain maximum velocity for short-range missions, or keep the second burn for just before interception during a long-range engagement.

SOVIET SYSTEMS

Latest-generation Soviet air-to-air missiles are the AA-9 Amos, AA-10 and AA-11 Archer. These are the main air-to-air threats which the F-117A and B-2 will face in the early to mid 1990s. AA-9 arms the MiG-31 Foxhound and seems to have been developed with cruise missile (and presumably low-RCS) targets in mind. During snap-down attacks it has successfully engaged drone targets at altitudes of down to (160ft (50m). Maximum range at high altitude is 25 – 28 miles (40 – 45km), falling to about 12 miles (20km) at low level.

The medium-range AA-10 Alamo arms both the MiG-29 Fulcrum and Su-27 Flanker and exists in three versions. Little is known about its performance but, in late 1980s USAF exercises, the head-on range of the Alamo was assumed to be 6 to 8 miles (10 13km), well below the 20 miles (32km) of Sparrow.

In defending the Soviet Union against the B-1, Moscow is having to spend about six times the sum the USAF invested in the aircraft, the USAF claims. Fielding the B-2 will make the problem even worse. While serving as US Defense Secretary, Weinberger stated that "To

Below: This MiG-29 Fulcrum fighter is armed with a pair of medium-range AA-10 Alamo missiles, plus four short-range AA-8 Aphid dogfight weapons.

cope with the ATB, the Soviets will be forced to make an enormous investment in new defensive systems over a span of many years, while their existing enormous investment becomes rapidly obsolete. The ATB will not only dramatically degrade existing Soviet air defences, but also those of Moscow's Warsaw Pact allies and Third World client states.'' He estimated the total cost of the current Soviet air defence programme as the equivalent of $120 billion (US).

General Larry D. Welch, Air Force Chief of Staff, has predicted that ''It would take an incredible density of radars'' to create a workable defence against the B-1B and B-2. In a war, the US bombers would fly through gaps in radar coverage, potential weaknesses which are plotted and regularly monitored by US intelligence-gathering.

Not everybody is convinced that stealth will live up to these claims. Critics include Dr Edward Teller — ''Father of the US H-bomb'' — who has stated that in his opinion ''The American people are being misled about the possibility of a practical and effectively invisible bomber...

Countermeasures seem so easy that even a couple of years — considerably less time than the actual production time requirement for stealth — would suffice for their deployment.''

THE FUTURE

He may perhaps be overstating his case but the fact remains that no weapon in history has remained unchallenged for long. In this century, the machine gun, the tank, the battleship, the piston-engined bomber, the nuclear-armed jet bomber, the ICBM and the ballistic missile submarine have all been seen as the ''ultimate weapon''. Only the ballistic missile submarine has kept its reputation near-intact, even so, the concealment which these vessels enjoy in the world's oceans is slowly being stripped away. In the long term, stealth technology will almost certainly share a similar fate.

Left: **The MiG-31 Foxhound is the only Soviet interceptor to use the AA-9 Amos missile. Despite its size, this weapon does not have active-radar guidance.**

INDEX

ACKNOWLEDGEMENTS

This book is the largest popular account of stealth technology to appear in print by 1989, but it could only have been written as a result of painstaking researches of earlier writers. Without their achievements as a solid foundation, I could have accomplished little. Credit is particularly due to the published work of Professor Allen E. Fuhs, Eugene F. Knott, John F. Shaeffer, Michael T. Tuley, Bill Sweetman, Bill Gunston, Ben Schemmer, Tony Devereux and Joseph Jones.

I have also drawn on material published in aviation and technical magazines such as *Air International, Aviation Week* and *Space Technology, Armed Forces Journal International, Defence Electronics, Flight International, Interavia, International Defence Review* and *Jane's Defence Weekly*. Other useful information was drawn from the pages of the world press, particularly news reports by the *Washington Post* and Associated Press.

The Publishers would like to thank all the official organisations, press agencies, commercial companies and private individuals who have contributed illustrations and photographs for this book. Picture research was undertaken by Military Archive Research Services (MARS).

PICTURE CREDITS

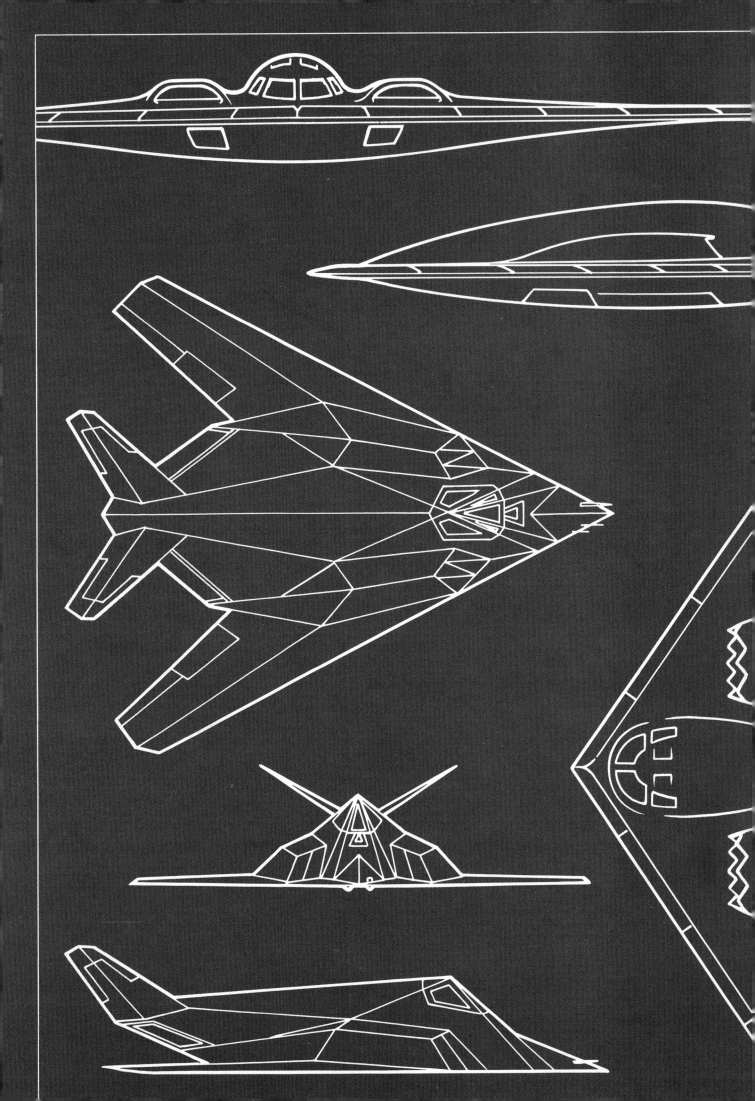